The Complete Idiot's Reference

Top Stressors in the Workplace

1. Commuting craziness: It's long, arduous, and decidedly unpleasant.
2. Environmental ennui: Your office is neither stimulating nor comfortable.
3. Interruption insanity: You can't concentrate on your job because of all the interruptions and distractions.
4. Job description dizziness: You're constantly being badgered to take on extra tasks above and beyond the ones you were hired to do.
5. Teamwork tribulations: If you don't do everybody else's jobs for them, your own work will suffer!
6. Deadline dementia: Your supervisor sets due dates that have no relationship to the realities of getting the job done right.
7. Resource ridiculousness: You're trying to do your job with inappropriate or inadequate equipment and data.
8. Input impotence: You have little or no say on decisions that have a direct impact upon your work.
9. Underappreciation consternation: You work your fingers to the bone and nobody ever seems to notice.
10. Oversight obnoxiousness: You've proved your competence and commitment, but your boss still insists on looking over your shoulder and second-guessing your actions.

alpha books

Rate Your Own Workplace Stress

Please circle one for each point.

Characteristics of your workplace	Rarely/Never (1 point)	Occasionally (2 points)	Often (3 points)	Always (4 points)
You feel secure in your job and role in the company.	1	2	3	4
You are committed to your job, company, and product.	1	2	3	4
Your creativity and individual initiative are recognized and rewarded by your boss.	1	2	3	4
There is a mutual respect for each individual in your department or division.	1	2	3	4
There is a strong sense of teamwork within your department; you share a vision of the common good.	1	2	3	4
You work within a clear and well-established chain of command, answering to only one superior.	1	2	3	4
You are inspired and motivated by your boss and his or her practices.	1	2	3	4
Your company's policies and procedures are fair, applicable to everyone, and enforced consistently.	1	2	3	4

Add responses for each characteristic.

Scoring:

17 or less:	A stressful work environment.
18 to 23:	It's tense, but survivable.
24 and above:	Lucky you! You enjoy a low-stress workplace.

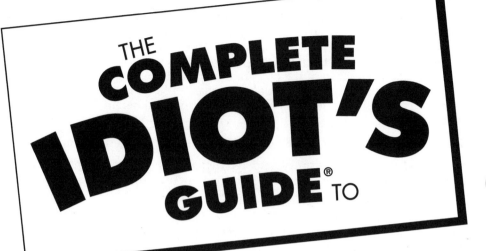

THE COMPLETE IDIOT'S GUIDE® TO

Managing Stress

by Jeff Davidson

alpha books

A Division of Macmillan General Reference
A Pearson Education Macmillan Company
1633 Broadway, New York, NY 10019

Macmillan Publishing books may be purchased for business or sales promotional use. For information, please write: Special Markets Department, Macmillan Publishing USA, 1633 Broadway, New York, NY 10019.

International Standard Book Number: 0-02-862955-8
Library of Congress Catalog Card Number available on request

01 00 99 8 7 6 5 4 3 2 1

Interpretation of the printing code: The rightmost number of the first series of numbers is the year of the book's printing; the rightmost number of the second series of numbers is the number of the book's printing. For example, a printing code of 99-1 shows that the first printing occurred in 1999.

Printed in the United States of America

Alpha Development Team

Publisher
Kathy Nebenhaus

Editorial Director
Gary M. Krebs

Managing Editor
Bob Shuman

Marketing Brand Manager
Felice Primeau

Senior Editor
Nancy Mikhail

Editor
Jessica Faust

Development Editors
Maureen Horn
Phil Kitchel
Amy Zavatto

PRODUCTION TEAM

Development Editor
Nancy E. Gratton

Production Editor
Scott Barnes

Copy Editor
Amy Lepore

Cover Designer
Mike Freeland

Photo Editor
Richard H. Fox

Illustrator
Jody P. Schaeffer

Designer
Scott Cook and Amy Adams of Design Lab

Indexer
Greg Pearson

Layout/Proofreading
Debra Kincaid
Linda Quigley

Contents at a Glance

Contents

Foreword

Serenity. Tranquillity. Peace. If you are like most people in this fast-paced, time-starved world, you long for these states of being. You crave a simpler, saner way to live. And you hope that a life with less stress is truly possible in these topsy-turvy times. Well, I'm delighted to tell you that, by choosing this book, all the help you need now rests in your own two hands.

We live in exciting times. Technology has never been so advanced, societies have never been so connected, and opportunities have never been so abundant. However, the dazzling change that has dominated our world over the past few years also has given rise to a modern plague—stress. At the office, we are expected to do more with less and to stay on top of all new developments. At home, we are expected to be great partners and ideal parents. In our communities, we are expected to offer real contributions and to make a difference. All these obligations and demands have left us exhausted, dispirited, and searching for real-world solutions to our real-life problems.

In this excellent book by Jeff Davidson, a leading authority on stress management and personal change, you will discover a wealth of sensible and immediately effective strategies that will help you restore balance, peace, and perspective in your busy life. You also will find, on the pages that follow, hundreds of simple yet powerful ways to deal with stress and to live a far happier life. I see this book as a manual for effective living in these turbulent times. I feel certain that, as you turn the pages and appreciate the lessons shared, you will feel the same way.

Jeff Davidson is well qualified to write a book about managing stress and successful living. A dynamic speaker of international repute, he is the acclaimed author of 25 books and is a highly respected conference and convention speaker. When Jeff was in his mid-20s, both his father and his sister passed away suddenly. This happened just a few years after one of his best friends died of leukemia at the age of 19. These events, along with a number of other personal challenges, forced Jeff to reflect on some of life's larger questions and to make some changes in his own life. He was determined to find ways to deal with the stress he encountered and to get the best out of life as he advanced along its path.

Through more than 20 years of research, study, and personal observation, Jeff has done just that. Fortunately, he has decided to share his wisdom with you and offers a complete system for stress management and self-renewal. This book is honest, fun, challenging, thought-provoking, and above all, valuable. Whether you are the CEO of a major organization, a teacher hoping to manage work pressures, an entrepreneur aiming to slow down and streamline your life, or a student seeking a guide to help you live better, you will be delighted by the information in this book.

In my book, *The Monk Who Sold His Ferrari,* I share the following story. Once a young student traveled many miles to find a famous spiritual master. When he finally met this man, he told him that his main goal in life was to be the wisest man in the land. This is why he needed the best teacher. Seeing the young boy's enthusiasm, the master agreed to share his knowledge and took him under his wing. "How long will it take before I find enlightenment?" the boy immediately asked. "At least five years," replied the master. "That is too long," replied the boy. "I cannot wait five years! What if I study twice as hard as the rest of your students?" "Ten years," came the response.

"Ten years! Well, then, how about if I studied day and night, with every ounce of my mental concentration? Then how long would it take me to become the wise man I've always dreamed of becoming?" "Fifteen years," replied the master. The boy grew very frustrated. "How come every time I tell you I will work harder to get my goal, you tell me it will take longer?" "The answer is clear," said the teacher. "With one eye focused on the reward, there is only one eye left to focus on your purpose."

Within the pages of this book, Jeff Davidson shows precisely how to stay focused on the purpose of your life while, at the same time, enjoying the journey. His purpose in writing this volume is to offer you his time-tested, ready-to-apply techniques for creating the results you want along with the high-quality life you deserve. Through the application of his ideas, principles, and tips, you will notice some very positive changes in your life during the coming weeks. By consistently applying his wisdom, these changes will lead to the development of a series of life habits and mental attitudes that will bring balance back into your life, will restore your passion for work, and will recharge your batteries.

You now have in your hands a tool that will help you master stress. I hope you will read it often and implement the concepts Jeff has worked so hard to discover and apply in his own life. I also hope you will share the book with others. After all, a world with less stress is a better world for all of us.

Robin S. Sharma

Robin S. Sharma is a professional speaker and is the author of *The Monk Who Sold His Ferrari*. He lives in Toronto, Canada.

Introduction

Stress: Handling the Intangible

If you hold any position of responsibility, are raising a family, serve as a volunteer, or care for others in any way, chances are you're experiencing stress—perhaps a boat load more than you'd like.

Even merely discussing your stress can add to it. That's not much help, right? To help you keep your stress level down while you're focusing on the subject, here's a trick that works for me: I envision the word encased in an ice cube. How stressful can the word "stress" be when there's cool ice all around it? If that doesn't work, try this: Whenever you see the word "stress," think of the word "stressbusters." You might even picture a little ghost with the word "stress" written across its chest and a red slash through it to mean "No Stress!"

No matter what technique you use to detoxify the concept, with this book you're embarking on a journey to alleviate the stress you face in your life. On the way, you need to get at the hard-core reality of why you experience stress. Actor/comedian Steve Martin once said, "Comedy is not pretty." Hard-core reality is seldom pretty, either. Once your feet are firmly rooted in reality, however, you have a better chance of taking effective action.

As I discussed in one of my other books, *The Complete Idiot's Guide to Managing Your Time,* Second Edition, the quest to reduce your stress is a noble pursuit. Up to now, however, you've probably been enduring a fast-paced and frenzied existence. With everything that competes for your time and attention, how do you modify the pace of your career and your life so you can achieve control over your stress? How can you enjoy what your career and your life have to offer and still have time to reflect, ponder, and be whimsical?

Together we'll explore how to do just that. You'll learn how to reduce your stress level and, hence, improve the quality of your life—for now and ever more. I know you're up to the task. To be victorious, you have to acknowledge that the changes you'll implement need to come without too much pain. They must be subtle, natural, and gosh, even easy.

Even before you get into the meat of this book, let me share one key observation: Easy changes are best. We've been told throughout our lives that we have to grit our teeth and plow through formidable obstacles to achieve lasting change. Yet, lasting and effective change also can come from small, incremental steps, as long as they're directed to a common purpose.

Suppose you place an egg in boiling water. After a certain number of minutes, it will become hard-boiled. Even if you place the egg in boiling water for 10 seconds at a time, taking it out for a minute and then putting it back in, the egg still will eventually become hard-boiled. In other words, you can get a hard-boiled egg either way—through one prolonged immersion or by doing the deed in small, incremental steps.

Small, incremental changes in the way you approach your workday and life can lead you to the desired result of dramatically reducing stress in your life. You can achieve an altered state, just like the egg in boiling water. (Fortunately, the changes you make won't result in you becoming hard-boiled!)

Why do I recommend making changes in your personal life in small steps? Simple—I want you to go the whole distance. When you're asked to make changes that are too painful, too upsetting, or too radically different from what you're used to doing, the changes won't last and they certainly won't be effective. This is an axiom of human nature. Therefore, ignore anything you read here that represents too much of a stretch for you—for the simple reason that it won't work.

On the other hand, whenever you encounter something that resonates within you, that gives you a little goose bump or a feeling of "Gee, I could handle that," then as hotelier extraordinaire Conrad Hilton said, "Be my guest," and give it a whirl. Little by little, with a solid framework of knowing what stressors impact you, methods for dealing with them, and a modicum of follow-up, you'll emerge as a less stressed, more balanced person. And people will notice.

How to Use This Book

You can proceed through each chapter of this book in chronological order, or you can tackle chapters at random. Each chapter is self-contained, and they all provide nuggets of wisdom and gems of insight for your cerebral grist mill. I'll move from all-encompassing, culturally based issues to in-your-face work and personal issues. All the while, I'll keep my main message before you: Most of the stress you face can be licked.

Part 1, "Where It All Begins," starts by acknowledging the reality that to be alive is to experience stress. Consider these questions: Is the pace of your life speeding up or slowing down? Are you being asked to do more each day or less? Do you handle more paper despite the advent of the Computer Age or less? Does anyone pass through this world without experiencing stress in one form or another? I'll discuss the curious phenomenon of how the direction of stress has changed. If this intrigues you, jump right now to Chapter 3, "Surveying Stress from Every Angle."

Part 2, "Your Workplace and Welcome to It," explores the angst of holding a job in contemporary society. Although your grandfather probably learned one skill or trade and was able to use it for a lifetime, this just ain't in the cards for you. Chances are you're scrambling for economic survival, and that in itself is stressful. I'll also examine the effects of escalating competition in the workplace, working too long, and being expected to do too much. You'll learn why there are so many workplace distractions and what happens when stress boils over—the increasing incidence of workplace violence.

Part 3, "From the Far Corners of the Globe," examines the sardine effect—why we naturally feel more stressed as population density increases. I'll also tackle what the news and information industry does to make your day more stressful and why the massive amounts of misinformation to which you're subjected can ultimately contribute to stress.

Part 4, "Empower Thyself," gets to the heart of what you're doing—and not doing—to affect the quality of your day, week, year, and career. I'll examine the impact of sleep on your stress level, what happens when you don't maintain control of the environment around you, and the effects of leaving too many tasks incomplete.

Part 5, "When Stress Comes, Tell It to Back Off," offers insights and recommendations for becoming the master of your environment, perfecting the strategic pause, and asking key questions of yourself to help keep you in control. I'll take you through a variety of age-old as well New Age techniques used by people throughout the world to alleviate stress.

Part 6, "Higher Order Measures," offers key insights for assessing the origins of your stress and, hence, taking control of it as well as making choices about your day, week, career, and life.

With what you learn from this book, the coming years are going to be good ones. After all, you've made it this far in life—presumably on your own—and you're now ready for something more. I'm excited for you. Get ready to go where you've haven't gone before!

Extras

The special boxed notes throughout this book were designed with you in mind to help you learn just what you need. Examples of these sidebars are shown here so you won't be alarmed when you encounter them in the text.

Stress Alert

These are warnings of the pitfalls you want to avoid as you take steps toward reducing your stress.

Tranquillity Terminology

These sidebars define new words and terms you'll encounter in the text.

Stressbuster

These are actions you can take to reduce stress right now!

Anxiety Antidote

These are helpful truths and realities you can depend on.

Calming Concept

These are anecdotes, observations, or interesting facts that will help you develop a better understanding of stress and how to relieve it.

Without any further ballyhooing, turn to Chapter 1, "Stress: A Very Old Phenomenon." You'll quickly learn why to be alive is to experience stress, about stressors everyone faces, and what you can do about them. Otherwise, let's roll some credits ....

Acknowledgments

Thanks to all the wonderful folks at Alpha Books and Macmillan General Reference. They gave me the support I needed to make this book the winner that it is. Thanks, particularly, to Gary Krebs in acquisitions, Nancy Gratton in development, and Scott Barnes in production for their careful editing, guidance, and all-around excellence.

Thanks also to Jennifer Hayes in international sales for getting the first edition of this book translated around the world. Thanks to Rachele Schifter in subsidiary sales for making sure that excerpts have been printed all over creation. Thanks to Julie Sanders in special sales for making mega-book buyers take notice and place mega-orders. Thanks to Margaret Durante in publicity for making sure that newspapers, magazines, TV, and radio stations knew where to find me. And thanks to Gardi Wilks for booking me on shows where the hosts were enthusiastic and supportive.

Finally, thanks to Randy Bullock, Anna Hayes, and Tom Seymour for crackerjack editing and proofreading of the early manuscript, to Sandy Knudsen for her super-fast hands and lightning-quick keyboard, and to Valerie Davidson, now age 9, who can de-stress an entire room at 50 paces.

Trademarks

Special Thanks to the Technical Reviewer

The Complete Idiot's Guide to Managing Stress was reviewed by an expert who double-checked the accuracy of what you'll learn here. This helps us ensure that the book gives you everything you need to know about managing stress. In addition to the experts mentioned earlier, special thanks are extended here to Jay Dunbar, Ph.D., of the Magic Tortoise Taijiquan School in Chapel Hill, North Carolina. He has studied and taught T'ai Chi for 20 years. He has led sessions at the Omega Institute, the New York Open Center, and the Southern Dharma Retreat Center. Also special thanks to Tracy Bogart, director, Triangle.

Part 1

Where It All Begins

Would you like to reduce the level of stress in your life? Welcome to a club with tens of millions of members in the United States and billions more around the world. Life, even from birth, is inherently stressful. Life's no fun when the amount of daily stress you experience is too high.

All around you there's evidence that you're experiencing stress. It hits you in the face, the gut, or wherever else you might personally experience it (maybe it's the base of your neck). If you learn to manage your stress now, the quality of the rest of your life will be better. Sure, new events—and new stressors—fall like rain into each life. If you're armed with effective coping techniques, however, your future will look brighter and brighter.

Enough opening banter—these first three chapters examine an array of factors that lead to stress in your life. The stressed-out club has the largest membership on earth! Stress wears many different faces, and many people find their domestic lives are more stressful than their professional lives! Armed with these pleasant notions, let's continue.

Chapter 1

Stress: A Very Old Phenomenon

In This Chapter

- Stressors we all face
- Stress through the ages
- Considering the big picture
- Getting off the worst-stressed list

Stress! The word itself is stressful for some people, me included. No one passes through this world without experiencing considerable stress in one form or another. From the dawn of human civilization to this very minute, each generation and each person has encountered his or her own set of stressors and stress experiences. Undoubtedly, you've heard that there's good stress and bad stress. (Chapter 2, "The Nature of the Beast," gets into the differences between the two types.) This book is about bad stress—the kind you don't want, don't need, and, by George, don't have to have. The kind that limits your effectiveness, diminishes your spirit, chews up your insides, and makes you feel like unrefrigerated chopped liver. In this chapter, you'll explore the sources of stress you face every day and *why* so many things can stress you out.

From the Prehistoric Era to the Present

Cavepeople (or to be more politically correct, the Neanderthals) lived on average to the ripe old age of 18 while experiencing a wide variety of stressors, some of which still confront humankind today. You're not being chased by saber-toothed tigers, but some of the stressors you encounter can be just as foreboding. In a way, stress is analogous to electricity. The right amount of electricity powers your radio, lights your light bulbs, and turns on your PC. *Too much* electricity blasts out your speakers, burns out your light bulbs, and causes a power surge that can fry your hard drive.

Racing in Overdrive: Your Brain at Work

What initiates a stress reaction? When your brain recognizes—or thinks it recognizes—danger, it sets a chain reaction in motion. Chemicals are released in your body that put your nervous system into high gear. Your heart starts pumping faster, and your breathing accelerates to take in the extra oxygen you'll need whether you fight or flee. In either case, you're wired for action. Either you and the saber-tooth duke it out, or you break the record for the hundred-meter dash.

Whether you fight or flee, you have to draw on your physical resources. In fact, so many systems in your body rev up to meet the need at hand, it would take pages and pages to cover them all. Your reflexes get sharper so you can respond more readily. Believe it or not, your blood actually clots faster so that, if you do get clawed, you won't bleed to death ... at least not on the first swipe!

Calming Concept

When a caveperson encountered a saber-toothed tiger, especially by surprise, he (or she) exhibited stress in much the same way as you exhibit it today. The caveperson's body and mind were prepared for either fight or flight. Your ancestors stood their ground and knocked that big cat for a loop—or they posthaste got out of striking range altogether!

Flash forward to the modern office. Suppose new software is introduced in your department, and you have to learn it in a matter of days. You're comfortable with the old program, however, and you don't want to take on the new, but the whole organization is changing over and you have no choice. So what do you do? You gear up. You put all your energy and intensity into this effort. The problem is, you're "on" the whole time. For the next three days—at work, at lunch, at home, and at all points in between—your internal systems are revving at inappropriately high levels to accomplish the task at hand.

You're not keen about feeling this way, but you don't know how to turn it off. You start swigging cups of coffee, aspirin, "miracle" mood modifiers, or whatever else is in reach. After work, maybe you belt down a couple drinks or—if you're wise—do a couple of laps around the park. Maybe you get enough sleep that night, maybe you don't. Regardless, the next day, whatever stress control you achieved the day before is quickly lost as you plop down in front of the PC and begin round two of doing things in a completely new and unfamiliar way. You don't like it, but you have to do it. Your body responds by operating in too high a gear for *way* too long.

Bet You Never Knew...

Amazingly (at least *I* find it amazing), in almost every situation you face, at least half the battle in alleviating your stress is simply becoming more aware of how you react to such situations. This sounds too good and much too simple to be accurate, but it is! We might as well face the biggest fact about stress right off the bat:

> For most people, most of the time, most of the stress they encounter is self-induced.

Unholy cow! Yes, I agree that this is a broad, sweeping, general statement, and no doubt you can come up with all types of exceptions. Still, for most people—and Bubba, I'm talking about you!—most of the time, stress is self-induced. Of course, there are traumatic incidents, deaths of loved ones, cataclysmic losses, and the like. For the most part, however, this book isn't about those things. For such events, you need case-specific texts or perhaps professional help—guidance that dwells extensively on the types of stress you're experiencing.

Stress Alert

It might well be adaptive, and even appropriate, for you to exhibit the fight or flight stress responses at the onset of a change in your environment. The problem for most people—need I say it, the problem for *you*—occurs when you stay in this high gear long after the initial surprise, shock, or bend in the road is past.

The primary focus of this book is the day-to-day, week-to-week types of stress that John Q. Public and Jane Doe experience simply from having lots of responsibility, living in a frenetic society, and operating at too rapid a pace—the good old-fashioned stress that comes from being alive; the stress that comes from commuting to work, from working for an S.O.B., or from having everyone give you grief.

Name Your Aggravation

Let's take a typical professional—someone like … you! What kind of stressors do you experience? The number can be staggering. In fact, almost *anything* in your environment can be a stressor. For example

- **Your boss.** A mean boss, an unfair boss, a disorganized boss, or a boss with whom you simply can't get along can be a major source of stress. Such a boss can make your daily work routine miserable. In extreme cases, such a boss can shorten your life, as can many other stressors.

Tranquillity Terminology

Downsizing is the current corporate trend to improve profits by reducing or eliminating much of a company's regular workforce. It has significantly eroded the employer-employee relationship and has mightily increased job insecurity throughout commerce and industry.

- **Co-workers.** Everything just said about bosses applies to co-workers as well.
- **Subordinates.** The people who report to you can be an extreme source of stress, especially if they're incompetent, tardy, unreliable, or untrustworthy.
- **Work-related stress.** Independent of any particular people involved, the workplace itself can be stressful. Moreover, work-related stress seems to be on the rise. Whether due to takeovers, *downsizing*, mergers and acquisitions, new organizations, or hypercompetition, today's professional is likely to be bursting with stress.

  This stress manifests itself in dead-end careers, emotional disorders, and families torn asunder. More employees at higher levels are turning to drinking and drugs than organizations would like to admit. Some employees even burst into uncontrollable fits of rage, abuse their families, or turn to suicide. (For more information about stress blowing over the top, see Chapter 9, "The Office Danger Zone: When Stress Leads to Violence.") Even in a noncrisis setting you can have too much noise, not enough privacy, too many distractions, and unrealistic deadlines. Hey, you probably already have a mental list of all these and more!
- **Occupational stress.** Some people, simply by virtue of where they work, experience oodles of stress—and not always in the industries you might guess. Airline pilots, for example, tend to live shorter lives. It is postulated that too much flying during the day leads to higher levels of radiation, which speeds up the body's internal engines and over many hours and years shortens one's life. Even sanitation engineers experience occupational stress. (A-ha, you didn't know that, did you?) They have a very high rate of accidents and injuries on the job. Think about all the sharp, dangerous, or otherwise harmful objects in garbage cans. So you see, you don't have to work in a coal mine to experience occupational stress. People who are around loud noises for too long each day or who are routinely in high-pressure situations, such as air-traffic controllers, have their work—and sometimes their livers—cut out for them.
- **Relationships.** Whether it's your wife, husband, mother, brother, father-in-law, mother-in-law, uncle, sister, second cousin twice removed, great-granduncle on your mother's side, or anyone else in your lineage, your kin often qualify as a source of stress.

  Relationship stress is something to which almost everyone can relate. Who hasn't had stress as a result of a relationship in their life? Even Abraham Lincoln had troubles with his father. David Herbert Donald, in his book *Lincoln*, writes that Lincoln had "not one favorable word to say about his father." He didn't even attend his father's funeral.

Stress Alert

When you're bombarded with more messages and more information than you can possibly respond to, the sheer volume you have to face can stress you out.

- **Poor nutrition.** You might not have considered this, but if you've been eating junk food all your life and are lacking vital nutrients, you might not have the physical stamina to support your needs. Do you eat at least two square meals a day? Do you eat any vegetables and fruits? Do you take vitamins? A lot of people don't and then wonder why it's so tough for them to get through the day.
- **Sleep.** Study after study shows that Americans, in particular, and professionals throughout the world, in general, consistently do not get the amount of sleep they need on a daily basis. Lack of sleep can weaken your immune system, can increase your susceptibility to disease, and most definitely can increase your susceptibility to stressors in the environment. Which leads us to ...
- **The environment.** You don't have to live near electrical power lines (which emit powerful electromagnetic waves, considered a deterrent to proper cell functioning) to experience stress arising from your immediate environment. Poor water, poor air, traffic congestion, noise, fear for your safety, and a range of other environmental factors can contribute greatly to the stress you experience.
- **Monetary pressures.** Meeting the monthly mortgage or rent when you're short on funds, being laid off and not having a bank account, putting your kids through college, getting that operation for your mother, and simply making ends meet have become continual sources of stress for the masses. Spending more than you take in and having what they call "champagne taste on a beer budget" also will do you in, time and time again.
- **Being alone.** Has your partner in life passed away? Has looking for a mate become a long-term struggle? Did someone who matters leave or get stationed far away? Being alone can be stressful and can lead to all types of aberrant, if not unhealthy, behavior.
- **Not having time alone.** Just like loneliness, the opposite also can stress you out. If you

Stressbuster

Breathing—that's right, just breathing—can help you offset stress. Take a deep breath, s-l-o-w-l-y. Count to three and then let it out, s-l-o-w-l-y. You'll be amazed how much calmer you'll feel.

never get a spare moment to think, relax, and reflect, the stress can start to mount. The prototypical "Super Mom" of today—she makes breakfast, gets the kids out the door, holds a full-time job, and barely gets home in time to make dinner, check the kids' homework, and do all the evening's household chores—can fall into this category. "Super Dads" have equally taxing challenges that result in long-term mounting stress.

- **Your physical self-image.** Do you perceive yourself as too fat, too thin, or too something else? Lots of people do. One poll showed that more than two-thirds of all men and even more women are fairly discontented with various aspects of their physical selves and would like to make major changes. (You'll learn more about this in Chapter 12, "Unreality Bites.") To compensate for perceived deficiencies in their physical appearance, some people starve themselves to death. Others eat themselves to death. Some go on binges; some go on feast-and-famine diets. All these behaviors are guaranteed to increase stress.
- **Chemical substances.** Do you smoke? Do you drink? Do you take drugs? Do you do any of them to excess? 'Nuff said.
- **Other stressors.** Add your own stressors here based on what you do, with whom you do it, when you do it, how long you do it, and so forth. The point is that there are many, many ways to experience major stress in this world.

The Nitpickers

As if the preceding list isn't enough, there's an endless number of situational stressors, many of which are highly familiar:

Time pressures. You're late for an appointment, or you're late for a date. Different situations, different sensations, but either way, it's hard to be at your best unless you're armed with tools for keeping your stress to a minimum.

Commuting. Maybe you haven't been lucky enough to be on the highway when the guy in the next car pulls out his ten-gauge shotgun. Being stuck in traffic—even occasionally—is upsetting, let alone crawling in a moving parking lot every day just to get to work. Which leads of course to …

Waiting in lines. Despite all the advances in technology, we seem to end up in lines—*long* lines—all too frequently. Whether you're at the bank, the supermarket, the movie theater, or God forbid, the DMV license branch, the post office, or any other government agency, it's a reasonable bet that you'll be waiting in lines for the foreseeable future.

As if these annoyances aren't enough, *Redbook* surveyed its readers and found that the following factors also can contribute to stress. Do any of these apply to you?

- Living in a rural area
- Having had a major health problem within the last year
- Having unsatisfactory child-care arrangements
- Having no close friends or relatives in the community
- Living in a high-crime area or an area you perceive to be unsafe
- Having a spouse who doesn't do his or her fair share of housework

Technology and the Accelerating World

Did something inherent in our culture lead to the development of a high-stress society? Or did we just luck out? I believe factors were at play that, in retrospect, are easily identifiable now. With each advancement in transportation, communications, and technology, human capability increased. In the next nanosecond, expectations also increased. (Chapter 6, "What Do They Want from Me!?" focuses on this in detail.)

The Tempo of Technological Advance

In 1803, Robert Fulton, disproving those who thought it folly, was able to propel a boat by steam power, sparking a revolution in transportation and commerce. A scant sixty years later, the railroad hastened the development of migration to the western part of America. In another forty years, the Wright brothers from Dayton, Ohio successfully flew a powered plane at Kitty Hawk, North Carolina (for which North Carolina later claimed "First in Flight" on its automobile license plate).

By 1911, Charles F. Kettering developed the first practical electric self-starter for cars. In 1923, Henry Ford, having already established the Ford Motor Company ten years earlier, developed the assembly line to produce the affordable Model-T. Today, 175 million registered motorists in the U.S. own, drive, or have responsibility for more than 400 million registered vehicles. In some sections of some cities, there are literally more vehicles than parking spaces. In all cities throughout the U.S., traffic has become a drag and a major source of stress.

Stress Alert

We are the first generation in history to experience change on such a rapid basis. None of us can comprehend the magnitude and ramifications of the changes we face. So on top of everything else, we've got the stress of facing the unknown.

In communications, Johannes Gutenberg printed a 42-line Bible at Mainz between 1453 and 1455. It was known, surprisingly enough, as the *Gutenberg Bible*. In 1729, Benjamin and James Franklin began publishing *The Pennsylvania Gazette*, confirming that colonial America could, in fact, support more than one newspaper. (Who'd have thunk it?) In 1844, empowered by Congress, Samuel Morse completed the first telegraph system linking Baltimore and Washington. By 1861, the system extended to California. In 1866, the Transatlantic Cable was successfully laid between

Newfoundland and Ireland. A scant 10 years later, Alexander Graham Bell invented the telephone.

And the Insistent Beat Goes On

You know what's happened since then. In the 1980s, we witnessed the development and enhancement of cellular phones, fax machines, voice mail, and all the rest. By the end of the 1990s, online communications via cable, ASDL, and ISDN lines sped images and data to us 28 to 30 times faster than the earlier, simpler modems. Capabilities for gathering and disseminating information will continue to be greatly enhanced with each passing year. At the same time, our expectations also will continue to increase.

Even the simplest breakthroughs, which might seemingly have no downside, contribute to increased expectations and ultimately to stress. Take the washing machine. Prior to its development and widespread use, people commonly wore the same clothes several days in a row (or at least several days in a week or a month) before washing them. With the advent of the washing machine, higher standards of cleanliness developed. Soon it became unthinkable *not* to wear a freshly washed shirt to work every single day. WISK detergent, the staunch defender against ring-around-the-collar, still sells today because of the sociocultural expectation that no one should dare be caught at work without a freshly washed shirt.

The list can go on and on and on. From innovative products in personal hygiene to chewing gum and breath mints, we're all making ourselves frantic in our quest to live up to social expectations and living in fear that we might slip up.

A Margin Call

In his book *Living On the Margin*, Dr. Richard A. Swenson says that there's a specific point at which we reach overload "… where the demands on us exceed our limits. We have, as a culture, crossed that line." Swenson points out that 268 million Americans are all "hitting the wall together." He believes that the demands on our time and energy—and our ability to cope with these demands—can be mapped and plotted with the same accuracy as the path of a comet.

Anxiety Antidote

It's important to learn measures of control that enable you to stay on an even keel throughout the day.

As science and technology vastly outpace our ability to keep up, we predictably find that our responses to our surroundings are not what they used to be.

Swenson says we're not simply facing time hurdles, we're expending mental, emotional, and physical energy. He points out, for example, that by the time your days are up on this earth, you'll have learned how to operate some 20,000 different devices from can openers to cam-corders. Name a generation in history that's experienced even $^1/_{20}$ of that.

Finding Comfort in Ultra-Rapid Change

Professor Charles Hardy, author of *The Age of Paradox,* has this to say:

> We stand at a crossroads, seeking our way to the future. It is a place of paradox, confusion of simultaneous opposites, of unexpected consequences, of altered meanings and oxymorons. What was once obvious, like the necessity of economic growth, is now hedged with qualifications. We thought we knew how to run organizations, but the organizations of today bear no resemblance to the ones we knew. We're confused because things don't behave the way we instinctively expect them to behave. What worked well the last time around is not guaranteed to work well the next time.

This paradoxical living could be stressful, but I tend to find comfort in it. Why? Because everyone is pretty much in the same boat. There's a certain equality among this flock of human beings as we encounter the brave new world. The changes will come swiftly and no one will have an edge.

We're All Equally Confused

Lowell Catlett, noted author and professor at New Mexico State University, says that the rate of change in the United States and Canada is such that a new high technology is introduced to the marketplace every 17 seconds. That's more than three a minute, more than 200 an hour, and well more than 5,000 a day. With each new high-technology product comes at least 100 related services. Yet, in just a few years, there will be 17 new high-technology products produced every *second.*

But you can't eat more than one dinner at a time (unless you're a real glutton), drive more than one car at a time, sleep in more than one bed at a time, or appreciably speed up bodily functions in some vain, ludicrous attempt to stay on top of "it all." Nor will you have to.

Everyone experiences stress—in some cases major stress, in many cases unprecedented levels of stress. It's not exactly the same stress you're experiencing, but on balance,

Calming Concept

Understanding that these broad, sweeping changes are perplexing everyone will help you see the larger picture: We're all in the same boat.

person to person, professional to professional, the nature and level of stress often is surprisingly similar.

Consider this. Years back, the Gallup Poll surveyed a cross section of Americans and asked, "How often do you experience stress in your daily life?" Forty percent of respondents said always; 39 percent said sometimes. This means 79 percent responded affirmatively to daily stress. By some estimates, stress-related symptoms now account for about 60 percent of office visits to doctors.

Who's in Charge Here?

When asked, "Would you take a 20-percent income cut if you or your partner could work fewer hours?" 33 percent of respondents said yes. (It would be interesting to know the results if it was only a 10-percent income cut.) During stressful times, almost half of respondents said that they prefer to be alone. Finally, when asked "Is the amount of stress in your life within your control?" 76 percent said yes.

I'm not surprised that three-quarters of respondents said stress was under their control. After all, with the amount of psychological babble we've been exposed to in the last several decades, some of it quite helpful, most people understand that they bear most of the responsibility for the quality of their lives. Of course, you knew that—that's why you picked up this book. The key to reducing stress to an acceptable level is to apply what you learn to make a difference in how you feel.

Handling Stress with Aplomb

The future will unfold at a rapid pace. Yet nothing is quite as stressful as attempting to be someone different from who you really are. It takes a great deal of energy—like a power surge too high for your radio, your light, or your PC—to maintain the posture of someone you're not. It's less stressful to give in to who you are. This is not such a bad thing.

Tales from Twindom

Research on identical twins separated at birth but reunited later in life shows that genetics might have more to do with personality than we previously believed. Lawrence Wright, reporting on the findings of twins research in *The New Yorker*, had this to say:

> The life experiences we think have shaped us are little more than ornaments or curiosities ... and ... the injunctions of our parents or the traumas of our youth, which we believe to be the lodestones of our character, may have had little more effect on us than a book we have read or a show we have seen on television.

Wright believes that if identical twins growing up alone can "sort through the world of opportunity and adversity and arrive at a similar place, then we may as well see that as a triumph of our genetic determination to become the person we ought to be." Do you get bent out of shape when traffic moves along at four miles an hour? Chances are you always will. The key is to not get so bent out of shape that it does internal damage or upsets your whole day.

After reading this paragraph, I want you to put down the book and participate in the following exercise. Sitting in your chair, notice areas of your body. Where is there tension? In the back of your neck? In your shoulders? This is common for people who work at a desk. Does your back ache? Is your stomach tied up in knots? Wherever you're feeling discomfort, be it a headache, a backache, or what have you, it's your body's way of signaling that you're not getting the rest, relaxation, nutrition, or some other element it needs to operate more effectively.

Anxiety Antidote

Does a typical baby walk around with a frown on his face, fretting over what he didn't get done today? The natural state of the human being is alertness, health, well-being, mental clarity, and—dare I say it?—a tinge of happiness.

So what can you do right now? Here are a variety of ways to reduce some of the stress you experience in your life, starting with simple maneuvers and then moving to the more involved or costly.

Drink water. Half the time when you're under stress, simply taking a sip of water will immediately make you feel better. A dry mouth seems to accompany many types of anxious situations. Hydrate, hydrate, hydrate.

Sit still. For the next minute, stare at your watch. If that's too boring, think about something pleasurable you're going to do today. Your perception of the length of a minute will differ vastly compared to using that minute to listen to the news or to read a page from a magazine.

Twist and shout. Physical movement can relieve tension. You can take a walk around the block, stretch right in your office, or use the stairs instead of the elevators. After work, blow off steam by going places where it's okay to yell—sports bars, baseball games, conventions, or pep rallies. By the way, when barreling down the highway alone in your car, some therapeutic singing also can help reduce stress. Yelling might even work.

Improve your posture. Have you noticed that you begin to slouch when you get a phone call? Or that you slink further and further into the easy chair when you watch television? The body was made to be upright and erect. When you talk, eat, walk, and sit with full and proper extension, your systems work better and minor stresses melt away.

Contemplate pleasant thoughts. Whether you think about a waterfall, the picnic you had last Sunday, what it will be like when you're with your lover next, or getting a $10,000 check in the mail, visualization can calm the mind and can soothe the soul. You don't have to get heavily into meditation or yoga. Simply develop the ability to take two to five minutes out of your day to peer out the window or to simply close your eyes. Get into a quiet space and feel good about aspects of your life.

Stressbuster

Envision interacting with others, going to lunch, conducting or attending meetings, using the phone, finishing up projects, and walking out the door in the evening. With this exercise alone, you'll begin to feel a greater sense of control in aspects of your job that you might have considered uncontrollable.

Use visualization. Tomorrow morning, as you get ready for work, rather than switching on the radio or TV, quietly envision how you would like your day to be. Include everything that's important to you—the commute, entering your building or your office, sitting down at your desk, handling tasks, and taking breaks.

Buy a hand-gripper. A tennis ball, a racquetball, or a hand-gripper at your desk is a marvelous stress reducer. Squeeze it when you feel tense to achieve a release.

Buy a joke book. If a particular author or joke-book series brings a smile to your face, keep such cartoons within easy reach. With one good laugh your whole temperament can change, plummeting the stress you feel back down to a manageable level.

Build slack into your schedule. A paradox among accomplished people is that the more they achieve, the more they believe they can achieve—and with less effort. If you think something is going to take two hours, plan on it taking three and schedule accordingly. This is a great stress reducer. If you finish in far less than three, fine.

Reduce some of your costs. Living beyond your means is one of the most stressful forms of existence in our society. What can you do right now to eliminate some onerous monthly expenses? Can you trade in your car? Can you sell a vacation property? Can you eliminate subscriptions? Take a look at what you don't need.

Volunteer. Serving others helps you increase your self-respect and sense of accomplishment. When you stay in isolation, your worries intensify. Choose one cause or one issue and take some kind of action outside your home. There's little use in sitting in your den with the channel-changer in hand and "intellectually resonating" with the world's challenges and problems. Action is customarily invigorating. Your ability to make a real, if minute, difference will immediately lessen your concerns about attaining some breathing space.

Now you should have a good grip on what stress is, its all-pervasiveness, and the fundamental truth that you *can* take control of the stressors in your life. In the next two chapters, you'll get to know this demon we call stress intimately. Then you'll move on to learning how to beat this devil down!

The Least You Need to Know

- Everyone in industrialized societies who holds any position of responsibility is experiencing the stress of dealing with increasing change.
- Changes in technology invariably lead to enhanced capabilities and, in the next nanosecond, enhanced expectations.
- Human physiology and psychology change very slowly, nowhere near the ultra-rapid pace of technology.
- Because everyone is in relatively the same boat, there's no need to worry excessively about the future.
- Awareness counts. Simply understanding this socially pervasive phenomenon that is impacting all humanity can be stress-reducing.
- You have at your disposal many techniques for minimizing stress, from taking a walk to visualizing something pleasant to reducing some of your expenses.

Chapter 2

The Nature of the Beast

In This Chapter

- The manifold manifestations of stress
- Determining whether your job is inherently stressful
- You and your personal stress style
- Discovering what your stress is telling you

If you want to be a lion tamer, it pays to first know something about lions. Dr. Hans Selye, one of the prominent psychologists of the twentieth century, undertook original and breakthrough work in understanding and defining stress. According to Dr. Selye, stress is the "single, nonspecific reaction of the body to a demand made upon it."

Hmmm .... A nonspecific reaction of the body—what did he mean by that? When there's some situation, irritation, or force confronting you, your body responds in a particular way. This response is entirely different, however, from your body's response if you step on a thumbtack with a bare foot, walk into a freezing meat locker, or get slapped upside the head.

So what's the difference? For the latter three events, your body's reaction is quite specific. You feel the pain of the thumbtack, the chill of the meat locker, or the sting of the slap in a specific location at a specific time. The pain or discomfort is quite specific and so is your response: You grab your heel and hop on one foot shouting "Owwwww," you pull your jacket tighter around your body, or you duck before you get hit again.

An irritating situation, however, is a more nebulous, nonspecific stimuli. Sure, it can cause pain, but that pain comes in the form of stress. In this chapter, you'll learn to recognize the many faces of stress and to decipher what they're trying to tell you.

Calming Concept

You usually get over a specific reaction to a pain-inducing event. A nonspecific reaction to a nonspecific irritant, however, such as the droning noise from the equipment in the next office or the fear that the bank might foreclose on your property, can actually do more long-term damage.

Stress: The Psychic Chameleon

In many respects, stress is the wear and tear your body endures. Author Marilyn Manning, Ph.D. says that stress is a by-product of the pressures, changes, demands, and challenges you face each day. Keep in mind that the pressures you confront every day don't have to be bad to cause stress.

You see, stress is the way your body tells you that you need to be more attuned to your environment. As Manning says, it's your cue to "become more attentive and permissive, to let go, and to relax."

Looking for Signs

Among the many signs of stress you might experience, a dry mouth and throat immediately come to mind. For reasons it would take pages to explain, your saliva becomes less abundant. You might find yourself clenching your teeth or holding your jaw very tightly. If you experience any kind of jaw pain or pressure, you'll know you've been doing this—perhaps in your sleep.

Belching, Yawning, and Getting Sick—It's All Stress to You!

When stressed, you're likely to swallow more air, which can result in bloating or belching. If you find yourself taking short, shallow breaths, it's a sign that you're anxious. You're literally depriving yourself of oxygen. Your body has no choice at this point but to request that you yawn—another major stress indicator—forcing you to take deeper breaths.

If all this weren't enough, stress can make you more prone to colds and the flu, headaches of all kinds, and even gas and heartburn. Stress also can constrict the blood vessels in your arms and legs while increasing your heart rate. This situation results in an increase in your blood pressure, perhaps to dangerously high levels.

The Good and the Bad

Have you heard that there's good stress and bad stress? Not surprisingly, the term stress often is misunderstood and misused. Even highly paid executives often have misperceptions regarding stress—some don't even believe it exists. What is good stress all about?

Good stress, or *eustress*, is what gets you up and running, what enables you to get to work, to get to the ball game on time, or to clean out the garage on Saturday. Eustress helps make your life enjoyable and even interesting. Such stress provides stimulation and challenges and is essential to development, growth, and change.

The other kind of stress, *distress* (bad stress), makes you anxious and irritable, dampens your spirits, and shortens your life. Distress is a reaction to a pressure of some type, either external or self-imposed, that prompts psychological and physiological changes of an undesirable nature.

Here's the totally amazing thing about stress: No single event categorically leads to stress. Dr. Selye says, "It's not the event but your perception of it that makes all the difference." Two people can be subjected to the same stimuli, and one might not notice it at all while the other is stressed out to the max.

Stress Alert

It threw me for a loop to learn that, under stress, you might actually feel fat within your body being deposited in your midsection. Gosh!

Tranquillity Terminology

Eustress is a word that means "good stress." It's opposite is **distress** (bad stress).

Four Spheres of Stress

Here is one of the best definitions of stress I've come across: Stress is the psychological and physiological reaction that takes place when you perceive an imbalance in the level of demand placed on you and your capacity to meet that demand. In plain English, you're up against something and you're not sure you have what it takes to meet the challenge. Or, what you're facing is so unchallenging or stimulating that you want to be somewhere else.

Managing stress, in many ways, means keeping the pressures you face at a challenging but containable level—the level you might term good stress. When you face a challenge that you perceive to be within your capabilities, you flourish and, more often than not, meet the challenge.

As you undoubtedly know, maintaining this level is easier to discuss than to achieve. If the pressures you face become excessive, whether real or imagined, you're likely to become distressed or, for short, stressed.

Attention reader! For the rest of this book, "stress" will refer to bad stress.

When you do things that don't stimulate and challenge you, you can get a backache, a stiff shoulder, neck pain—you know the feeling. What you're doing is too boring to focus on and, therefore, it's difficult to get through. Thus, there's always a fine balance to be achieved.

To be sure, stress itself is not something lurking out there, waiting to get you. You have to perceive and recognize it. Your background and upbringing—and your own personality—determine whether a potential stressor has the capability to rub you the wrong way. As a framework for classifying the types of stress you might experience, C. Leslie Charles, a management trainer and the author of *Why Is Everyone So Cranky?*, categorizes stress into four basic areas:

- **Anticipatory stress** is stress caused by concern over the future. Another word for it is worry. You concern yourself with endless stressful possibilities, stewing over something that hasn't happened—and might not. A better strategy? Plan. Planning is different from worrying. If you're concerned about a pending event, figure out how you would handle it and quit worrying. If it happens, you're ready for it; if not, even better!
- **Situational stress** is stress of the moment. It's an immediate threat, challenge, or agitation—something that demands your attention right now. How do you deal with it? Breathe! Take a nice deep breath from your diaphragm (not your chest) and let it out slowly—it *will* relax you. Keep your hands open (avoid making fists) and relax your shoulders and jaw muscles. Tell yourself you can handle this (because you can). Stay as calm as possible, do your best, and give yourself credit for coping when it's over.
- **Chronic stress** is stress that persists over time. It might stem from a tough experience over which you have no control such as the loss of a loved one, an illness, an accident, or another trauma. It could be from a strained personal relationship or an unfortunate work situation. Its defining feature is that you cannot escape the stressor—you need that unpleasant job, for example.

  Chronic stress is best handled one day at a time with patience, personal strength, support from others, a daily plan, and few projections into the future.

- **Residual stress** is stress of the past. It represents our inability or unwillingness to let go of old hurts or bad memories. Come to terms with the fact that you cannot rewrite history, change the past, or magically make things recur the way you want. Let them go.

Often, by simply recognizing these different faces of stress, you can plan an appropriate response. For example, if you can recognize that the stress you're experiencing at the moment is of the situational type that will pass rather quickly, you can immediately "turn down" your internal stress level because you know the stressor won't be around two hours or two days from now.

Stressful Work, Nerve-Wracking Workplaces

Is your job or office inherently stressful? Inquiring minds want to know. A growing number of professionals believe they're in a profession that uniquely contributes to stress. Insurance agents think their industry is inherently stressful. Taxi drivers, especially in urban areas, know they're in a stressful job. Recent statistics showed that theirs is the most dangerous profession in America, what with all the robberies and assaults that occur right in the cabs!

Even mild-mannered accountants feel the pinch. A study by the New York State Society of Certified Public Accountants (CPAs) found that most CPAs agree: Public accounting is a high-stress profession. Anyone in the collections department of a major organization can tell you there's a plethora of built-in stressors that arise when you attempt to collect money from others.

Stressbuster

View stress as beneficial. When you do, it starts to lose its power. When you see stress as a problem, you remain in conflict. But when you see it as a cue to take action to make yourself feel better, it becomes a stepping stone to opportunity.

Are there indicators that tell you when your industry, your career, or your position is too stressful? Try these on for size:

- Do you have a difficult boss?
- Are you constantly asked to put in overtime, particularly at the last minute?
- Do you face role ambiguity? That is, do you lack a clear definition of what's expected of you?
- Do you face conflicting demands? If you have more than one boss, and many people do, sometimes to please one you have to displease the other.
- Do you deal with excessive job requirements—tasks and assignments that clearly exceed your ability or training?
- Do you lack job security? Are you working somewhere not knowing from day to day how stable you are within the organization?

- Do you have an inflexible work environment? Do you have to be in by 8:30 a.m. on the button? Are you allowed to leave early to pick up your son when necessary? If not, stress might be predictable.
- Is there a healthy career progression? Do you have enough opportunities for advancement? Does hard work earn rewards?
- Are your talents underused? As I mentioned earlier, a job that doesn't offer enough of a challenge can be as stressful as one that offers too much of a challenge.

Stress Alert

Do you have responsibility for the performance of others? Have you ever had to fire someone? Even after many years, top executives who've fired dozens of people still find this to be a highly stressful aspect of their position.

Other indications might include:

- Insomnia
- Persistent fatigue
- Irritability
- Nail-biting
- Intestinal distress
- Rapid pulse
- Frequent illness
- Lack of concentration
- Increased use of alcohol and drugs
- Hunger for sweets

Following the Chameleon's Movements

Some of the stress you experience probably exhibits itself in subtle ways. You don't have to be sucking down a cigarette every three minutes or climbing the walls to be showing signs of stress. If you manage a department or lead an organization and you're under stress, chances are you'll abandon the judgment and calculated thinking that got you the job, and fall back on reflex methods that worked well in the past but might be inappropriate to current circumstances. Unfortunately, this lack of dynamic flexibility might yield less than optimum results. This is a subtle but predictable display of stress among leaders and managers. Some of the more subtle signs of job stress are

Focusing on the trivial. Many professionals focus excessively on insignificant minutiae when working under stress. This causes them to miss important deadlines and to overlook problems in the making. If you think you're the only one who falls into this trap, guess again.

Absenteeism and tardiness. And you thought you were just late.

Combativeness. One of the emotional fallouts of working under stress is that you're likely to become irritable or perhaps aggressive with others. This affects people around you at work and at home as well as your ability to perform effectively.

Low concentration. If you're experiencing excessive stress, don't be surprised if you're less rational, more forgetful, and not quite your usual self. The mental effects of working under stress for a prolonged period can lead to indecisiveness and poor decision-making. You might even find yourself reading lines in a book over and over. You might even find yourself reading lines in a book over and over.

Presenteeism. In a study of workers in the United Kingdom, which now averages a longer workweek than most of the rest of Europe, many professionals are suffering from what is called *presenteeism.* This is analogous to being among the living dead.

> **Tranquillity Terminology**
>
> **Presenteeism** is when you're at work and appear to be doing your job, but in reality, you're too tired or unfocused to be effective.

How else can stress dress itself up as something else?

- If you've got a poor attitude or are feeling lethargic, achieving low productivity, beating yourself up mentally, or frequently letting your mind wander, you're showing potential signs of stress.
- If you're encountering unexplained depression or are subject to fits of nervous giggling or foot-tapping, you're probably stressed.
- If you find yourself wishing you could just run and hide, are having bad dreams, or are experiencing heightened anxieties, you're showing signs of stress.
- If you've come to feel that there's no meaning, direction, or purpose in your life or if you're feeling shallow, uncharitable, cold, or uncaring, you could be exhibiting signs of stress.
- If you notice that you're resenting others, finding it difficult to trust others, or feeling depersonalized and getting upset over little things that normally wouldn't have any effect on you, you're showing signs of stress.
- Losing interest in sex or developing an inability to achieve intimacy are really big signs of stress.
- If you notice that you're clumsier than usual; that you're under- or overeating; that you're suffering migraine or tension headaches, indigestion, or irritable-bowel syndrome; that you're getting too much or too little sleep; or that you're becoming easily fatigued, you're probably stressed.

- If your menstrual cycle becomes irregular or if you have to make frequent trips to the bathroom, begin displaying nervous twitches, or suddenly develop a racing pulse, you're showing possible signs of stress.

Is My Stress Unique to Me?

The probability of encountering stimuli that result in stress is high. This much we can bank on. But is your stress unique to *you*?

The answer is "Yes." After all, what stresses me out might have no impact on you whatsoever, and what I breeze through might stop you in your tracks.

Here's an exercise to help you understand what's stressful to you and why. It involves tracing back to the origins of your belief system. Suppose being late for an appointment is stressful for you. Could it be that you attach a lot more to the event than it actually warrants? Let's break it down.

Okay, you're late for a sales meeting. What does this mean?

It could mean that you'll incur the wrath of the prospect.

You might not make a sale.

If you don't make a sale, your income could suffer.

You might not make quota this month.

Your boss might lean on you even harder.

You might lose your job.

You might not be able to take care of your family.

If this goes on for too long, you might find yourself in poverty.

In extreme situations, you might even starve to death.

Starvation, egad! If this scenario seems a little overly developed, consider this: Some people actually respond to the stress of being late for an appointment as if they really *were* faced with the prospect of starving to death. Who knows, maybe it's embedded someplace in their genetic makeup.

Here's a second example: Consider the potential stress of being rejected by someone. You ask someone to go out with you. The other person says "Sorry." You feel rejected, but it goes deeper than that.

You ask someone out, but the answer is "Sorry."

Maybe they didn't find you attractive or desirable.

Maybe you're not worth their time.

What if they're right and you *are* unattractive, undesirable, or worse, unlovable?

Maybe you'll never find a mate.

You'll never have sexual satisfaction.

You won't be part of important social circles.

You won't have children.

No heirs. Nothing to leave behind.

There will be no heritage.

You'll have lived a drab and despicable existence.

You'll die alone and lonely.

Historians will reflect on these shortcomings in your life if you become famous.

Does this sound a bit far-fetched to you? For some people, the stress of being turned down is synonymous with being lonely for the rest of their lives.

Here's a final example: You're a high school student, and you just got rejected by one of your top college choices. It's still early in the year, however, and you've always been a good student. Nevertheless, what kind of scenario might ensue?

You've applied to colleges, but your first choice school turned you down.

Maybe they'll all reject me.

Maybe I won't get into college at all.

Then I won't get the proper education.

I'll get a low-paying job.

I'll live in low-cost housing.

I'll fall out of my circle of friends.

I'll be old before my time.

I'll have to live off Social Security.

But Social Security is going bust.

What's the use? I'll probably starve.

Not so curiously, getting rejected from a college, although probably more significant than getting rejected on a sales call, can invoke the same type of response in people. For some, the underlying fear is that they'll starve to death or be a social reject.

If these are the kinds of equations hard-wired into your consciousness, even minor events can provoke highly stressful reactions within you.

Listening to What Stress Is Telling You

When you experience undue stress about, say, being late or being early, being rejected or being accepted, look at the situation at hand, experience the stress in all its magnitude, and then consider it your best friend. Best friend?

Calming Concept

Avoiding or attempting to avoid the stressful information you receive doesn't give you any power. That power only comes from confronting and overcoming your stressors.

Stress is Nature's Way...

Author Robert Fritz, who wrote *The Path of Least Resistance*, observes that the sensations you experience—problematic stress for seemingly minor events—can be viewed as dynamic, creative forms of information.

Viewing your problematic stress response as a friend, from Fritz's perspective, enables you to benefit from what he calls the "Law of Reversal." Use the negative energy surrounding the problem to propel you to positive forces available to achieve a solution. The more stress you experience in a particular situation, the greater your potential to one day alleviate that stress and to live a more balanced life.

To employ the law effectively, keep asking yourself, "What is this reaction forcing me to learn or to do? Do I need to read up on this, to involve others, to let go of my tendency to over-control, or to simply take things more slowly?"

...of Telling You to Let Go!

What if you need to be in control and become discombobulated if you're not. Lack of control is a key issue that causes stress for many people. It's easier to feel successful when you're in control. When you're not feeling in control, any little thing can become stressful. The less in control you feel, the more you want to be in control, which makes you feel even more out of control. This spiral adds to your stress.

An irony about control is that, to feel like you have more of it, you have to let go of your need for it. To successfully reduce your need for control, take a different path and attempt counter-control measures.

Develop some perspective. Step back from the problem. A week from now, will you even remember what was bothering you?

Be realistic. Can you make a difference in this situation? Maybe not.

Look at the big picture. Having a sense of purpose or a mission in life routinely offers peace of mind independent of the nitty-gritty problems you face on a daily basis.

Channel the Negative Energy

Being adept at keeping your stress at an acceptable level is vital to your health and well-being, to your career success, and to your personal quality of life. Like the electricity example in the last chapter, when you have the right amount, everything clicks. When you have a short circuit, you're going to suffer in one or more ways.

Anxiety Antidote

The way you respond to the environment around you can actually give you the ability to keep your level of stress in check all day long, day in and day out.

Imagine a spectrum with numbers ranging from 1 to 100 (100 being your highest level of stress). When you're above 80, your entire being is under stress, and you're unable to operate effectively, either mentally or physically. When you're at a score of 30 or below, you're calm, relaxed, and have a rare peace of mind. When you're between 40 and 70, you're the most productive at work. If you're an athlete, you'll turn in your best performances in this range. Two researchers ranked common stressors on a 1–100 scale and called it the "Social Readjustment Rating Scale," showing the relative impact of known stressors in one's life. First published in 1967, it remains a classic:

Social Readjustment Rating Scale

Number	Life Event	Mean Value
1.	Death of spouse	100
2.	Divorce	73
3.	Marital separation from mate	65
4.	Detention in jail or other institution	63
5.	Death of a close family member	63
6.	Major personal injury or illness	53
7.	Marriage	50
8.	Being fired at work	47
9.	Marital reconciliation with mate	45
10.	Retirement from work	45
11.	Major change in health of a family member	44
12.	Pregnancy	40

continues

Social Readjustment Rating Scale (continued)

Number	Life Event	Mean Value
13.	Sexual difficulties	39
14.	Gaining a new family member	39
15.	Major business readjustment (reorganization, bankruptcy)	39
16.	Major change in financial state (a lot worse or better than usual)	38
17.	Death of a close friend	37
18.	Changing to a different line of work	36
19.	Major change in the number of arguments with a spouse (many more or less than usual)	35
20.	Taking out a mortgage or a loan for a major purchase (a home, a business)	31
21.	Foreclosure on a mortgage or loan	30
22.	Major change in responsibilities at work (promotion, demotion, lateral transfer)	29
23.	A son or daughter leaving home (marriage, college)	29
24.	Trouble with in-laws	29
25.	Outstanding personal achievement	28
26.	Spouse beginning or ceasing work outside the home	26
27.	Beginning or ceasing normal schooling	26
28.	Major change in living conditions (building a new home, remodeling, deterioration of a home or neighborhood)	25
29.	Revision of personal habits (dress, manners, associations)	24
30.	Trouble with your boss	23
31.	Major change in working hours or conditions	20
32.	Change in residence	20
33.	Changing to a new school	20
34.	Major change in the usual type or amount of recreation	19
35.	Major change in church activities (a lot more or a lot less)	19
36.	Major change in social activities (clubs, movies, visiting)	18
37.	Taking out a mortgage or a loan for a lesser purpose (for a car, a TV, a freezer)	17
38.	Major change in sleeping habits (more or less than usual or a change in the part of the day when you sleep)	16
39.	Major change in the number of family get-togethers (more or less than usual)	15
40.	Major change in eating habits	15
41.	Vacation	13
42.	Christmas	12
43.	Minor violation of the law (traffic tickets, jaywalking, disturbing the peace)	11

Source: Holmes and Rahe, "Social Readjustment Rating Scale," Journal of Psychosomatic Research, November 1967.

Curiously, you actually have a choice of where you want to be on the spectrum, almost independently of whatever potential stressor is immediately confronting you.

Perhaps you know someone who exhibits such power and never realized that he wasn't just born under a lucky sign. He's participating in the process of keeping his stress under control.

> **Tranquillity Terminology**
>
> **Type A** personalities are characterized as hard-driving workaholics. **Type B** personalities are more laid-back.

You might have read that Type A personalities are likely to be more stressed than others. This isn't necessarily true. Some people are quite comfortable being Type A's all the time. It isn't harmful as long as they don't exhibit overly aggressive or hostile behavior. If you're operating the controls and levers of your career and life, whether you're Type A or Type B, you're likely to avoid this type of stress.

Shake Up the Routine

Are you convinced you're part of the proverbial rat race and the rats are winning? Here are some suggestions that offer a change of pace, something away from the ordinary that might help you achieve lower levels of stress. The later chapters in this book will provide even more suggestions for dealing with stress.

Undoubtedly, not all of these are for you, and I don't suggest for a moment that you attempt to do them all in a relatively short period of time. If even a few interest you, I suggest you give them a try. Often, simply changing your routine a little is a great help.

- Plan a vacation. Get brochures, pamphlets, books, and advice from friends about where to go for a relaxing week or weekend.
- Go through your bookshelf, pull out the books you know you'll never want or need to read again, and make a donation to your local library.
- Challenge yourself to make small improvements in your daily life such as leaving the house on time or putting on your seat belt before starting your car.
- Celebrate an upcoming holiday (really celebrate) by getting together with friends or family members.
- Eat dinner early one night each week to make time for family conversation.
- Eliminate all extraneous noise that competes for your attention at dinner. Turn off the TV and radio and find out what's really going on in your family members' lives—talk to each other.

Winning the war on stress requires only small steps applied consistently. Sure, you can head off to the mountains for a weekend and hang out with the peace and love gurus, but hey, then you gotta come back to the same world. (Weekend retreats are discussed further in later chapters.) You might as well make small, incremental changes right where you are!

The Least You Need to Know

- Stress wears many faces, and not all of them are easily recognizable.
- There's good stress and bad stress. The good kind works naturally *for* you; it's only the effects of bad stress you need to minimize.
- Stress at work can show up in many different ways, but its effect is always the same: It makes you less effective than you could be.
- The stress you experience is unique to you because of the uniqueness of your background, upbringing, and experiences.
- Methods for alleviating stress, from treating it as a best friend to learning to let go of some control, are simple techniques that can work for anyone.

Chapter 3

Surveying Stress from Every Angle

In This Chapter

- Even your happy home can be stress-inducing
- The top 10 stressors
- Fighting stress through forging stronger families
- Starting your day stress-free

Most people's lives are not likely to get spontaneously less stressful in the near future. As you proceed in an ever-changing world, life, itself—both at work and away from work—seems to be getting more stressful.

A feature article in *Time* magazine about stress and anxiety, "The Evolution of Despair," discussed the views of evolutionary psychologists, specialists in a field suggesting that modern life itself causes the stress we are all experiencing. Human beings, the article observed, seem to be "hard-wired for a different way of life than offered by modernity." In this chapter, you'll learn just *where* in life your stress is coming from and what you can do to relieve it.

Your Castle Besieged

Traditionally, you could count on Dad or Mom to bring stress home from his or her job. Home was supposed to be the place of refuge from stress. Now, however, we know that the reverse often is true. In fact, researchers at the University of Chicago report that people actually feel more creative, focused, and happy at work than at home. The researchers say, "There's a perfect middle zone, often achieved at work, when a task is challenging enough to compel your full attention, yet not so challenging that it completely outstrips your ability."

What are people saying about the sources of stress they experience? In a mid-90s study conducted by *Prevention Magazine*, the top 10 stressors as reported by survey respondents, in order, included:

1. Personal finances
2. Career
3. Too many responsibilities
4. Marriage
5. Health
6. Children
7. Loneliness
8. Sex
9. Relatives
10. Neighbors

Stress Alert

Today, the typical American carries about nine credit cards. Merely keeping track of that many monthly payments can stress you out!

Hmmm .... It seems that the first three items are all related to work, so how can these Ph.D. types assert that the dominant direction in which stress travels is now from home to work? The answer is simple. Although the first three items are work-related, people are likely to spend more time *worrying about them* at home.

The Root of All Evil? Personal Finances

Personal finances are directly related to your work—how much money you make. The number of Americans with money troubles or stress about money is rising. Even millionaires are losing sleep over their future finances! A *USA Today* survey of the wealthiest one percent of Americans, who have net worths of several million dollars, found that most of them are concerned that they will not have enough money in retirement.

Why do most people have stress related to money? The lack of a high income is not the predominant reason people experience financial stress. Not living within their means is. Too many people, for example, are overwhelmed by credit card debt because they are turning to plastic to pay for things they can't afford. Some people even take the debt they rack up on one card, pass it on to a new card, and continue to use both cards.

Debilitating Debt

From the largest and most successful nation to the individual household, no one can run up huge deficits over a prolonged period of time—without making an effort to reduce them—and hope to achieve any measure of economic or psychic prosperity.

Getting your finances under control is the first step to reducing stress away from work. Yes, I realize that depends on how much you make at work. Whether you make a lot or a little, the task ahead of you is to get your checkbook and your finances in order—to live within your means.

Stressbuster

If you're running a financial deficit, place a moratorium on nonessential spending until all your credit cards have zero balances. The moment you get your head back above water, begin saving.

Many people are too caught up in making a living and making ends meet to pay attention to their financial health. Too many people count their earning power as their major asset but fail to apply those earnings to their financial security in any meaningful way. If this sounds familiar, perhaps it's time to come to terms with your tendency to avoid or deny financial matters.

Calming Concept

When Albert Einstein was asked what was the greatest miracle he ever encountered, his answer was the compounding interest of money.

A Shortcut to Serenity: Financial Planning

Many articles in major periodicals indicate that financial planning is more important to baby boomers and Generation Xers than it was to previous generations. Why? Because people are living longer (see Chapter 21, "Can We Talk?"). You might not have just 35 or 45 years left; you might have 55 or 75 more.

A financial planner will tell you that achieving suitable income and savings requires discipline—something neither baby boomers nor Gen Xers seem to have mastered. The earlier you begin saving, the greater your benefits from the wonders of compound interest.

Suppose you're 30 years old and you want to retire at 65. You calculate what you think you'll need, and you figure you need to save $200 a month to reach it. If you wait until you're 40 to start saving, you'll need to save $600 a month to achieve the same results. If you wait until you're 50, you'll have to save $1,200 a month to accumulate the same sum at age 65.

Nevertheless, this is not a book about personal finances! If personal finances are an issue for you—and there's a good chance they are—check these wonderful books: *The Complete Idiot's Guide to Managing Your Money, The Complete Idiot's Guide to Getting Rich,* and *The Complete Idiot's Guide to a Great Retirement.*

The Workplace—Career Stressors

Work and career are intertwined, and as you saw in Chapter 2, "The Nature of the Beast," concern about job security is epidemic. I'll address career concerns in spades in the next chapter and beyond, so let's move on. Having too many responsibilities also is largely work related, but it also might represent a blend of work-related responsibilities and domestic responsibilities.

The Worst of the Rest of the Stressors

Stressors 4 through 10, which encompass marriage, health, children, loneliness, sex, relatives, and neighbors, are all "away from work" categories. Considering what's happened to the average man and woman away from work in the past 25 years, it's not hard to see why getting to work can be a relief. First, traffic is worse everywhere. If that's not bad enough, you might be wearing a beeper and be on-call all the time. If your health isn't an issue, chances are the health of your children or your aging parents is.

Let's look at stressors 4 through 10 in detail.

Happily Ever After—Marriage

It's tough today to maintain a committed, vibrant relationship. Consider your own! Among the litany of problems and obstacles that marriage partners face today are personal finances, career and dual-career concerns, too many responsibilities, raising children, health, sex, and many more. (All of these made the top 10 list.)

Anxious about the onslaught of responsibilities, more couples are finding it exhausting to have to "be" with one another—to converse, to empathize, to be responsive. Also, the number of families headed by a single adult—usually female—is growing. This places inordinate strains on working individuals with children. Dual-income spouses might have more money, but they invariably experience the stress of two careers.

Astonishingly, millions of couples have no friends even though many wish they did. Many people are too busy juggling family and career to make and keep friends, so they rely entirely on their spouse to meet their needs for companionship.

Let's Get Physical

The health-related concerns of people today—from AIDS to Alzheimer's disease to breast or prostate cancer to irritable bowel syndrome—literally can fill volumes. In large measure (as a manner of speaking), to understand society's health concerns all you have to do is step on the scale. The number of overweight Americans has increased steadily in the past two decades. More than one half of people over age 20 tip the scales in the wrong direction, according to statistics in the Journal of the American Medical Association. Studies now popping up indicate that the typical individual in other societies such as Brazil and Great Britain also are experiencing mass increases in body mass. It seems that the more affluent a society becomes and the more its people are surrounded by creature comforts, the greater their girth.

Stress Alert

Today you're likely to bring more stress from home to your workplace than you'll bring home from the job at the end of the day.

More weight can put stress on your heart and can make your vital organs work harder. Unfortunately, many weight charts in America have been adjusted upward, making people believe their weight is OK because they're part of the norm.

For the Children

What's the matter with kids today? Children mean family, and families, it has been widely rumored, are in turmoil.

Many people have constant anxiety regarding their children, no matter what age their kids are. If they're young, there are all types of safety issues. If they're older, there are potential problems related to sex, drugs, alcohol, driving, and so on.

The decline of the nuclear family hasn't helped make home life less stressful. U.S. Bureau of the Census statistics show that 4 out of every 10 U.S. children no longer live with both biological parents, and the number of single-parent families has more than doubled since 1970. What's more, the number of children born outside of marriage has increased by more than 500 percent in one generation.

Worldwide, families aren't faring much better. Journalist Tyler Marshall, writing for the *Los Angeles Times,* found that in Eastern Europe "Communism has been replaced by a mixture of economic uncertainty and social confusion, producing what some analysts call a values vacuum that frequently leaves parents incapable of addressing their children's questions on what to do with their lives." In one part of India, where many fathers spend months working overseas, the divorce rate jumped 350 percent in a single decade. On the relatively tranquil island of Male off the coast of India, the divorce rate exceeds that of the U.S.! Similar phenomena are starting to occur around the globe.

Marshall says, "Against the backdrop of shifting economic conditions, which have brought millions more women into the labor force" and have generated a competition for jobs that frequently sends potential breadwinners away for months at a time, it is getting tougher to raise a family.

Flying Solo

Anxiety Antidote

Turn off the tube and pick up the phone or head out the door. Make contact with *real* people, and your loneliness will disappear like magic.

Loneliness is a solid fixture on the list of the top 10 stressors. More people live alone in the U.S. now than at any time in history, and the trend is beginning to take hold in Europe and other parts of the industrialized world. For many people, television and the Internet serve as the most human interaction they have throughout the day away from work. Some of that interaction is merely online psychobabble in a chat room.

Is it any surprise that thematic television shows such as *Friends*, *Suddenly Susan*, and *Ally McBeal* become instant hits from their first airing? Do you personally receive vicarious pleasure from visiting with your electronic *Friends* every week? (You know—Ross, Rachel, and the others.)

The following are but a few observations about loneliness and its potential relationship to stress.

- Single or divorced men, on average, live much shorter lives than married men.
- On any given night, by about 9:30 P.M. Eastern time, most if not all of the commercial online chat rooms are filled to capacity.
- The personals (advertisements for companionship) in urban and suburban publications are thriving. The ads themselves are placed by a vast range of individuals representing all races, ages, lifestyles, occupations, and sexual orientations.
- Being jilted by a lover continues to be cited as among the most prevalent reasons for taking one's life.

As contemporary society is currently configured, loneliness is a stress-inducing epidemic affecting people from all walks of life.

The Mating Game

Wait a second. Sex is a stressor? Despite inroads in the battle against AIDS, it might linger as a major health issue for years to come. Has there ever been before a generation that was constantly reminded of the specter of death for doing what people have been doing since the beginning of time?

Before the outbreak of AIDS, herpes was regarded as an epidemic, one that merited continual mainstream press coverage. And it still is an epidemic, with upwards of one in six of the population having some variety of herpes simplex. Because it doesn't kill—it merely agonizes people for years on end—you hardly ever read about it.

Even if sexually transmitted afflictions did not exist, it's still likely that sex would be high on the list of stressors. The number of harassment cases filed every year is increasing. What about the quest of homosexuals, bisexuals, and others to gain respectability in mainstream society? Think about the pressure on preteens and teens who would prefer to remain celibate. They incur incredible peer pressure when surrounded by legions of others who think and behave very differently.

Relative Measures

Relatives as a source of stress are nothing new. As comedian Henny Youngman used to say, "Take my wife—please." Whether it's husband or wife jokes, mother-in-law jokes, or what have you, behind the witticisms are age-old grains of truth. When you consider that people are living longer and that many people, perhaps even you, now have to care for their parents as well as their children, it's easy to understand the strains that might ensue.

You might be among the thousands of readers who have had to become "parents" to their parents. Here are some of the many organizations that might be of service to you.

- Elder Locator is a program that helps you find community-assistance programs for your elderly parents (1-800-677-1116).
- The Jewish Board of Family and Children's Services offers a wide variety of programs and services (1-212-582-9100).
- Local libraries in nearly every community have a variety of announcements, pamphlets, and other information about community groups for the elderly. You might be surprised at the resources in your town.
- The National Alliance for Caregiving has programs to train family and professional caregivers to care for the elderly (1-301-718-8444).
- The National Association for Homecare offers a list of home-care providers and a free booklet. Their address is 228 7th Street SE, Washington, D.C. 20003.
- The U.S. Government's Medicare Program offers information about what expenses for your elderly parents might be covered by Medicare (1-800-638-6833).

Stressbuster

Senior centers and similar organizations are springing up in many communities. They offer social programs, medical screenings, field trips, and much more. These programs are great for your elders, and they also provide respite for you if you're the main caregiver for your parent.

Neighborly and Not-So-Neighborly Types

On the list of stressors, neighbors should come as no surprise. As you'll see in Chapter 12, "Unreality Bites," regarding population density (at least in industrialized nations), the more crowded an area, the more people tend to grate on each other's nerves. And it's not as if the folks in rural areas don't have their feuds. After all, the Hatfields and the McCoys weren't feuding in a thriving metropolis.

Nine out of 10 Americans say that incivility is a serious social problem, according to a survey conducted by KRC Research and Consulting for *U.S. News & World Report.* When asked how various institutions affect people's ability to get along

- 73 percent said that political campaigns have a negative impact.
- 69 percent indicated that prime-time TV has a negative impact.
- 67 percent felt that rock music has a negative impact.
- 52 percent said talk radio has a negative impact.

A whopping 33 percent feel that schools have a negative impact on people's ability to get along.

In my little town of Chapel Hill North Carolina, it seems as if every other household of the 44,000 in town has a dog. Not just any dog, a big dog—the kind that barks at over 90 decibels, rapidly, and for long periods throughout the day and night. If the noise weren't enough, these very same large canines are "walked" each morning by their masters in search of places to poop other than the dog owner's yard.

Enough about my neighbors, we could fill a chapter or two on your neighbors! Some play music way too loud. Some pull in and out of their driveways too quickly. Some have other annoying pets. Some borrow things and never return them. Some leave things with you and never reclaim them. The list of neighbor-caused irritants is endless.

The Workplace as a Rest Stop

Your nonworking life, indeed, can be quite stressful. To close out this chapter, let's examine what you can do to at least minimize the stress you bring to work. In the next six chapters, I'll walk you through making your workplace a little saner. Then we'll look at both external and internal stressors that impact you regardless of where you are, and I'll lead you in the right direction for getting and keeping your stress level down.

Calming Concept

Given all that occurs away from work, you might be among the masses who come to work, essentially, to rest. Or you might supervise those who do. If this is the case, it's time to realize that you can't do your best work unless you square away your domestic life. The two are part of a system—a system called your life.

Is it vital for you to personally mow the grass? Do you need to make pickups when many stores deliver at no extra charge? The larger question behind all this is, do you use the same care and smarts in managing your domestic life as you do in your work life? I'm not suggesting that you turn your home into a branch of your work. By getting the rest you need, however, and by marshaling the resources that will help keep you vibrant, you can come to work more energized, can leave work more energized, and can have a happier home life. It's a victorious circle.

The following are some ideas to help you get to work ready to work.

Grocery delivery. Many supermarkets and groceries will deliver for a nominal fee of five to seven dollars. You also can order from some produce catalogs by phone or by fax. For items you buy frequently, you can establish a standing order in which every week the market delivers eggs, milk, and other staples.

Gift wrap it please. If you're buying presents and the store offers wrapping services, pay the extra dollar and have them wrap it.

Pickup and delivery services. Get in the habit of using vendors and suppliers who come right to your door. Use any neighborhood or community services that will free up your task list. Here are types of services that might exist in your community (but they might be called something else).

The Sparkling Touch—House cleaning

Mr. Fix-It—House repairs

Paul Bunyan & Company—Tree-trimming, hedge trimming

The Butler Did It—A catering service

It's On Its Way—Pickup and delivery

Pooch Takes a Walk—Takes care of your dog when you're gone

Anxiety Antidote

If you get a big raise, don't immediately elevate your level of expenses. A far better idea is to give some thought to reinvesting a portion of the new income to *maintain* your current quality of life.

Gutters 'R Us—Clears your gutters, saves you from roof duty

The Jetsons—Airport shuttle service

Part-time workers. Students (high school, college, and grad school), retirees, foreign-exchange students, and interns from colleges can help you with deliveries and pickups, cleaning, yard work, typing, and so on.

If you're earning $10,000 a year more than you did a couple years ago, save most of it for your future but also take $2,000 or $3,000 of that money and reinvest in yourself. Spend it on services that enable you to stay rested and relaxed (rather than down payments on fancy cars or other items that will lead to bigger bills) so you can go into work and do your best work.

Traffic Wars

Perhaps you see benefit in getting help with some domestic chores so you can get to work less stressed. Is your commute maddening, however? The answer to this question for most people is an emphatic "Yes!" If you let your stress boil over on the way to the top or on the way to and from work, you're likely to be shortening your life. Your *joie de vivre* is certainly killed a little more each day.

You don't need a doctorate in psychology to understand the effects of being trapped every day for an hour or more in your car or on buses, subways, and trains.

To make your commute as pleasant as possible, try these techniques.

Stressbuster

Do some stretches in your seat—move some from side to side, rotate your shoulders, lift one buttock and then the other, stretch out one arm past the steering wheel and then the other, and so on.

- Spend as little time on the road as possible by becoming a contrarian. Leave earlier in the morning and earlier in the afternoon to do your commuting.
- Keep your car in top condition. Take it in for servicing if anything is askew.
- Make your seat as comfortable as possible. Do you need a mat, a cushion, or wooden beads like New York cab drivers use that supposedly massage you while you drive?
- Schedule a health club visit before you head home. This can help make you more relaxed during rush hour.

- Add some leeway into your plans. Tightly scheduled commuting only leads to continued frustration.
- Install a tape or CD player to control the sounds in your environment as you travel to and from work.
- Close your windows and turn on the air conditioner. You'll get the same miles per gallon as with the windows open and the A/C off, and your ride will be much quieter.
- Use drive time to consider what you'd like to do or how you'd like your day to go.
- If you're part of a carpool, ride to work with people you like.

Here's looking forward to Monday morning!

The Least You Need to Know

- Modern life itself might be causing the stress everyone is experiencing.
- You are likely to bring more stress to work than you leave with at the end of the day.
- The 10 top stressors are personal finances, career, too many responsibilities, marriage, health, children, loneliness, sex, relatives, and neighbors.
- Strive for a balance between how much you earn and how much you keep. This will help you achieve some relief from financial stress and a sense of security about your financial future.
- By getting the rest you need and by marshaling the resources that keep you vibrant, you can come into work more energized, can leave work more energized, and can have a happier home life.

Part 2

Your Workplace and Welcome to It

At a Meadowlands exposition in New Jersey in December 1990, I met Alvin Toffler, the renowned author of Future Shock. *He told me that the contemporary office is a terrible place to get any work done. But I guess you knew that all along!*

Work is a big part of your life and indeed can be stressful, so it deserves serious attention. This section has six—yes six!—chapters. Chapter 4, "Making Your Career Work for You," looks at competition in the workplace and how to survive it. Chapter 5, "Beating Back the Grind," explains why simply working long hours will not propel you further or faster. Chapter 6, "What Do They Want from Me!?" discusses what happens when you try to perform beyond your limits and shows you how to tap into the "cycle of productivity." Stay tuned, you'll want to know about this.

The rest of the chapters in this section concentrate on transforming your work life into something less stressful and more fulfilling. Chapter 7, "Get Out of Jail Free," focuses on how you can harness emerging technologies to become more effective, to get out of the office, and to lead a more balanced life. Chapter 8, "Dismantling Workplace Distractions," offers you many ways to stay focused and to minimize interruptions. Finally, Chapter 9, "The Office Danger Zone: When Stress Leads to Violence," discusses the life-threatening increase in workplace violence, how to spot potential powder kegs before they blow, and general strategies for defusing your workplace.

Chapter 4

Making Your Career Work for You

In This Chapter

- Competing with yourself, not with others
- Distinguishing yourself from the pack
- Is self-employment on your horizon?
- Hanging loose when nothing seems to be going right

Your grandfather had the good fortune of being able to learn some basic skills that could generate a lifetime of income. Your dad knew he could progress up the job ladder and set the cruise control. Today, however, John and Jane Doe are scrambling for economic survival. With the dissipation of traditional career paths, you're facing an adulthood unlike anyone else's in recent history. In this chapter, we'll take a look at how the workplace—and the workforce—has changed and what this means for your stress level.

Career Confusion

Today, when you ask others, "Where will you be in five years?" you're often told, "I have no idea." Likewise, many companies have no idea where *they'll* be in five years. Organizations of all sizes are being hit hard by sweeping changes. This is forcing them to place increasing pressure on employees—higher expectations for every job and an environment of rapid employee turnover. Employees are getting the message to hustle or hit the road. Job security today is less and less of a given.

Competition in the work place is stressful with a capital S. Some experts believe it's harmful and deleterious to progress. Top performers often thrive, but others who might have made a substantial contribution are placed under tremendous pressure and question their future with the organization.

Some companies, particularly in their sales division, have a "forced distribution of rewards." Standards are set so high that only 5 or 10 percent of the workforce has any hope of earning an outstanding grade. Recognition systems in many organizations offer too little recognition too late and can promote unhealthy competition for the scant recognition that's available.

Let's look at these new competitive stresses in the workplace and learn about strategies for dealing with them.

Your Most Challenging Competitor—Yourself

How much control do you have over your organization's way of doing things? Perhaps little or none! You're in charge of how you treat yourself, however, and how you compete with yourself. But what exactly does it *mean* to compete with yourself?

Anxiety Antidote

Small, incremental steps applied to improving your work routine will help you rise to the top.

You compete with yourself when you challenge yourself to perform better than you have in the past—when you accomplish something you never have done before.

Be careful! You don't want to engage in unhealthy, workaholic efforts that deplete your mental, physical, and emotional energy. Instead, you should seek to lessen your focus on what others are doing and increase your focus on how to be the best you can be.

Consider the example of John Wooden, the legendary former UCLA basketball coach, who guided his teams in the mid-1960s and 1970s to 10 NCAA championships in 12 years. This is a feat that will likely never be duplicated. Wooden maintained the curious custom of *not* discussing the other team in practice sessions with his own team.

His record bears out the wisdom of his approach. Wooden found it far more effective to have his players primed and focused, confident in their ability and skills, and ready to execute the right plays as the game evolved.

Whether in sports or business, other examples abound of people who chose to carve their own path with little or no concern for the competition. Michael Dell in PC manufacturing, Jeff Bezos (Amazon.com) in online bookselling, Charles Schwab in the brokerage business, and Fred Smith (of Federal Express fame) in overnight express services are among the many career achievers who not only paid little heed to what the competition was doing, they carved out new territory for themselves.

All right, you've heard some of these stories before, but what do they have to do with the stress you feel right now? Plenty. On an ongoing basis, think about the ways you can make improvements in what you do. The Japanese call this *kaizen*, which literally means "small but continual." Remember, small incremental steps can lead to wondrous results—and can lessen stress.

An Authorial Aside

In my own career, competing with myself—rather than against others—has proven to be a superlative way to proceed in work and in life. In the early 1980s, when I worked for a management consulting firm in Washington, D.C., everyone was handwriting reports, This was in the prehistoric days long before personal computers. I learned how to dictate (usually from an outline or from notes) and condensed six- to eight-hour assignments to 30 minutes.

Nowadays, I dictate everything. I even dictated this sentence, this book, and 25 previous books. It's not rocket science, but it works. I complete articles all day long—sometimes two or three per plane ride. This is one area in which *not competing*, but simply seeking to get the best from myself, has paid off in wondrous ways.

A Peter Principle to be Preferred

In Boston, Massachusetts, my best friend Peter also has achieved his fortune by not competing with others. He's in the commercial real estate business and never answers advertisements in the paper. He says that by the time something hits the market, it's already too late. There will be lots of bidders, and the competition means he's not likely to get a good deal. How did he get wealthy? He competed with himself. He compiled data on the key buildings in a certain radius from his location in the Boston area. Over the years, he has added to his database.

Stressbuster

No matter what your industry or profession, keep your eyes open! If you do, you'll easily spot opportunities that will let you forge ahead by virtually eliminating competition—without confrontation or direct competition.

Peter now maintains current data on the size and number of units, and square footage of these key properties. He sometimes will submit an offer to an owner who had no idea anyone was interested in purchasing the property. Often enough, he makes a purchase at a good price because there are no other buyers.

Understanding the Big Picture

You can eliminate your competition on the job and not even go to jail for it. All it takes is a little initiative.

The Tale of Terrence

Consider the case of Terrence. He was just hired yesterday as a bag boy, the lowest level of employment in a supermarket. If anyone is likely to be fired first, it's him. His is not a glamorous job, and Terrence's career prospects don't seem that promising. Let's explore what Terrence can do to make himself more valuable to his employer.

During break time, Terrence might walk over to the head of shipping and say, "I'd like to put in some overtime in shipping to understand how your department works." Sure enough, he'll probably be allowed to put in a couple hours there. Another time, he might go to the manager of the meat department and say, "I'd like to work with you a little to understand how you wrap the meats and preserve them." At other times, he might go to the bakery, security, cleanup, even the credit department, each time offering to help out in return for the chance to learn how the department works.

In as little as three months, Terrence will have worked in a dozen different areas. When someone from another department is delayed or calls in sick, guess what? Terrence can substitute.

Terrence Takes Charge

Let's say a couple more months pass, there's a downturn in business, and the store has to lay off some people. Who are they going to lay off? It's not going to be Terrence—you can count on it. Or suppose there's an upswing in business, and they need to make someone a manager. Who are they going to consider? You guessed it!

Each time you take an unwanted job or pinch hit for others, you can benefit from the same principle that Terrence uses. Put in a little overtime, learn a little more about your organization, and gain a greater understanding of overall operations. In a matter of months, you can become one of the most valuable employees in the organization—with no exaggeration whatsoever.

Terrence essentially has eliminated the competition without killing anyone—least of all himself. If the operation expands, who will top management want to participate in the expansion phase? Terrence, Terrence, Terrence.

Calming Concept

Moan and groan all you want about the relentless grind of the competition—you're on the wrong track. Constantly trying to ace someone else out of a promotion is the least efficient way to get ahead. The most efficient? Challenging *yourself* to do the best you can, no matter what the job.

Standing Out from the Pack

Whether the economy is strong or weak, job security remains the number one concern of most workers. With everything going on in the world contributing to a potentially stressful environment, who wants to work under the constant fear of losing one's job?

If you're not self-employed and you want to make your current job more secure, I suggest you distinguish yourself from others. It's a highly worthwhile strategy.

Making yourself indispensable is a relatively simple but surefire way to improve your job security. Here are some basic tactics you can use to do this. They're drawn from my book, *Marketing Yourself and Your Career*. Don't just apply them blindly, however. You want to avoid creating more work—and more stress—for yourself. The trick is to integrate the strategies you can most comfortably initiate, those you can "piggyback" on top of what you're already doing.

- Take on the task no one else wants.
- Go the extra mile.
- Work harder when the cat's away.
- Give credit to the group.
- Make your boss look good.
- Become a mentor to junior or new members of your company.
- Be aware of a boss who is feeling professionally threatened and be supportive.
- Figure out what's needed, not what's expected, and do it.

Let's take these strategies one at a time to see how they can work for you in your own, real-world workplace.

The Skills that Pay the Bills—Taking on Unwanted Tasks

Brendan was the latest hire in a consulting firm. He was brought in as one of a well-established group of trainers and instructional designers. Rather than melting into the pot of professionals versed in education, Brendan became an expert in the company's intranet, which up to that time had been underutilized by project and staff members. Then the company announced that its resource base, case histories, executive memos, question and answer forums, and staff schedules would be put on the intranet!

Suddenly, Brendan had a niche for himself. Few others understood how to make the most of this new information, resource, and communications tool. The president of the firm needed someone who could explain the system and its features to the others. Brendan stayed after work twice a week to act as the company's intranet expert. Soon everyone with a question was referred to Brendan. He became indispensable.

Like Brendan—or Terrance, the once but not future bag boy—you can develop your niche by picking up a skill or technical knowledge that is vital to your company yet hard to learn. If you can be the best at something no one else wants to do, you will dramatically raise your level of importance to your organization.

Smile All the While and Go the Extra Mile

To get ahead in your company, take on more work than you are assigned—but make sure it's work you enjoy. (After all, you want to avoid adding to your feelings of stress.) Volunteer to help on a project that's running over deadline and make yourself available for extra projects. You'll be highly visible.

Stress Alert

Don't showboat! If you volunteer for so many extra tasks that your regular work suffers, you won't be doing anyone any favors.

Haven't you noticed? Companies *need* assistance with rush jobs. Consider, for example, the problem a company faces when it needs to produce and submit a proposal on deadline. With quick turnaround necessary, volunteers are *always* greatly appreciated. In addition, working on proposals can expose you to both information only available outside your department and people with whom you don't usually work.

Be Productive Each Day the Cat's Away...

Is this a familiar scene? The boss is away on business or a vacation. A great sigh of relief goes up the minute he or she is out the door. People drift into each other's offices, the telephones light up with personal calls, and lunch hours are stretched to the maximum.

Many managers report that productivity is only about two-thirds its normal level when they are not in the office. That's why, when your supervisors are away, working even at your *normal* place will look impressive.

During such times, always stay productive. The boss is more likely to monitor employee performance during periods of absence than when he or she is in the office.

Would you like to add to your reputation of being indispensable? When supervisors are away, try to complete jobs they assigned before their departure. There's nothing a supervisor appreciates more after a trip than hearing, "Here's the job you wanted. It's done." The subtle message you convey is long lasting.

There Is No "I" in Team—Give Credit to the Group

Some people will never get this concept. Giving credit to the group of people you work with can work wonders. This seeming irony—standing out as an individual by praising the group—makes sense in the overall business context. People who make it to the top levels of management are able to motivate others to do their best and to work well in group situations.

When you say "My team did a great job," you're actually imparting something much more important about *yourself*. People above you know that, when a group does well, it's because someone exhibited leadership. If you take the time to praise the group, you stand out as the likely leader of it. It also indicates your ability to facilitate good work.

Building Goodwill That Pays Off—Make Your Boss Look Good

When you give credit to the group of people you work with or manage, you make them look good. This, in turn, has the happy effect of making *you* look good—to them! But there's another question to consider as well. What about making your *boss* look good? The best way to make your boss look good is to handle your own work efficiently and thoroughly. If your boss is fair, you'll get credit, increasing your chances of promotion. The beauty of this is that it's a win-win situation. Even if your boss doesn't do his share of the work, leaning on you unfairly without giving you the credit, you're still likely to be promoted when he is.

Anxiety Antidote

Few experiences lead to stress like the feeling you're falling behind in your work. Avoid procrastination! Do the annoying, nitpicky tasks as soon as they come up, and you'll always feel on top of your work.

Why is this likely to happen? It's simple. Your boss knows that you've been doing part of his work and that he can't take a new position without your help. Making your boss look good can only reflect favorably on you. Both your boss and his or her supervisors will appreciate this.

Helping the Rookies—Become a Mentor to Others

Perhaps you're young—only 28 years old. Or maybe you've only been in your job for a year and a half. No matter. Regardless of your age, with your previous experience and achievements, you might already be in a position to serve as a mentor or informal advisor to others.

Don't wait for someone to officially ask you to teach your co-workers. You can be a mentor informally, and you can choose how much energy you're willing to commit. Helping junior members of your organization *always* looks good to those above you, especially at performance-review time.

Send Praise Upward—Be Aware of Your Boss's Needs

Everyone appreciates praise—even your boss. Yet how often do you do this? Hey, bosses are people, too (most of them anyway). If your boss has been extra supportive of you, tell him or her you appreciate it. Remember to honestly praise your boss to your co-workers and other supervisors. It'll pay major dividends when bonus or promotion time rolls around.

Know the Score—Figure Out What's Needed

A superior method of becoming indispensable is to be on top of your job, your department's goals, and your company's objectives. Knowing your job description and following it or amending it if necessary protects you from misunderstandings. It also gives you an idea of the part you play in the whole organization—an important factor in your job satisfaction and your chance for promotion.

Calming Concept

Does your job description adequately detail your responsibilities and the information you need to know to do your job? If not, change it! Take it upon yourself to learn your department, division, or project team's goals. This will give you the "big picture" perspective that is so important if you want to guide your actions in a way that will move your career forward.

Also consider that any organization, from the smallest business to the multibillion-dollar corporation, has objectives. The objectives could be to expand sales, to increase mergers, to solidify a market already captured, or to make a specific contribution to research. By making yourself familiar with the larger goals of your company, you can better plan your own work so it directly addresses your company's goals.

If you lack direction on a particular project and are not receiving sufficient guidance, look at the problem in light of your company's objectives. Is what you're doing in line with these objectives? Will it be good for the company over the long haul?

Commanding Your Own Ship

An increasingly popular strategy for distinguishing yourself from the pack is to prepare for the day when you're not employed by others. (If you're already self-employed, skip this section.) In his book, *Job Shift*, William Bridges discusses one of the curious realities of our time. He says, "What is disappearing today is not just a certain number of jobs or jobs in certain industries or in one country—or even jobs in the developed world as a whole. What is disappearing is the very thing itself: the job."

There's ample evidence to support his contention. In recent years, large and highly visible organizations such as General Motors, IBM, and GTE have eliminated tens of thousands of positions. Indeed, hundreds of thousands of jobs are cut each year by other major employers.

What will your options be if, sometime in the future, you do not have a job? You can start your own business. You can become a consultant. In some cases, you can even become a consultant to the organization that previously employed you or to similar organizations.

Here are some steps to facilitate such a transition:

- If you don't already own one, buy your own PC and develop more computer skills. Get online and become a whiz at navigating the Internet.
- Set up a rudimentary office in a corner of your home.
- Take a course or two in marketing, finance, record-keeping, or entrepreneurism.
- Talk to others who have gone the self-employment route.

Many people today who work within organizations do so under arrangements that you wouldn't call a "job." They work as contract employees. If you're released due to corporate downsizing, your previous organization or others might begin to rely on your capabilities, and you can charge a premium per hour for your services. More and more companies are willing to work with former employees on an as-needed, contract basis. You might even end up making more and working less than you did before.

Becoming a consultant gives you the opportunity to structure your life in more supportive, balanced ways. You can earn an income *and* have a life. That's more than some 10 million people experience crawling along superhighways on their way to and from the big city and their more conventional jobs.

Anxiety Antidote

Armed with your PC, modem, fax, copier, printer, scanner, and online services, you might be able to carve out the niche you've always wanted. You can cut your commuting time to nothing, can maintain a decent income, and can have a life. Such a deal!

Some New Tools For New Adjustments

Whether you work at a conventional 9-to-5 job or as an independent contractor, it's important that you take steps to reduce your stress levels. During the workday, when your head starts pounding, your insides start shaking, or you feel like you're simply going to explode, you'll find there are many tools at your disposal. Here are just a few.

Maintain a sense of humor. Humor can take you a long way. The ability to laugh at yourself or any situation can defuse almost any stress you're experiencing. Laughter also can help lower your blood pressure. It can mean the difference between blowing up over a situation or sailing past it. Having a sense of humor in the face of tough challenges can make the difference between dead-ending in your career and rising to the top.

Stretch. I don't mean you have to join a yoga class (although I do talk about that in Chapter 22, "Let's Get Physical: Yoga and Exercise"). Instead, stretching means engaging in *any* type of activity that enables you to shake out the kinks during a long work day.

Right now, right where you are, stand up, close the door to your office (if you have an office and a door), and reach toward the ceiling. Then look right and look left. Extend your right leg to the right and extend your left leg to the left. Do deep knee bends.

If you can, bring your knee to waist level and then alternate legs, it'll only take about 10 or 20 seconds before your derriere and posterior side feel somewhat toned. And although you're feeling the physical effects of this little workout, you'll also feel mentally sharper, more alert, and ready to take on the next task.

Don't sweat the small stuff. Ray Perez, an ordinary guy from Gainesville, Florida, believes there are two major events in a person's life. The first is when you're born. The second is when you die. "Everything in between," according to Ray, "is small stuff." Too many people have a tendency to *catastrophize* daily obstacles. Accept the day-in and day-out stuff that *is* going to happen—just don't let it get the best of you.

Tranquillity Terminology

To **catastrophize** is to commit the common error of emotionally inflating simple negative events into major setbacks. Most problems can easily be handled as long as you keep a sense of proportion, break them down into their component parts, and deal with them as they arise.

Take a walk. Walking is one of God's many gifts to homo sapiens. It's relaxing, energizing, and easy to do. The key is not being in a hurry. Walk purposefully, stretching out your legs and swinging your arms as you go. Maintain your best posture. Take deep breaths while you walk. Notice your surroundings.

Take a drink of water. Notice I said water—not coffee, not tea, not alcohol. Just good ol' plain H_20. Undoubtedly, you've learned at some point that your body is mostly water. You need to replenish it once in awhile, particularly when you're feeling stressed. I suggest keeping a bottle of spring water in your office or nearby.

Change your posture. Good posture enables every one of your body's systems to function more effectively. You can't be as stressed when you're standing up straight as when you're slouched over. It's a physiological impossibility.

Keep a hand-gripper nearby. This could be a tennis ball or a mechanical hand gripper sold in any sporting goods store. Squeeze it a few times throughout the day to release tension. Squeezing the gripper can actually provide a release that satisfies your body's fight-or-flight response mechanism.

Listen to a relaxation or subliminal tape. Most health food stores carry these today. There are tapes for releasing stress, relaxing, visualizing a pleasant scene, and so on. The tapes run anywhere from 20 to 45 minutes. Sit back in a chair, pop the tape into your cassette recorder, and follow the instructions.

Take a hot or cold shower. Do whichever feels better to you. Simply being under running water changes your outlook. Something about going from air to water makes all the difference.

Leave nice notes for yourself. If you have a rough working environment, for example, sometimes it's refreshing to come home and see a note that says you did a great job today despite all you had to put up with. You can leave these notes on your car dashboard, in your calendar, and in your gym locker.

Little Victories Add Up!

Regardless of what you do, you'll still have days when nothing at work seems to go right. You want to throw up your hands, jump out the window, or do something equally unhealthy. When nothing is going right, *look for something you can do*—anything—that represents forward progress.

Stressbuster

String together two or three small tasks for which you can get a few easy "wins." It will improve your outlook, and any stress you're experiencing will begin to subside.

Suppose you've got a big project due in several days and you're roadblocked. The essential people are not in the office, you can't get the approvals or the resources you need, nothing's working as planned, and you're ready to scream. Look for a small victory. It might be as simple as reorganizing the project's materials, putting them into the proper file folders, or making a couple phone calls you'll eventually need to make anyway.

By successfully completing small but worthwhile activities, other roadblocks seem to dissipate. You can continue motoring down the highway of your day. For a further anti-stress boost, always conclude your day with these positive steps.

- **Leave your work at the office.** As the day winds down, even if it was a near disaster, give yourself the mental, emotional, and physical break of separating from your work. Make a clean break at least for the evening. Have a life for the rest of the night. It'll all be there the next day, and mercifully, you'll probably have a better perspective with which to tackle it.
- **If the spirit moves you, take a different way home, perhaps along a more scenic route.** Stop and get an ice cream cone if it'll make you feel better. When you get home, change from your work clothes into whatever you wear around the house.

- **Talk to people at home.** Especially before dinner, give everyone at least five minutes of your complete attention.

The Least You Need to Know

- No one knows where they're going to be professionally in five years.
- An effective form of competition is to compete with yourself, not with others.
- Making small, continual improvements in what you do can lead to fabulous results.
- To distinguish yourself from the pack, take the job no one else wants. Go the extra mile, give credit to your group, and become a mentor to others.
- Learn some simple procedures for staying limber while in your office. Keeping your good humor, stretching at your desk, and taking a brief walk are just a few steps to beat stress at work.

Chapter 5

Beating Back the Grind

In This Chapter

- Avoiding workplace overload
- The overwork quotient—what's yours?
- Working longer and feeling less stress
- Self-help antidotes for common workplace stressors

Do you put in long hours and feel tired to the bone? Have you been feeling overwhelmed and perhaps under-served? Have you been making gallant efforts on the job, but you're still feeling underappreciated? If so, take a number and get in line! The official results are in. Too many hours on the job can yield disastrous effects mentally, physically, and emotionally.

In the United States, the typical man and woman are indeed working longer hours. According to some surveys, men spend an average of 50 hours each week on the job, while women average 42 hours. Worse still, many people feel constantly rushed on the job, and surprising numbers of people take no vacation over the course of a year. In this chapter, you'll learn just how overworked we've all become and what each of us can do to reduce the stress that comes from spending too much time on the job.

Where Do You Draw the Line?

"In the last 20 years the amount of time Americans have spent at their jobs has risen steadily," observes Dr. Juliet Schor in her book, *The Overworked American.*

Would you believe that U.S. manufacturing employees today work over 320 hours per year more than their counterparts in France or Germany?

320 hours = 8 more work weeks!

Much Pain, Any Gain?

For the record, there have been some productivity gains in the last 20 years. However, most people don't use any of this productivity "dividend" wisely. Instead, the average American owns and consumes more than twice as much as his counterpart in the late 1940s, but has less free time.

"One-fifth of Americans don't even take the vacation time allotted to them," according to Joe Robinson, editor and publisher of *Escape* magazine. They're too busy working and guzzling laxatives and potions for indigestion. "They can't stop, because if they did, they'd have nothing else to do." Robinson says it's not easy to learn to relax in a culture in which identities are based solely on jobs.

Tranquillity Terminology

Vacation deficit disorder is the inability to take time off even when you've earned it and it's offered to you.

Perhaps *vacation deficit disorder* will be a feature story on *Dateline* one of these days. It's certainly a social phenomenon and a threat to your nervous system, your quality of life, and your potential holiday plans. America's vacation record is dismal. Most European countries and Australia rank ahead of America in how much time their citizens vacation per year.

How to Know When You've Been Working Too Long and Too Hard

Watch out for these indications that you need to take some time off (in Letterman-style reverse order)!

10. You've become good pals with the nightly cleaning crew.
9. You're so out of touch with the world outside of work that you think that Janet Reno is the nickname for a card shark from Nevada.
8. You and your PC have become one.
7. You've filed for an extension to complete your taxes for the third year in a row.
6. *Eyes Wide Shut* sounds like your kind of movie title.
5. You have equipment in your office that you've never had time to learn how to use, and you can't recall what it does.

4. You've installed a cot in your office and keep forgetting to bring in a pillow, so you roll up your jacket.
3. The word "vacation" has no meaning to you.
2. Your company has honored you with a gala awards dinner at a splashy hotel, but you were too busy to attend.
1. You got lost on the way home last night.

Too Many Hours, Too Much Stress

In Chapter 3, "Surveying Stress from Every Angle," you learned that stress now flows from home to work. It's easy to see that there are some built-in incentives for you to stay longer at work. What's more, many modern organizations both here and abroad no longer give you a choice. People are simply *expected* to stay late. But how can you tell if you, personally, are working too many hours?

- During the winter months, you arrive at work while it's still dark and leave work at the end of the day when it's dark again. In other words, you're not commuting during daylight.
- You have no expectation of leaving at normal closing time; 4:30, 5:00, and 5:30 P.M. come and go, and you're still at your desk.

Calming Concept!

Human beings are creatures of habit. What you do now reinforces that behavior for the future. In other words, if you're in the habit of leaving the office at 6:30 P.M., you're reinforcing the likelihood that you will leave on future evenings at around 6:30 P.M. as well. But you *can* take advantage of your habit-forming tendencies. To reinforce the probability of leaving work at 5 P.M. in the future, start by leaving at 5 P.M. *today.*

- When you get home, you don't have the energy to be a full participant in your household. You want to plop down in a chair and take it easy.
- You don't converse with members of your family, you don't help make dinner, and you sure as heck don't want to listen to anybody's problems.

- You've started to abandon hobbies, and worse, you don't even miss them. You spend less and less time with friends and more time with electronic media such as television, videos, or the Internet.
- You're not only eating lunch at your desk, you're also eating some dinners there as well.

The High Price of Overwork

If you've experienced any of the following, you not only have been working too much, you might be reaching the danger level. You need to take immediate action so more damage is not done.

- You experience chest pains on the job for no apparent reason.
- You've experienced any kind of dizziness, fainting, or blackouts.
- You have difficulty digesting food or swallowing.
- You get through the day through chemical dependence.
- You've started to experience near misses while driving.
- You begin to bump into things, cut yourself accidentally, or are more accident prone, in general.

Overwork and Underperformance

Canadian author and trainer Dan Sullivan, who runs seminars for entrepreneurs, believes you'd actually be better off, in terms of job performance, if you only had *half as much time* to spend on your job. Why? Then you'd be forced to do the following.

- Focus on what's important
- Streamline your operations
- Assemble the appropriate resources
- Stay on target more of the time

Sullivan contends that, when you allow yourself to pour 50 to 55 hours or more per week into your job or business, you're virtually setting up a situation *in which you will not work efficiently*.

Calculating Your "Overwork Quotient"

If you're thinking "Buzz off, buddy, I have no choice," think again. You *do* have choices. But first, you need to know how many hours you *need* to do a good job.

You're the only one who can determine what amount of work is comfortable for you. Some people thrive on 60 hours; some people are wasted after 35. If you're an entrepreneur running your own show, you might actually gain energy from the time you put into your business. Some people find it stressful to be *away* from their work, at least if they're away too long.

A simple calculation will enable you to determine your *overwork quotient*—how many extra hours per day and week you can work before it becomes counterproductive.

Tranquillity Terminology

Your **overwork quotient** is the total number of extra hours—beyond your normal work day and work week—that you can comfortably put in before your work begins to suffer.

Let's assume that working an eight-hour day is well within your capabilities. Notice, then, how you feel on days when you work 8.5 hours, 9 hours, 9.5 hours, and perhaps 10 hours. For many people, somewhere between 8.5 and 9 hours begins to feel uncomfortable. Certainly, beyond 9 to 9.5 results in noticeable differences in energy level, enthusiasm, and *joie de vivre*. The easiest way to pinpoint your own limits is to start keeping a log of your working hours on both a daily and weekly basis.

A Day-by-Day Accounting Helps

My workday usually begins at 7 A.M. and ends sometime a little after 5 P.M. During that time, I eat a good lunch for 30 to 40 minutes and usually sleep about 20 minutes. Thus, my average workday is nine hours. On Fridays, it's probably closer to eight hours. Occasionally, I also will work one to three hours early on a Saturday morning. So my typical workweek is 46 hours. The following table summarizes my normal daily and weekly work schedule.

Jeff Davidson's Average Workweek

Day	Sun	Mon	Tues	Wed	Thurs	Fri	Sat
Start time		7:00 A.M.	6:50 A.M.	7:20 A.M.	7:00 A.M.	7:30 A.M.	9:00 A.M.
Lunch		30 min.	30 min.	30 min.	40 min.	30 min.	—
Breaks		20 min.	30 min.	20 min.	30 min.	20 min.	20 min.
End time		5:30 P.M.	5:50 P.M.	6:00 P.M.	5:10 P.M.	4:00 P.M.	11:50 A.M.
Daily Total		9:40	10:00	9:30	9:00	8:40	2:30

Weekly Total = 46:20

A simple recounting of the hours I work tells only half the story, however. The other half is *how I feel when I alter my normal schedule.* I've discovered, for example, that if I work an extra half hour on Monday alone, I'm fine. But if I add that extra half hour every day from Monday through Thursday, I immediately begin to feel it in terms of energy loss. In other words, although I'm fine working a 46-hour week, at 48 hours I register a slight—but noticeable—difference. At 50 hours, there's a distinct difference. And when I work more than 50 hours, life takes on a different—and more stressed out—perspective for me. Working too much upsets the delicate balance I need to remain happy in both my working and nonworking life.

Personalizing the Chart

What about your workweek? Perhaps a standard 40-hour workweek is your cup of tea, and even a half-hour beyond that throws you out of whack. On the other hand, you might be one of those people who can put in a 50-hour week—or more—with no discernible downside. It isn't dedication or intestinal fortitude that determines your limits. Sometimes, it's just a matter of what you've gotten used to. People in government positions, for example, or in any job in which they punch the clock, easily fall into this category. After years of working a fixed number of hours per week, your body and temperament become accustomed to it. A variation in the pattern could cause problems.

The blank chart in the following table is for you to add up the typical number of hours you work per week. In the coming weeks, take note of your overwork quotient.

Your Average Workweek

Day	Sun	Mon	Tues	Wed	Thurs	Fri	Sat
Start time							
Lunch							
Breaks							
End time							
Daily Total							

Weekly Total =

Overwork for you might be as little as 15 minutes a day, although for most people that won't register much on the Richter scale. More likely, you'll find that it falls between two to four hours per week.

Figuring in the "Expectations Effect"

When you've determined the number that seems right for you, you can align your week and days so you stay within your comfortable range. But there's one more factor to consider—the effect of your personal expectations. It's not only the sheer number of hours you work that causes stress; it's how productive and satisfying those hours can be. Your goal, therefore, is to work productively within the hours you've designated as your workday and workweek. You don't want to increase stress trying to get more done in less time.

Stress Alert

On days when I intend to put in nine hours of work but only get six or seven hours completed, my stress increases. On the other hand, when I only intend to do six or seven hours of work in a day and I succeed, I feel fine. The moral of the story? Match your work expectations to the hours you can devote to completing them.

Regaining A Foothold

When you consistently exceed your overwork quotient, you're setting up a situation in which the demands of your job can become overwhelming. In other words, you're a prime candidate for stress. If this sounds like you, it's time to take steps to get your work life and your nonwork life back into balance. Here are just a few activities and resources that professionals rely on to bring everything back into synch.

- Seek the support of family or friends.
- Share problems or feelings with others who can identify with them and understand.
- Use work and leisure time as wisely as possible.
- Actively engage in hobbies for relaxation or recreation.
- Eat at least two wholesome, balanced meals a day.
- Designate a quiet, private place at home as a sanctuary.
- Maintain a faith or belief system.
- Exercise at least three times a week for 20 minutes or longer each time.

Don't simply pick one or two of these strategies. It's far more effective to make three, four, or more a part of your routine. The more weapons you have in your arsenal, the more effective you'll be at handling the tough challenges you face. Let's take a closer look at a few stress-busting strategies that belong in everyone's repertoire.

Establishing Harmony Between Body and Mind

One of the best ways to fortify yourself for the demands of your job is simple exercise. I stay calmer during the day if I've had a vigorous workout the evening before. I'm better able to put in my nine hours—as long as I get a nap—and finish in the evening with enough energy to still have a life. But what kind of exercise is right for you?

Calming Concept

It sounds contradictory. If you're feeling overworked, won't exercise just make you *more* tired? Exercise is energizing, not energy-draining. Exercise causes your body to produce endorphins—natural chemicals that effectively boost your energy and make you much better fitted to face the demands of your day-to-day life.

The National Sporting Goods Association has conducted an annual sports-participation survey for several years. According to their survey, the most popular sport in America by far is exercise walking, with more than 20 million participants. Exercise walkers engage in this activity an average of 110 times a year, or almost once every three days.

In terms of popularity, exercising with equipment is close on the heels of walking, with more than 11.3 million people participating. People who exercise with equipment do so nearly one day out of every three. But you don't have to choose only one exercise outlet. Some people combine equipment exercise with regular walking. Whatever form of exercise you choose, you'll be improving your health and reducing stress—as long as you make the commitment to exercise regularly.

Do you already exercise regularly? If so, wonderful. If not, there's no better time than now to get started. Walking is the easiest to initiate and yields the greatest benefits, so why not start this evening?

Tranquillity Terminology

The designated **dress-down day** adopted by many companies is a day when employees are allowed to come to work in casual clothes. It's a popular innovation among employees, and it often results in higher productivity than on normal, "formal" office days.

De-Stressing Through Denim

It might sound trivial, but *dress-down days* are becoming popular at many organizations and for good reason. Nearly everyone agrees it's a great tension reliever. Many people are more relaxed when they can come to work in the clothes they consider most comfortable. In addition, you save on dry-cleaning bills and get to see your fellow workers in a whole new light. If you're a supervisor or a department head, this is a no-cost way to reduce stress among your employees.

Manipulating the Time Frame

As previously mentioned, it's not just the number of hours you work that causes stress. Other factors come into play as well, factors that can best be described as "time pressure." This is when you feel as if you're always racing the clock to get things done, and the clock seems to be winning. Most of this type of pressure is self-induced. You're engaging in activities that tend to speed up your sense of time. Here are several ways your sense of time might be distorted during the workday. If you can minimize some of these, the long hours you put in might not be so onerous.

Laboring in front of a clock. When you're constantly facing a clock, time seems to go by more quickly. Hide the clock and work at your own pace. You'll accomplish more in less time than if you monitor yourself. (Of course, you still have to loosely keep track of time: If you have kids to pick up from soccer practice, you can bet they won't be sympathetic when you're 45 minutes late!)

Maintaining an unrealistic time frame. Many otherwise accomplished people often set unrealistic time frames for the completion of tasks. If you think a project will take one hour to complete, you're probably underestimating. Examine all the contingencies and allow enough time to accommodate them. After estimating the time it will take to do something, multiply that number by $1^{1}/_{2}$. This usually provides a more realistic time frame for completion, with less chance of getting stressed by a looming deadline.

Toiling under pressure. Whenever you face a deadline, time will seem to run faster. In some cases, you can't do anything about deadlines. What you *can* do, however, is try to arrange your work schedule so you don't face them as often. You'll gain a greater sense of control over your time.

Working without the right equipment. If you don't use the right equipment (especially compared to your competitors), you'll be at a loss. Many people put off upgrading their equipment under the mistaken impression that they're saving money. But think about it. Let's say there's a software upgrade that will improve your efficiency but will cost you $200. If using the upgrade will save you as little as an hour a day, that's 250 hours a year! This is a return that will pay for your new acquisition many times over. Acquire equipment as the need is apparent and when you can comfortably absorb the cost.

Anxiety Antidote

The hour you spend each morning reading the newspaper—if you have no immediate use for the information at that point in the day—might be better spent on other tasks. By freeing up this time, you won't feel so rushed later on in the day.

Adhering to unchallenged workplace rituals. Look at the rituals you do during your workday that might no longer be supportive, productive, or efficient. Some tasks could be delegated, not done at all, or done a different way.

You'll be amazed at how your sense of time will stop racing and will be reduced to a more normal pace if you simply make a few of these adjustments to your workplace and schedule.

Innovation Is Key

The best way to handle seemingly time-consuming duties often is through discovering innovative strategies. I once counseled a pastor who was trying to find a new way to organize his schedule so his work life and home life were not at odds with one another.

This man had a very hectic life. He put in a full workday, and his duties frequently required him to visit members of his congregation who were ill or hospitalized. He spoke about the difficulties this presented in his marriage because his duties made it difficult for him to give his wife the attention she deserved. When I asked him how long his hospital visits generally lasted, he said usually no more than 15 to 20 minutes. My suggestion? I told him to make a date with his wife for the nights he knew he'd be making a hospital visit. His wife could accompany him to the hospital and could either stay in the car and listen to music or perhaps come into the hospital lobby to wait for him.

Because the typical hospital visit was relatively short, the pastor's wife actually found them enjoyable. She knew that, if she could simply weather the 20 minutes her husband needed, he'd then be totally available! Her resentment and the stress it caused were reduced, as was the stress the pastor faced when he felt the demands of work and family were constantly at odds.

The point of the story? Whenever you face conflicts between competing demands on your time, some innovative thinking usually can help you devise a way to reconcile the conflicts—and reduce your stress!

Routine Maintenance

Whenever you find yourself working late, you might encounter any number of common stressors. Here's a quick rundown of the usual culprits, along with some immediately applicable antidotes.

- **The problem:** You've been at your desk so long that you're no longer able to concentrate—you're even becoming indecisive.

  The antidote: Take some long, deep breaths. It might take a few minutes before you're able to breathe slowly and deeply. Let your abdomen expand with each inhalation. You'll soon feel calmer and better able to concentrate.

- **The problem:** You've got the sniffles and suspect a cold or the flu is coming on. When you've been working long and hard, your body can be low on vitamin C, making you susceptible to illness.

  The antidote: Keep some vitamin C tablets in your desk. You can safely take up to 1,000 milligrams each day, perhaps even 2,000. (Be careful—for some people, stomach irritation can result from high dosages of vitamin C.)

- **The problem:** After hours hunched over your desk, your neck and shoulders are aching.

  The antidote: Tilt your head down so your chin touches your chest. Roll your head gently left and right to loosen your neck muscles. If you can, let your neck go limp. Reach to the back of your neck and slowly and gently knead it. In a few minutes, you'll feel looser. Knead each of your shoulders with the opposite hand—left hand to the right shoulder, right hand to the left shoulder.

- **The problem:** The deadline you're facing has you clenching your jaw. This has made your muscles tight.

  The antidote: Make a fist and place it under your chin. Then, while resisting the jaw movement with your fist, try to open your mouth. If you can hold this for several seconds, the tension around your jaw should soon subside.

- **The problem:** You're experiencing heartburn, gas, or cramps.

  The antidote: You might be grabbing too many meals on the run, taking in too many carbonated or caffeinated drinks, or consuming too much alcohol. Eat more slowly and switch to water on occasion for your beverage during meals.

- **The problem:** The muscles in your lower back are tight or sore.

  The antidote: Clasp your hands in front of you and rest your arms on your knees as you squat down. Hold this for several seconds. If you've been sitting for an especially long period, repeat this a couple of times. Your muscles will start to loosen up.

- **The problem:** You feel fidgety and ill at ease.

  The antidote: Whenever you feel the urge to get up and walk around, do so. It's best not to ignore such urges. It's your body's way of telling you when it's time for a stretch.

- **The problem:** Your mouth and throat are dry.

  The antidote: Keep a bottle of water nearby. Nonsugared cough drops, a piece of fruit, or a vegetable also can help. Baby carrots are a great "munchie" to keep on hand. They're healthy, they don't need refrigeration (over a two or three day span), and they're edible right out of the bag.

- **The problem:** You've been in front of your computer screen too long, and your head is pounding.

The antidote: Get some fresh air away from anything that emits electromagnetic waves. When you return to your desk, make sure you sit at least two feet from your computer terminal. (Also see Chapter 4, "Making Your Career Work for You," which discusses staying in shape in front of your PC.) If you have an older monitor (earlier than 1994), you might need to get a screen to place over it. This can help limit the amount of electromagnetic rays to which you're exposed. Newer models have reduced these problems.

The Least You Need to Know

- You're working too much when other important aspects of your life are getting extremely short shrift.
- Determine your overwork quotient—how many extra hours a week you can work before you start to feel crummy—and then don't exceed that limit.
- Consider working fewer hours per week, and instead focus on what's most important. This will give you the mental and emotional strength to let go of lower-priority items.
- Rely on self-administered remedies right at your desk when you know you've been working and sitting for too long.

Chapter 6

What Do They Want from Me!?

In This Chapter

- Coping with the boss's increased expectations
- Recalibrating your expectations of yourself
- Going down in flames: the danger of job burnout
- Plugging into productivity cycles
- The best companies for which to work

Business executives everywhere are voicing the same lament—the pace of business has become incredibly fast. It moves at the speed of voice and e-mail. And although people are using all kinds of new tools and technology, still the paper mushrooms. Instead of one phone number, some people now have as many as seven—office, fax machine, car, home, administrative assistant, voice mail, pager, and who knows what else?

Any way you cut it, today you're facing more challenges and more situations in which you're balancing many tasks. All the while, you're unconditionally expected to do more. In this chapter, you'll learn how to stem the rising tide of expectations that threaten to overwhelm—and overstress—you.

That Was Then, This Is Now

Back in the old days—just a couple decades ago—you and your trusty typewriter could generate three or four items of correspondence per hour (if you were really fast).

Because that was the limit of your technology, that was how much you were expected to do. With the introduction of the PC, however, you can generate hundreds of pieces of correspondence with a few keystrokes. As a result, expectations regarding your output are noticeably higher than they used to be.

That's also true outside the office. People everywhere are expecting you to do more once they realize that you *can*. Fellow employees, family members, neighbors—in sum, everywhere you turn—you're finding more and more demands on your time and your productivity.

It's not just rising expectations of productivity. As society gets more complex, unfortunately, more stringent documentation often is required by your company, your customers, the government, and (it seems) just about everyone else. It seems harder and harder to do anything without documentation.

There's a time lag between the introduction of new ways of doing things and the actual implementation of these new methods ... not to mention all the unresolved mental clutter, resistance, personal agendas, and attachment to how things used to be done.

Stress Alert

People frequently resist change, not because of change itself, but because of their attachment to doing things the way they always have.

Faster, Further, Higher—The Opening of the Expectation Floodgates

The "ever-increasing expectations" phenomenon might well have begun shortly after the birth of Federal Express. Don't get me wrong. I'm not blaming FedEx founder Fred Smith. He spotted an important need and found a way to fill it. I've personally used his and other overnight courier services at least a dozen times each year since the mid-1980s.

It's clear that the FedEx notion of delivering a package "absolutely positively, overnight"—along with widespread use of PCs and growing competition from foreign manufacturers—raised the performance-expectations bar, if you will. It prompted more progressive businesses throughout the world to increase their own levels of service. When everyone got e-mail, well, there were no time-outs anymore. And if you're chained to a pager, yikes—there's no place left to hide.

Who isn't in favor of improvements in efficiency? It's certainly hard to argue against the value of having companies dispense better service. But these services come at a price, paid by the employees who are responsible for *delivering* that improved service. When you look at particular industries, it becomes obvious that expectation levels everywhere are rising, probably with no possibility of declining.

I Need It Right and I Need It Now

You're part of the mix as well. Let's face the music—your own level of expectations regarding the goods and services you acquire also has increased markedly, hasn't it? Don't you get impatient if the phone rings more than twice before someone answers? Don't you find your frustration rising when your computer takes that moment or two to boot up? More and more, people are finding it hard to wait even just a little while to get their needs satisfied. The following table shows just how people's expectations have increased.

Increased Expectations Resulting from Goods and Services Provided at Record Speeds

Near Instantaneous	
✓ Telephone directory information	✓ ATM Machines
✓ Tele-banking fund transfers	✓ Photocopiers, printers
✓ Fax machines	✓ E-mail
✓ Web sites: news, weather, updates	✓ CNN Headline News
✓ Air phones on planes	✓ Fast-food restaurants, drive throughs
✓ Microwaves	✓ Pay-per-view television
On Demand	
✓ Pizza delivery	✓ Gourmet-dinner delivery
✓ Groceries delivery	✓ Courier service
✓ Oil change	✓ State car-safety inspection
✓ Motor club response	✓ 911 response
✓ One-hour glasses, contact lenses	✓ 24-hour print shops
✓ All night restaurants, supermarkets	
Next Day, Same Day	
✓ Express delivery of packages	✓ Laundry, dry cleaning services
✓ Office-supply delivery	✓ Morning-after pill
Close to Perfected	
✓ Education on demand	✓ Just-in-time manufacturing
✓ Universal cellular telephone	✓ 100s of techno-breakthroughs

The following table illustrates how the pressure for speed might increase even further in our lives.

Great Expectations: A Chart of Future Attitudes

Current Expectations	New Expectation
An electric can opener	A laser-driven can opener
A portable iron that heats up in 30 seconds	A portable iron that heats up in a second (and wondering why it takes so long)
Pressing "Select" and "Enter" on your cable tuner for a video on demand	On-demand holographic or virtual TV available wherever you are
High-speed modem uploading and downloading of data via the Internet, taking perhaps an hour for longer files or those with heavy graphics	Immediate Internet transmission of even the most complex files
Phone, fax, or e-mail shopping, with delivery due within 4 to 6 weeks	E-mail shopping with overnight or same-day delivery
Twelve-hour flight to travel halfway across the globe nonstop	Forty-five minutes from Houston to Sydney, Australia on a half-orbital shuttle flight

Your increased expectations aren't confined to receiving products and services quickly. Communications also are now expected to be instantaneous. Suppose you send a letter or an e-mail message to your congressional representative and you don't get a quick reply. You're likely reaction is "What's taking so long?" But consider this: The number of e-mail messages coming into the House of Representatives system increased by eight times within a three year period. Many representatives already were deluged *before* e-mail. Today, we all know that checking your e-mail account can yield hundreds of new messages every day. Who among us can respond to that kind of volume?

Confronting Your Own Worst Critic—Yourself

After all is said and done, the expectations you have for yourself might be the highest of all and certainly the most stress-inducing. After all, you can escape a demanding boss or a customer at the end of the day, but you can't run away from yourself. It's no wonder, then, that guilt and perfectionism are rampant among today's professionals. Along with perfectionist demands on the job, Dads feel guilty that they're not spending enough time with their kids. Working moms feel guilty that they're not successfully juggling work and child rearing.

Scads of people report feeling as if they are not living up to company standards, even though the current climate of downsizing means they've been asked to do more with fewer resources. "I am worried that I'm not living up to my boss's expectations," says a

34-year-old director of marketing at a financial brokerage in Cincinnati. Never mind that this person lost two people from his staff and endured a 10-percent budget cut.

On a Wing and a Prayer

It's important to maintain your sense of equilibrium, especially if you're a survivor in an organization in which many people have been downsized. People around you might resent the situation they face—having to do almost twice as much as before—although they're thankful to be among those retained. To flourish in an environment in which you're asked to do more with less

Pace yourself. In the short term, you can work extra hours, you can work faster, and you can throw yourself at your job. In the long run, regardless of the situation, pacing is the order of the day. You're better off, for example, working a regular schedule, even if it's long days, rather than pulling all-nighters and around-the-clock efforts—crashing, getting up, and expecting to be at your best.

Treat yourself with care. Too many professionals under heavy stress abuse their gastrointestinal tracts, their hearts, and their heads. They fill up on fatty foods, alcohol, cigarettes, and worse.

Maintain perspective. The higher-ups know they've reduced your staff, reduced your budget, and reduced your resources. If you turn in a superior performance, they're probably all slapping each other on the back, knowing they have such a rare talent in their stable.

Calming Concept

If you maintain the same quality or level of effort as before, your superiors know you're actually working more efficiently.

Why get stressed if you're truly doing the best that you can do? If you're rewarded for your efforts, this invariably offers some release. If your efforts are ignored, there's a reliable way you can bring credit to yourself for the good job you're doing.

Your own organization's in-house newspaper or newsletter is always looking for news and tidbits to fill their pages. If you can develop even a two- or three-paragraph summary of your accomplishments, you probably can get it published. Here's a mere subset of all the topics suitable for a small blurb on what you've accomplished.

- **Services.** New service introduction, new projects, new uses for existing products, unusual service offerings, and new contracts.

- **Your professional activities.** Speaking engagements, travel abroad, noteworthy accomplishments, civic activities, courses completed, certificates, degrees, seminars attended, mentions in trade and professional journals, awards, citations, honors, and affiliation.
- **Research.** Survey results, trends, projections, and forecasts.

Hey, Who Needs It?

Has this ever happened to you? You're asked to do more with less and then you get no credit for it. In such cases, your path is pretty clear: You'll have to move on. Any group that asks you to do more with less and then is dissatisfied with your best efforts will never be happy with your performance. If you remain in that situation, you'll be a prime candidate for burnout.

Burnout: Near Lethal Doses

Tony Alessandra, Ph.D., author of *The Platinum Rule,* asks: What happens when you run a machine too hard and too long. Answer: It burns out. The same thing happens to an overworked human machine. "When people strive too hard and too long to reach a goal, they burn out," he says. "*Burnout* is a state of fatigue and/or frustration brought on by an intense pursuit of a goal or devotion to a cause. It brings on a series of physical, emotional, and psychological problems."

Actually, the term "burnout" has made the rounds in business and general literature over the two decades. It's a unique type of stress that involves:

- Emotional exhaustion
- Depersonalization
- Diminished personal accomplishment

Burnout is widely regarded as a distinct type of stress related to demands on the job. Burnout is costly to organizations. Ironically, however, the organizations in which employees are most prone to feeling the effects of burnout often do little to help—so their employees have to handle the problem on their own. How do you know if *you're* heading for burnout?

Tranquillity Terminology

Burnout is the state of fatigue and frustration that arises from pursuing a goal or an effort too long with little or no reward for the effort.

Exhaustion, Emotionally Speaking

Emotional exhaustion often is the first component of burnout to make its appearance—the feeling that you don't have the capacity to respond emotionally to others. Your energy level is so low and you are so irritated and tense that you know you can't give of yourself like you have in the past. Even after a long weekend or time away from work, you still dread the thought of going back to your job Monday morning.

"I Am Robot!"—The Danger of Depersonalization

A second strong indicator of burnout is depersonalization. This is when you still manage to do what you're supposed to, but you've withdrawn emotionally from the process. Among health-care workers, this could manifest in a nurse who follows correct medical procedures and is cordial with patients but no longer cares about them personally. In business, depersonalization can appear as detachment, a blasé attitude toward peers, clients, or customers, and perhaps a lack of interest in the organization in general. If you begin to see others as objects rather than as human beings, beware! You might be on the burnout path.

Stress Alert

If you begin to find it difficult to share in the normal emotional highs and lows of people close to you, watch out! This can be a sign that you're disengaging emotionally *and* that you're depersonalizing your normal human contacts. *Both are serious indicators that your stress level is getting out of hand.*

Slipping Standards

How have you been stacking up in terms of your own personal evaluation? Are you coming up mostly negative? Does it seem like you're not making any progress—or even that you're losing ground? If you feel you're not as competent and successful doing your job as you have been in the past, you're experiencing the sensation of diminished personal accomplishment—the third aspect of burnout.

Likely Candidates for Burnout

Who is most susceptible to burnout? People in the helping professions or in positions that have significant amounts of interpersonal contact. This includes people in customer service departments, municipal services, health care, and the travel industry.

It's not just *what* you do. Your attitude as well can predispose you to burnout. People who initially are optimistic or idealistic about what they can achieve on the job are particularly susceptible to burnout—particularly as they experience setbacks and frustration.

Dr. Alessandra says high achievers might be especially prone to burnout. "They usually have overly full schedules and yet still find the time to take on more," he observes. "They have a difficult time saying 'No!' to the requests of others. When working on projects, they usually do more than their share." Part of their problem, he suggests, is their inability or unwillingness to delegate things to others. "They like things done right and done on time," he says. "Consequently they do almost everything themselves."

Burnout-Fighting Basics

Dr. Alessandra offers the following activities to help prevent you from becoming a burnout victim. They're also useful when recovering from burnout you already are experiencing.

1. **Limit the number of hours you work.** Classic burnout victims work excessively long hours 6 or 7 days per week. Even when they're home or out socializing, they can't stop thinking and talking business. They wear themselves down physically and mentally.
2. **Set goals—and *write them down*.** A list of clearly defined goals is your best protection from burning out because it gives you perspective. Most burnout victims work so hard and so long because they get bogged down in too many trivial tasks because they can't see the bigger picture.
3. **Learn to say "No!"** Burnout candidates have a difficult time telling people they are not able to take on another task. Ironically, taking on too much puts so much pressure on you that the overall quality of your work decreases. When you feel you have more than enough to keep you busy, politely refuse to take on more.
4. **Learn to delegate.** One of the major problems afflicting burnout victims is their inability or unwillingness to *delegate* tasks to others. You must resist the tendency to try to do everything yourself. Train others, especially your secretary or assistant, to do routine and low-priority tasks. If they make mistakes, that's okay, too. That's how people learn, after all. Give your subordinates the space to do things on their own while you spend your time planning and completing your high-priority tasks.
5. **Get enough exercise.** One of the most effective ways to relieve tension and stress is through exercise. It not only helps you avoid burnout, it also helps you circumvent many other physical ailments. Don't complain that you don't have time to exercise. By taking a little time out of a busy schedule to exercise, you'll feel less fatigued while you're working and will actually increase your level of awareness and productivity on the job. Force yourself to get at least 200 minutes of physical activity per week, spread out over at least five separate days.
6. **Break your routines.** Too much structure gets you into a rut. In the field of nutrition, experts recommend rotational dieting. This simply means not eating the same foods all the time and adding variety and flexibility to your eating habits. The same advice holds true for your daily and weekly work schedule.

Tranquillity Terminology

Delegating means handing off a task and its attendant responsibilities to another person. Efficient workers and managers know how to prioritize and turn low-level tasks over to helpers. They're then free to concentrate on higher-level problems.

Purposely go out of your way to do some tasks differently, to do some new tasks, and to do them at different times.

7. **Kick back every so often during each day**. Let your mind wander from your business concerns every so often. These are necessary recharge breaks. Once home, take long hot baths to relieve tension. You'll find that this is an ideal way to relax both your mind and body.
8. **Eat lunch *away* from the office**. This is an excellent way to combine many of the preceding suggestions. For example, the walk to and from the restaurant or the park is an excellent source of exercise, eating lunch outside or in the park gives you a chance to relax and to cleanse your mind, and leaving the office for meals breaks the routine of being in the office all day.
9. **Take vacations**. Most burnout victims rarely take vacations. Even when their company or spouse forces them to go on a vacation, they load one suitcase with books, reading materials, and work. If the vacation consists of more than three days in the same location, burnout victims start climbing the walls. If this sounds like you, take a series of three-day vacations throughout the year instead of trying for a single long one—but discipline yourself not to bring any work with you.
10. **Spend more time with your family and/or friends**. Get to know the important people in your life. They'll help restore your perspective on why you're working so hard in the first place.
11. **Take time for yourself**. Get away by yourself every once in a while. Meditate. Relax. Read light, enjoyable material. Pursue a hobby that has absolutely nothing to do with your line of work but that's relaxing and enjoyable. Treat yourself—you deserve it.
12. **Lighten up**. Believe it or not, you're not indispensable. Not to the world. Not to your country. Usually not even to your company. Yes, you do make a contribution, maybe even a major one. But don't overestimate your own value and worth. Let up on yourself and others. Do what you do and do it well. Don't diminish yourself in the process because then you're of no value to the people and causes for which you're working. Take care of yourself and enjoy all aspects of your life—not just work. Everyone will be better off for it, especially you.

Dr. Alessandra's suggestions are all valuable, but he cautions that you shouldn't try to change *too many* of your behaviors at once. It's better that you attempt one new behavioral change at a time. Wait until you've comfortably mastered one before taking on another.

Know Thyself!

I find that the ability to engage in self-evaluation can be an enormous help in spotting stressors and alleviating them. Self-evaluation involves looking at what you do with some measure of objectivity. A chart, checklist, or scale that includes the key components of your job description and responsibilities can be a useful tool for achieving objectivity. Here's a chart that you might find helpful.

What I Accomplish					
What I'm Asked to Do	MON	TUE	WED	THU	FRI
Task A					
Task B					
Task C					
Task D					

Simply fill in the left-hand column with the tasks you face on a daily basis and use the day-to-day columns to record your performance for each. You can simply check off tasks as they're completed, or you can employ a scale (say, from 1 to 5) to evaluate your performance of that task.

Listen to the people around you. When your spouse, co-workers, and friends notice changes in your behavior that might be detrimental, heed their warnings. Listen up when somebody says, "Take it easy."

Handling an Unreasonable Workload

Despite the prevalence of stress and burnout in the contemporary working world—and its well-documented dangers—too many organizations continue to ignore the problem. Too many managers have the misguided notion that only wimps get stressed out. These are the same managers who tend to give out stress in abundance, but they don't provide help or support to stressed employees.

Who knows, one day organizations might be held responsible, both socially and legally, for the mental health and well-being of their employees. It only takes one little lawsuit .... Until that day comes, however, you're really on your own in finding relief.

Just Saying No—Politely

What if your boss unduly heaps piles of stuff on your desk with little warning? How can you maintain your relationship with your boss yet not be overwhelmed? Here are some tactful and professional responses:

- "I'm really overcommitted right now, and if I take this on, I can't do it justice."
- "I appreciate your confidence in me, but I wouldn't want to take this on right now, knowing my other responsibilities would prevent me from doing an excellent job."

- "I'd be happy to handle this assignment for you, but realistically, I can't do it without foregoing some other things I'm working on. Of tasks a and b, which would you like me to do? Which can I put aside?"
- "I can do that for you. Will it be okay if I get back to you in the middle of next week? I currently have blank, blank, and blank in the queue."
- "The number and complexity of the assignments I'm handling is mounting. Perhaps we could look at a two- or four-week scenario of what's most important to you, when the assignments need to be completed, and what I can realistically handle over that time period."

Meanwhile, remain as flexible as possible. In most jobs, your responsibilities and assignments change frequently. As you learned in Chapter 4, "Making Your Career Work for You," your ability to adapt to your boss's needs will go a long way toward helping you flourish at your position. It also will help diminish the feelings of being overwhelmed that you might be experiencing.

Figuring Out Your Cycles of Productivity

Consider the following office scenario:

Amy is a transcriptionist who has established a personal week-long productivity cycle that works for her. She won't transcribe tapes late in the day or anytime on Friday. Brad, Amy's colleague, also maintains high productivity by personally prioritizing assignments and scheduling his tasks. Each has different strengths and weaknesses, and their energy levels peak and decline at different times throughout the work week. Each has long since gauged these factors, so they know what can best be undertaken at which times. In short, they "go with the flow" of their energy levels.

Stacey, Amy's production supervisor, rarely interferes with Amy's or Brad's cycle unless an urgent report or letter has to be completed.

Are Amy and Brad obstinate employees, undermining the production needs of Stacey's office?

❑ Yes ❑ No

Is Stacey deficient as a production supervisor?

❑ Yes ❑ No

Should any of these employees be given the heave-ho?

❑ Yes ❑ No

Amy and Brad are extremely effective members of the production staff, and Stacey directs the production department skillfully. Both Amy and Brad have determined their production peaks and valleys over the course of the normal workweek and schedule their regular work to take advantage of them. For all but urgent assignments, Stacey acknowledges her subordinates' ability to maintain high productivity by handling assignments on those days and at those hours. This achieves a relatively constant effort-to-task ratio. By tuning in to their natural cycles of productivity, the depart-ment's members form an efficient team.

Everyone Has Their Cycles

If you supervise others and want more assignments completed faster and more effectively, it's wise to give your good employees every opportunity to establish their own productivity cycles. Even if you report to others, you're well advised to see how you might implement this arrangement. In either case, it makes sense that good workers should schedule their assignments according to their productivity peaks and valleys whenever circumstances allow. It's more efficient and by far less stressful for all concerned.

Calming Concept

Enabling employees to respond to job-based demands according to their personal cycles of productivity results in higher job satisfaction and yields a greater long-range output.

Allowing productive people to follow their own schedules means they will be less fatigued and less stressed. It's draining to continually meet arbitrary deadlines. Productive employees that are allowed to pace themselves can accomplish more and can remain vibrant. They'll also take pride in consistently maintaining a high level of output.

Keep the Cycle Flexible

Productive employees have an internal "time grid" that charts their cycle of productivity even if no formal sketch or chart is ever made. When your best staff members tell you they'd "rather not handle the XYZ report right now" because they "can do a better job on it tomorrow morning, and the ABC assignment could be better undertaken now," believe them!

To help your productive employees recognize their cycles of productivity, try these two suggestions.

- Provide enough and varied assignments so the cycle can be used. If an employee only has one assignment, there's obviously little leeway in undertaking the assignment at the most personally opportune time. With numerous assignments, a productive employee can strategically arrange his/her schedule.

- Be flexible with deadlines whenever possible. Productive employees will make every effort to finish important jobs on time. Assignments of lesser importance will be finished as soon as possible.

The more flexibility you give productive employees to complete assignments, the better they can execute assignments in accordance with their cycle. More often than not, given flexible deadlines, productive employees will complete many assignments *sooner* than you anticipated.

Tampering with the Cycle

In the short run, good employees can "reprogram" their cycles to handle a crisis. If you need a report finished within four days, good employees will prepare themselves and will generate the requisite energy to successfully accomplish the task. Don't tamper with their cycles too often, however. You'll risk sending them into the "stress zone."

When All Else Fails

If you work in an organization that provides no good role models for you and, to top it off, your immediate boss is just plain nasty, things might become so stressful that you'd like to quit—and maybe tell your boss a thing or two. Before you storm into the boss's office, however, consider how you can make the situation work *for*, rather than *against* your best interests.

You can gain some long-term benefits from the experience of working for a tough boss. Knowing this can help shore up your withered work ethic. After all, if you can weather the rigors of working for an onerous boss, think how much easier it will be for you to work with others in the future. Then, too, you might be a better boss yourself someday for having had the experiences you're having now.

Stressbuster

If you can work with a nasty boss for a four- or six-month period or longer before leaving for good, do so. You might actually be strengthening your capabilities to work with a wide variety of people—including difficult ones—in the future.

Here's a sampling of other "successes" you might experience in one form or another for having worked with a difficult boss.

Consider The Bright Side

Regardless of the specifics of your work situation and the various reasons for your lack of satisfaction, one point remains clear: It probably could be worse. You could be working for someone who practices exploitation, is dishonest, makes exaggerated promises, or misrepresents the company. All things considered, your personal dissatisfaction with your work situation, particularly your relationship with your immediate boss, is probably tempered with positive as well as negative factors.

There's also the ultimate "worse" to consider: Toiling in a crummy situation is undesirable, but it's better than being unemployed, right? Statistics indicate that it's far easier to obtain new employment *while presently employed* than to land a job while unemployed.

Take the Opportunity to Toughen Up

If you make the best of a bad situation by learning to peacefully coexist with people you don't care for, your ability to deal with *all sorts* of people will improve. You'll learn how to successfully undertake tasks and responsibilities in difficult situations—an ability that will serve you well in other business and professional relationships.

Consider Your Boss's Perspective

Before you fly off the handle, take a moment to think about what might be behind your boss's attitude. You don't exactly know what it would be like to undertake each and every responsibility that confronts your boss, so perhaps you could try developing a sense of empathy. Maybe he or she has a reason for the behavior you find so difficult to work with.

Taking Comfort in Your Impending Departure

Your dissatisfaction in your job might be well founded. Let's assume you are totally in the right, and it's really only a matter of time before you're out the door. You just can't make that big break just yet.

You can always take comfort in knowing that you're leaving. If you've ever debated about leaving a position for months or even years, you know the utter relief you feel once the decision is finally made. There's now a light at the end of the tunnel. The daily trials and personal conflicts you've sought to minimize are now, at least, tolerable. As long as you're still employed in "doomsville," however, commit to doing a good job and to upholding the good name of your organization. To do anything else would be a strong reason to lose respect for yourself.

Rising Above It All

If you know it's only a matter of time before you leave your current position, stay professional and take your experiences in stride. Don't waste your energy rehashing past dissatisfactions, evening up the score, or trying to fulfill your personal sense of justice. This is a waste of time, regardless of any minor satisfaction. The long-term personal satisfaction of getting revenge is nil, and the possibility of such strategies backfiring is high.

Sharpen Your Diplomatic Skills

A far better choice is to use this time constructively. Making do where you are, even though you'd prefer to be elsewhere, helps you refine your diplomatic skills even if you're not aware of it. In a work environment, a little experience with the art of diplomacy can go a long way.

Just ask Andrew Carnegie, the multimillionaire steel magnate. Carnegie observed that he could easily hire the functional or technical skills necessary for any business venture. The one skill for which he would (and did) pay most dearly, however, was the ability to deal with people.

The Best Companies to Work For

The top business organizations and industries to work for generally recognize that the needs of their work forces are changing. These organizations also know that retaining good employees today means offering them the kinds of programs and benefits that make for vibrant, balanced workers.

The Wave of the Future?

Top executives at E.I. Dupont de Nemours and Company, for example, have developed "work-life programs" designed to help their employees handle issues such as elder care, child care, and other demands of holding a job and raising a family in contemporary society. Enlightened companies acknowledge that pressures away from work have a definite impact on employee productivity, so they design programs and benefit plans accordingly.

At Dupont, staff members who participate in three or more work-life programs report that they would "go the extra mile for Dupont." Observers both inside and outside the company agree that such employees are better able to approach their jobs with creativity, energy, and a sense of urgency.

We All Benefit

To be sure, benefit initiatives such as those offered by Dupont are business-driven. They're based on improving productivity and competitiveness rather than on some squishy notion of "social responsibility." Meanwhile, the end result is that the company becomes more socially responsible.

Companies deciding to employ work-life programs need to assess the particular circumstances their employees face. If your organization is progressive, thank your lucky stars. They value you as an employee and want to make sure you achieve results while maintaining balance and peace of mind. If you're not working in such an organization, you have two basic options.

1. Seek to initiate change in your current environment. Perhaps you can get top management to notice the long-term benefits of installing work-life programs.
2. Find employment with a company that already has instituted such programs (albeit this might be a long shot). You'll then be able to meet high expectations without experiencing diminishing returns.

Where do you find such paragon companies? Since the late 1980s, several books have been published on the subject such as *The 100 Best Companies to Work For* and *The 100 Best Companies to Sell For. The Best Jobs in America for Parents*, by Susan Dynerman and Lynn Hayes, shows you how to go about searching for a good, flexible job whether you're an attorney who wants to work a reduced schedule of "only" 40 hours a week or a pair of secretaries who'd like to share a job. It also outlines negotiating methods that ensure you get the kind of job you want and explains how to make sure everyone (especially you) is satisfied once you get it.

The Least You Need to Know

- As more and faster tools of technology are developed, you are asked to do more.
- Your own expectations in terms of acquiring goods and services also have increased markedly.
- To flourish in an environment in which you're asked to do more with less, treat yourself well and maintain a healthy perspective.
- Emotional exhaustion often is the first of the three characteristics of burnout to appear. One of the best safeguards for avoiding burnout is to accept input and advice from trusted others.
- Recognizing your own productivity cycle and the cycles of your subordinates is the key to developing an efficient and low-stress work environment.

Chapter 7

Get Out of Jail Free

In This Chapter

- Coping with the onset of techno-stress
- Taming the telephone
- Claiming a little professional distance from your stressors
- Shhh! A little quiet, please

Let's go back in time. Grok, your typical Cro-Magnon, is exploring the far side of a hill. He finds some caves and, upon entering, discovers some untouched walls. He gathers up some art supplies—sticks, stones, mud, red clay, and anything else he can find—and starts to create a colorful mural. Hmm, what can we paint today? How about a hunting scene or maybe a dance? Or maybe some of the sacred animals? This is going to be one of the better murals! There's nobody around, oodles of time, and lots of space on the cave wall.

Suddenly, a pterodactyl flies by and drops off a message. It's from Mamuk, his common-law wife. Hmm, wonder what she wants? Let's see, she wants him to get some of those elderberries on the far side of the hill, some more kindling, and oh, try to get home early today?

Today, interruptions like the message from Mamuk come two or three at a time. The automatic, electronic gadgets of today present new paths to stress. Faxes, e-mail, voice mail, and (jeepers, creepers) beepers ensure that anyone can be reached anytime. In this chapter, you'll learn how to use the same technology that exposes you to all types of disruptions to create some sanctuary for yourself.

The Information Lockup: Paralysis by Distraction

It's not simply your perception—more potential disrupters exist today than ever before. We are the most distracted generation in history. By 2010, technical knowledge will multiply at a frightening pace, doubling perhaps weekly. As technology infiltrates every aspect of life, it's easy to understand why some people view the onslaught with trepidation. Will anything be left of the world we knew? Will there remain any semblance of the privacy we once enjoyed?

Tranquillity Terminology

The **Luddites** were a group of people who smashed machines during the early days of the industrial revolution. They feared the machines would steal their jobs and destroy their lives.

The *Luddites* among us, and they're growing in number, want to smash PCs, stamp pagers and cell phones into the ground, and rip out Internet connections. All these technological intrusions, they feel, are destroying the quality of our lives. Keeping it all in perspective, however, technology has both simplified and complicated life.

Question: What's it called when you make a telephone call, encounter an automated reception system, and have to keep pushing buttons to climb the options menu, only to discover that the option you want isn't reachable and you can't even get to a human operator?

Answer: Phone mail jail. An inane voice-mail system with redundant messages and endless options is merely one of many examples of technology run amok.

Today you can send messages and information around the globe with the push of a button. At the same time, however, you're often prevented from reaching others because of technology's inherent capability for fouling up what it was designed to improve. Take the voice-mail system. It was designed to speed up access to commonly requested information. The "menu trees" have become so complicated, however, people often hang up in frustration long before they get the answers they need.

Theodore Roszak, Ph.D., a professor of history at California State University and the author of *The Cult of Information,* observes that "data merchants have shamefully promoted the importance of bits of information …." Paradoxically, "master ideas," he observes—the moral, philosophical, and religious teachings that are the underpinnings of our humanity—are not based on information at all.

What can he mean? Take the statement, "All men are created equal." This is a philosophical truism widely accepted by millions if not billions of people around the globe. But it's not based on "information"—on empirical data. It's a conceptual truth, and no amount of simple factoids can add up to such a powerful proposition.

Calming Concept

In the affairs of humanity, that which is universally held to be true is the product of original, creative human thought. It is not the by-product of a hardware system's configuration or any form of data processing.

When and Where to be Available

This much I know is true—no one works effectively when they're continually interrupted by faxes, beepers, phone calls, and office visitors. The few simple principles explored here will enable you to stay connected, to stay productive, and to keep your stress at a manageable level.

Telephone—For Your Convenience, Not Theirs

The foremost tool of communication among people at a distance is the telephone (cell phones included!). It has become all-pervasive, and it's capacity for causing stress through interruptions has increased dramatically. Depending on the flexibility you have in your current position, I suggest implementing the following suggestions to control telephone interruptions.

- Carve out at least one or two hours a day and let it be known that you are not accepting calls. If you have an answering machine, simply record a message that says "I'll be available today from one to three," or "I'll be away from the phone from nine to eleven," or something similar that gets your point across. The same goes for recording a voice-mail message.
- If you have a receptionist, stipulate that you're only accepting calls during certain hours of the day. He or she should take messages at all other times (except in cases of emergency).
- If you have a cell phone, turn off your call-forwarding for several hours each day. Ditto for those of you with pagers. Instruct people who page you most frequently that you want no interruptions for a few hours.

Many people worry that carving out a few hours when they can't be reached by phone will cause problems. Maybe a would-be caller will be upset! That's unlikely. If I happen to discover that Mr. Higgins likes to be telephone-free from 8 A.M. to 10 A.M., I don't get into a huff. Instead, I make a point to call after 10 A.M. I don't think any less of him because he carves out this time for himself, and I don't see it as an impediment to getting in touch with him. Indeed, I'm glad to know the best time to call because I want him to be receptive when I reach him.

Here are some other phone tips that can reduce stress.

Stress Alert

Interruptions don't have to actually be major disruptions of your time. All they need to do is break your concentration. Loud but avoidable distracting sounds such as your phone bell (when you've set it for your answering machine to pick up) can be just as bad as the phone call itself. Turn the ringer off if you want some uninterrupted time!

- If your work allows it, avoid Caller ID unless you know you can resist the temptation to spend time tracking down all the "mystery" numbers that might ring through. I've held off getting Caller ID myself because, for the brief time I had it, I spent too much time on trivial pursuits such as trying to determine who called and didn't leave a message.
- Decrease the phone volume to its lowest practical setting. The simple jangling (or beeping or buzzing) of the phone can be irritating whether you answer it or not. But make sure the setting is right for your workplace. If you're in a noisy machine shop and it's your responsibility to get to the phone, you might need the volume turned up all the way. If you work in an office and need only the most subtle ring, beep, alarm, or chime summoning you to the phone, you can turn it way down. (Inexpensive devices also are available that provide a flashing light in place of a sound when a phone call comes your way.)
- If you have two lines, dedicate one as your inbound line. It's usually best to use the one on your business card, stationery, or literature as the inbound line. Use the second line for outbound calls. Why? This keeps you from missing calls while you're on the line. It also enables you to monitor calls and to keep working, if you want.

  Most importantly, it enables you to offer a measured response to the calls you receive. Often it's best not to receive calls when they first come in. You might already be on another line with a client or a customer, and this means you won't be free to consider your response to the new call carefully. It's better to let the incoming line's answering machine take a message so you can call back. Sure, it's more costly to call someone back long distance, but the inconvenience is offset by your ability to handle your first party's request and then plan what you're going to say to the incoming callers when you're ready to deal with them.
- Avoid sleeping with your home telephone by your head. I know people who think there has to be a telephone in their bedroom. The usual argument people offer is that there might be an emergency call late at night. They have an aging

mother, a teenage son, and so on. But here's the issue: Such calls rarely, if ever, actually come. You have to weigh 10 or 15 years of good sleep versus being able to field that one emergency call that might never come in. Most of the time, those midnight calls aren't emergencies at all—they're wrong numbers!

- When you're on the road, unplug the phone in your hotel room (see Chapter 16, "Mastering Your Environment," for more on this).

One Call at a Time

Of all the modern telephone technology, *call-waiting* is probably the least productive, the most offensive, and the most stress-inducing service currently available. Do not subscribe to it—now or *ever*! No matter what the phone company says, it does *not* provide a convenience, and it is *not* professional.

I've spoken to top professionals in many fields, and they tell me they would not consider using call-waiting professionally. Why? When you use call-waiting, you're in essence telling *both* of your callers that they're not important and that you're not resourceful. Each caller on the line is fully aware that you're keeping your options open and might drop them whenever somebody more important calls. Call-waiting also is a dead give-away that you don't have a receptionist or the proper telephone configuration in your home or office to treat parties with any semblance of respect.

The most common argument people make to justify call-waiting is something like this, "I have a teenage daughter who will be calling around this time, and I don't want her to get a constant busy signal if I'm on the phone with someone." Fine. If you receive a call around the time you're expecting another call, keep your conversation short.

> **Tranquillity Terminology**
>
> **Call-waiting** is a technological innovation that caters to our fears of "missing out." While you're on the phone with a client (or a friend or a colleague), anyone else who chooses that moment to call you interrupts your current conversation. Speaking on behalf of your interrupted caller, "How rude!"

Employ Call-Forwarding with Prudence

Having the ability to receive a critical call when you're out of your office *can* be a blessing. You only want to use call-forwarding, however, when it's appropriate both for you and for any other parties with whom you'll be interacting when the call comes through. Otherwise, the interruption caused by call-forwarding can be as intrusive and disrespectful as call-waiting. On a more personal note, call-forwarding means you can never really escape the phone. That alone just adds to your stress.

And I Was Just About to Sink that Putt

If you're chained to your beeper on constant call, I feel for you. Doctors and emergency-service workers, among a few others, simply have no choice. But beepers are everywhere now. High-powered executives, low-powered executives, and all manner of professionals in between seem to be sporting a beeper.

The onslaught of beepers largely is analogous to the introduction of the PC, 20 or so years ago. Whereas only a few people had them at first, it suddenly became impossible to imagine a household without one. People were buying PCs when all they needed was a word processor. Same thing occurred with the beeper. People who had no need to be constantly on call suddenly felt the need to be reachable even while they were just taking a 15 minute walk to the corner store. Most beeper calls are unimportant, however. Every time you field an unnecessary message via your beeper, you add equally unnecessary stress to your life.

And so it goes .... Whenever a new technology is introduced, its overuse comes soon afterward, followed by a long-term era of abuse. (You see this even with PCs. How many people *still* only use them to type personal correspondence?) When it comes to breaking the beeper habit, my strongest recommendation is this: If you have a receptionist who can field your calls, the receptionist should be among the *extremely few* people who have your beeper number. He or she should get in touch with you only when it's necessary.

Calming Concept

In these go-go-go days, it's hard to imagine being out of touch with your boss or your customers. After all, someone else might take advantage of your absence, right? Not necessarily. Unless you're employed in one of the few fields in which round-the-clock, on-call availability is a justifiable necessity, you have every right to insist on maintaining private time as an assertion of self-respect.

Being on-call around the clock is highly stressful to many people. Outside of perhaps the president of the United States or a high-ranking diplomat, there are few professions in which you have to be reachable *all* the time. If your job requires you to wear a beeper and be on call, at least recognize the importance of being beeper-free every once in a while. Even brain surgeons, chiefs of police, heads of universities, and other high-profile professionals can carve out one day a week, or three or four days a month, when they are not electronically chained to the world.

On the Road Again

If you have children, a car phone or mobile phone (also called cellular or cell phones) can enable you to stay in touch at critical times during the day. Some cell phones also can double as a security device. They allow for speed-dialing, have some type of anti-theft alarm, and can even dial your home or office when an intruder attempts to make a call. Many offer wide display screens (brightly lit for easy use at night), speed-dialing, speed-redialing, and one-touch dialing. They *do*, admittedly, provide certain advantages.

When you add a cell phone to your automobile or start carrying one around with you, what happens that perhaps you *don't* want? Here are a few consequences of keeping a cell phone in your car.

- Anyone can reach you at any time.
- One of your last sanctuaries—your car during your commute—can be easily disturbed.
- The unexpected bleat of the phone could startle you, causing an accident.
- While talking on the phone, you might become distracted and thus begin driving less safely.
- Your cell phone causes added expense as you engage in unnecessary conversations.
- You're beset with another invoice to examine at the end of the month and another check to write.

For the purpose of keeping your stress level in check, use your cell phone for outbound calls only. At least then you're in control. As with a beeper, how often do you urgently need to be contacted while you're motoring down the highway or eating in a restaurant?

All the Spam You Can Stand

The telephone is but one of the intrusive technologies introduced to modern life. With the growth of America Online, other commercial online services, and Internet navigation software, the use of e-mail has proliferated to the point where many people log on to find dozens, if not hundreds, of e-mail messages per day. That would be great if all the messages were worthwhile. But that just isn't the case.

Many companies are in business to send you (and a few million others) unsolicited e-mail, promoting products and services you never even heard of. On the Internet, this is known as spamming—using

Stressbuster

You always have the option of getting a private e-mail address, one you dispense with great reserve to maintain a bastion in which you can receive high-quality messages—and not too many of them.

the Internet for promotional purposes—and it is widely frowned upon. These companies and other junk e-mailers can quickly make checking your e-mail inbox a high-stress event. Any message that has one or more of the following characteristics might qualify as junk e-mail. Be wary of spending your time on messages that

- Contain an unfamiliar e-mail address or one with symbols, Xs, or unlikely letter combinations.
- Appear in all capital letters.
- Are prefaced with junk openers such as "FYI" or "First, some background."
- Take longer than a minute to read.
- State that the message is being sent in compliance with some arcane or bogus reference to legislation.
- Appear to have arrived in your inbox by mistake.
- Refer to deals that are too good to be true.

Once you get rid of all such unsolicited messages, the chances are pretty good that what's left might actually be worth reading.

Faxing Can Be Taxing

E-mail's older cousin, the fax, is still alive and kicking in business communications. When it comes to fax machines, my personal pet peeve is the extensive waste of paper because most senders aren't clever enough to submit a concise fax. This means I get much more verbiage than I want or need to plow through and a stack of unnecessary paper I've got to store, recycle, or otherwise dispose of. Do you really *need* one full page announcing that a fax is coming, a second one saying that this represents page two of three, and a third that simply contains a one-inch paragraph at the top of the page? I think not.

You can't control the length of faxes being sent to you, but you do have the ability, to pare them down once they've come through. This cuts down on the paper you need to deal with as well as the space they take up in your desk or file cabinet.

When you receive a three-page fax, but the vital information you need is in one paragraph on page three along with a 3" × 3" square on page two with the sender's information, retain what you need and chuck the rest. A single file folder with the pared down, relevant faxes you receive helps keep your desk neat and you in control—and less stressed.

How overwhelming can faxes get? Consider this: Employees at one division of American Express had to field faxed requests for information at a rate of one almost every couple minutes. That was bad enough, but each fax represented another five or ten minutes worth of work—fulfilling the request, assembling the information, and getting back to the party who sent the fax. One supervisor remarked that her staff wanted to "rip the fax lines out of the wall."

American Express is not alone. A solution to the problem is *fax-on-demand,* a system in which callers are given a menu of information that they can receive at any time of day by simply pressing a few digits on their phone.

Dan Poynter in Santa Barbara, California maintains an elaborate fax-on-demand system. Dan is an author, publisher, and seminar presenter on book publishing and promotion. In fact, he has a fax-on-demand number that will automatically send your fax machine information about the *topic* of faxes-on-demand.

The beauty of fax-on-demand is that you can incorporate hundreds of documents into a file and assign each one its own telephone extension, thereby cutting your fax-related workload at least in half and your fax-related stress immeasurably. (Another way to make information available to your consumers is to put it on a Web site and encourage people to visit. But not everyone has Internet access—yet—so the fax will be with us for years to come.)

Tranquillity Terminology

Fax-on-demand is a system that unites telephone, computer, and fax technology in such a way that a caller can simply dial into a voice-mail system, select an informational topic of interest from a menu, and—with the touch of a few buttons—set up an automated info-retrieval system that faxes back the data requested with no human customer-service intervention.

The Sound of Silence

Let's face it. Throughout your entire career, there will be no one as concerned about it as you. As you saw in Chapters 4 and 5, you must continually take charge of your career if you want to make sure you advance at a comfortable and rewarding pace. One key way to achieve this is to establish mental and physical sanctuaries for yourself—sanctuaries to which you can turn on a daily, weekly, and monthly basis.

After all, who can do their best thinking when they're surrounded by noise and interruptions? Are you able to achieve dramatic insights when people are knocking on your door every couple minutes? Can you plan a merger or acquisition, a new product or service line, a new branch or store location, or any other major undertaking in the midst of high rabble? Few people can.

Gordon Hempton has recorded wildlife around the world. He's also a staunch advocate of quiet. He believes the environment is being degraded by noise and that each of us needs a quiet place for a little time each day to truly relax, to lower stress levels, and to hear the world.

Stress Alert

Most people do their best thinking when it's quiet. Yet, in contemporary society, the sounds of silence are elusive.

Years ago, Hempton identified 20 locations in the state of Washington that had more than 15 minutes of silence at a time. He returned five years later to find that 17 of the 20 had been infected by noise pollution such that the noise-free interval had decreased to less than three minutes. Only three locations still had noise-free intervals of 15 minutes or more.

Even some national parks don't represent a haven for quiet anymore, with bulldozers, jackhammers, chain saws, small planes and helicopters flying over hourly, car and other engine noises, and, oh yes, loud campers.

When surrounded by noise and other impediments that your organization or your work setting impose on you, how do you create sanctuaries for yourself so you can do your best work and achieve breakthrough or conceptual thinking? How can you be your most productive self with the least amount of wear and tear on your being? Here are some hints to make it happen.

- Barricade yourself in a room and post warning signs.
- In advance, identify the places where you will be able to work steadily when you choose to, such as the company conference room. You'll know when you've found the right spot. You will feel good, productive, and unhurried.
- Choose the far cubbyhole on the third floor of the library.

The notion of becoming the master of your environment is examined in greater detail in Chapter 16, "Mastering Your Environment." For now, suffice it to say that the observations of Alvin Toffler ring true in office suites worldwide. The contemporary workplace is a terrible place in which to get work done. Nevertheless, stress is a response to your surroundings, not the surroundings themselves.

If you feel that your office and the surrounding technology are deleterious to productivity and personal balance, let any disturbances hereafter serve as a reminder that, although you can't control everything, there are ways to turn situations to your advantage.

The Least You Need to Know

- Although every new technology offers both benefits and detriments, it's up to you to make the new technology work *for* you rather than against you.
- To reduce telephone-induced stress, set aside an hour or two each day when you will not receive phone calls.
- Leave the beeper behind when you can and keep your call-forwarding to a minimum.
- Most people need quiet to do their best work or conceptual thinking.

Chapter 8

Dismantling Workplace Distractions

In This Chapter

- Dealing with disruptions
- Systematizing interruptions to stay in control
- Timing isn't everything, but it's a lot
- Mental methods for reducing distractions

Early one morning you're ready to start work when your PC monitor starts fading. It flickers back on and then goes off for good. Instantly, your frustration level zooms up. Certainly, you'll be delayed in whatever you're going to do that day. You call your company's tech support staff. They can send someone up in 20 minutes to fix or replace your monitor. You fume a little in frustration while you wait.

Stop and think a minute! This time is valuable, but it's not a lifetime. Once it's over, you won't even remember this as a significant event.

Nevertheless, this incident is frustrating. After all, before it happened, you had a good notion of what you wanted to accomplish that morning. Waiting for tech support wasn't among the activities you'd planned. In the last chapter, you learned how to minimize distractions caused by communications devices. This chapter helps you deal with annoyances in your work life.

Disruption Happens

Suppose you just finished a business trip to the West Coast, and it went rather well. As you're waiting for your plane in the Los Angeles International Airport (you already have your boarding pass), you realize that you've lost your wallet—or perhaps it was stolen. You attempt to retrace your steps to see if you can find it.

You go back to the ticket counter, but they haven't seen it. At the lost-and-found office, you are told that the wallet might show up anywhere from a half hour to a day later. You leave your name, address, phone, and fax number and leave the office with few expectations that they'll be able to help.

Luckily, you didn't lose anything vital. Your wallet only contained about $11 in cash, one credit card, your driver's license, and a bank card. You still have your plane ticket and other valuables, so you'll still get home on time. For now, you don't need your credit card, and you don't need cash. No one can use the bank card because they don't have your personal identification number. You're not sure what someone might do with your license, but it won't affect you. You've already taken steps to cancel your credit card, so you're protected there.

But knowing all this doesn't turn down your frustration level. Why? It's simple. You've let yourself skip ahead to worry about how this loss will play out over the next several days.

- You'll have to make a visit to the motor vehicle department to get a new license.
- You'll have to wait a couple days until the credit card company sends you a new card with a new number.
- You'll have to make contact with all the places that already have your credit card number so they can bill you automatically on a monthly basis while you change over to the new account number.
- You'll have to get a new bank card, so it won't be easy to withdraw cash for a couple days.
- Oh yes, you'll also have to replace the photo of your spouse and child. Do you even know where the negative is?

Anxiety Antidote

You can't plan for every unexpected contingency, but you *can* recognize that what throws most people is the element of surprise. Learning to be flexible—to take things as they come—makes you much less likely to be "thrown for a loop" when the unexpected happens.

Losing your wallet certainly represents a disruption of activities, although the mere incident itself is not particularly upsetting. Rather, it is the interruption of your routine and the resultant newly imposed activities that bother you. It will take some recovery time to get over being distracted by something you hadn't counted on. By understanding this concept, you'll be better prepared to take the interruption in stride and to work through the consequences.

Interruption Corruption

What would you nominate as the most significant workplace stressor? Of more than 15 workplace stressors identified by managers, simple interruptions came in first on a list that included demands on time made by others, work load, organizational politics, responsibility for subordinates, firing someone, reprimanding someone, balancing work and personal life, dealing with upper management, conducting performance reviews, and trying to work within a budget.

A study conducted by *Industrial Engineer* magazine revealed that the average interruption sustained by a manager lasted from 6 to 9 minutes. That, in itself, doesn't seem so bad, but consider that the average time it took the managers to recover from interruptions was from 3 to 23 minutes.

Calming Concept

Interruptions aren't always avoidable, but you can learn to turn them to your advantage. Treat each interpersonal encounter as an opportunity to learn as well as to teach. If your subordinates are always turning to you for advice or information, for example, this might mean that your company is less than successful in giving them what they need to know. Is there a workplace innovation you might suggest to rectify the situation?

You don't have to be a math whiz to determine that it only takes a couple of interruptions an hour to consume the whole hour and a couple of interruptions a day to throw off your entire day. Is it any wonder that professionals find interruptions the most stressful aspect of their jobs?

Managing to Be Interrupted Less!

Does the phrase "interruption management" sound like an oxymoron to you? That's only because you haven't had a chance to give it much thought (perhaps because you're always being interrupted!). Consider the following story:

> A supervisor in Minnesota had six employees. These employees came to him with questions every couple hours. It seemed harmless enough, but look at how it built

up. If each employee asked a single question every two hours, he asked an average of 4 questions each day. Multiply these 4 questions by six employees, and you get 24 questions a day or 120 interruptions each week. Suddenly, it becomes clear that the manager's work was interrupted three times each hour for every hour in a 40-hour week!

If you throw in how long it took the manager to recover from each interruption, you can see that his whole day—his *every* day—was consumed by them!

What's a manager to do? When I consulted with this manager, I suggested a simple system to help him cope with the interruptions and to regain control of his time. I called it the J-4 system ("J" for Jeff).

The J-4 Way to Interruption Reduction

Simply put, the J-4 system calls for you to assign the types of questions you normally receive to one of four categories of manageability, as follows.

- **J-1 distractions**. Questions in this category have already been answered in print somewhere within the company—in the policy manual, perhaps, or in widely circulated reports or memos. These questions don't need a personal reply from a supervisor. Employees can simply be told, "Please don't concern me with these kinds of questions; review the manual (memos, reports) you already have to find the answer for yourself."
- **J-2 distractions**. Many questions can easily be answered by a peer or a worker in another department (the bookkeeper or personnel officer, for example) and don't require the input of a manager. As soon as you identify such a query, you can simply refer the employee to the appropriate person, or you can specify that "all health-plan questions go to Mary in the personnel department."
- **J-3 distractions**. These questions need only a straightforward yes or no answer. They require interaction with the supervisor but not much—just a quick phone call or a buzz on the intercom.
- **J-4 distractions**. These are the questions that *do* require a supervisor's input. The supervisor has to and wants to answer them.

Classify, Classify, Classify

Of all the questions that typically interrupt your day, how many are the J-4 level of importance? Think back to the manager I mentioned earlier. If you assume each person asked him two J-4 questions per day, this would total 60 interruptions each week. This cuts the number of interruptions in half! In real life, he actually achieved an even greater reduction in his interruptions. More importantly, he was able to better use his time and to reduce his level of stress. So can you!

Multitasking: Good For Machines, Bad for Humans

Do you work in a position in which constant interruption is the norm? Are you in charge of a switchboard, for example, a customer-service counter, a take-out lunch counter, or a taxi service? In such cases, you have to learn to practice the art of doing one thing at a time. (For a complete treatment of the subject, you might want to read my book *The Complete Idiot's Guide to Managing Your Time*.)

I wonder how many automobile accidents and mishaps can be attributed to people attempting to do two things at once—put on makeup, shave, eat, smoke, talk on the phone, or listen to 200-decibel music?

Stressbuster

No matter what your job, prioritization of tasks is one key to reducing stress. Learn to evaluate the tasks you face in order of urgency or importance. Once your priorities are sorted out, your path is clear. You can handle the most important tasks first and take on the rest as time allows.

The Dangers of Doing Too Much at Once

You do have the capability to safely engage in more than one activity at a time. Psychologists tell us, however, that only one activity can command your *sharp attention* at any given moment. Everything else gets a much lesser degree of your focus. So you never want to talk on a cell phone (even the hands-free variety) while driving. Crash statistics bear this out.

From the standpoint of managing stress, engaging in multiple activities makes a stressful life even more stressful. That's true not only in the office but when you try to combine work and personal time as well. It ruins vacations and diminishes the positive effects of leisure time. If you're a high achiever, it also can cripple your productivity.

Rather than trying to do too much at once, you're better off keeping your focus on the task at hand. This is the key to keeping your stress level in check, despite the number of tasks that compete for your attention. Don't waste time or energy lamenting over something that happened in the past—even if it happened just moments ago. And don't indulge in anxiety about what's coming up. Simply focus on the present.

Tranquillity Terminology

Sharp attention is the close, careful attention you pay to the details of a task. You can't spread such close focus to several things at once.

One Thing at a Time

Regardless of how quickly you proceed from task to task, you'll do your best work on *all* your projects if you give your complete and undivided attention to the individual task currently at hand, for however brief a time that might be. In other words, develop your concentration so that, even if you only have 10 to 15 seconds to focus on what confronts you, those 10 or 15 seconds are highly directed to the task at hand. Let me give you an example:

> You're sitting by the airport gate waiting to board when your flight is suddenly canceled. A swarm of angry customers surrounds the gate agent looking to quickly reroute their passages. How does the gate agent handle the throng? One passenger at a time, intently focusing on that passenger's previous itinerary, looking at the computer monitor to see what options are available, and making arrangements that satisfy the customer's needs. Only then does he turn to handle the next customer's complaint. Whether it takes one minute per customer or five, a skilled gate agent stays relatively unflapped.

What's Worth Your Precious Attention?

If you have five tasks confronting you and you're stymied as to how to proceed, what is the fastest and easiest way to tackle the five tasks and keep your stress in check? The answer is to prioritize! Put the tasks in order of importance and handle them one at a time. Child's play, you say—anyone could have figured that out. Anyone could—but hardly anyone does.

Calming Concept

Handling one customer or tackling one project at a time rubs up against the very nature of modern society, which seems to demand that you do as many things at once as you can. The modern-day work ethic seems to be telling you to just get it all done *now*. Never mind how stressful it is—jump on your horse and ride off in all directions.

The modern tendency to try to do everything at once turns up everywhere. Consider your last visit to your health club, for example. You no doubt saw lots of people getting on the stair climber while wearing headphones. They're listening to their favorite tunes, a lecture, or perhaps simply the radio. What they're *not* doing, however, is tuning into the rhythm—and therefore the relaxation—of their physical exercise.

They're not focusing on the moment. Some people take it even further. I once saw a headphones-wearing woman get on the stair-climber and then whip out a book to read. All she needed to bump her multitasking into truly high gear was to take a call on her cell phone as well.

Would you surmise then that, back at the office, our multitasking stair-climber tackles tasks one at a time? Probably not. But she's not alone. Management sage Dr. Peter Drucker once conducted his own survey of top executives. He found that they, too, attempt to do too much, resulting in a loss of productivity and an increase in stress.

Drowning in Paper

Another key source of distraction can be found in the sheer volume of paper that confronts us all. Personal computers, fax machines, laser printers, and personal copiers combine to produce a larger outpouring of paper to inundate your life than anyone could have predicted 20 to 25 years ago. Paper gluts the offices of industry, government, professionals, retailers, you name it.

F.D.R.'s Personal Paperwork Reduction Act

Is all this paper really necessary? I once heard an anecdote, the veracity of which I cannot verify, attributed to Franklin Delano Roosevelt, president of the United States from 1933 to 1945.

Supposedly, F.D.R. commissioned a special task force to determine the answer to a question critical to his administration. The task force met for a period of eight days and generated a voluminous report. The task force spokesperson brought the report to F.D.R., who was busy at the time. He told the messenger, "Please, boil it down." The spokesperson left, returning in a couple hours with a slimmer version of the report.

F.D.R. looked at it and said, "No, I mean *boil it down.*" Again the spokesperson left, this time returning in about an hour with a concise, executive summary of eight pages.

Even that, however, was not enough. Two more times, F.D.R. was presented with an ever-decreasing handful of papers, and two more times he asked for greater concision. When the aide returned with a single paragraph, F.D.R. finally said, "Can you give it to me in a sentence?"

The moral of this story? Everything—and I mean *everything*—can be communicated more succinctly and with greater precision if you try.

Stressbuster

Drowning in a sea of long-winded memos? Just for laughs, take the next half dozen you get and "boil them down" to their informational core. You'll probably find that most can be summed up in 20 words or less.

Pulling the Plug on the Paperwork Overflow

How can you do your part to cut back on the volume of paper you cope with regularly?

- Quickly reduce books to their essence by scanning the entire book. Copy the key pages you want to retain along with the title page and the table of contents. Recycle the book when you're done.
- With other printed information such as catalogs, fliers, and brochures, scan them quickly, break out the few scraps of information relevant to your needs, and recycle the rest.
- If you don't have time right now to assess incoming papers, books, catalogs, or brochures, at least get them off your desk. Set up a drawer to temporarily house them *out of sight* (where they're out of mind). When you have time, go back to the drawer, take out the items, and as F.D.R. would say, "boil them down!"
- For each item of paper that crosses your desk, ask yourself the following questions:

  "What is the issue behind the document?"

  "Should I have received this at all?"

  "How else can this be handled? Can I delegate this?"

  "Will it matter if I don't handle it at all?"

  "Can I file it under Things to Review Next Month?"

Why is cutting back on the paper you face each day a stress-reducing strategy? Because the volume itself can be overwhelming—and because it's hard to find the few valuable nuggets of information you need when they're buried in all the extraneous paper that usually surrounds them.

Timing Is (Nearly) Everything

If workplace distractions still seem insurmountable even though you've taken to heart the words here and in Chapter 7, you might need to examine the concept of timing. In other words, sometimes you can cut back on the destructive effects of distractions by simply adjusting the timing of what you do.

Getting Up with the Early Birds...

Could you, would you adjust your schedule so you go to bed earlier, wake up earlier, and get to the office before everyone else? Many top executives do, and they remark that this is one of the bright spots of their day when they get the most done. In the early morning, the phones haven't started ringing, and no one even knows they're in the office, and there's no one to wander by "just to chat."

Calming Concept

We're all supposed to know our job inside out, current events (political *and* economic), the top 10 pop culture hits (movie, music, and whatever else), and the tag lines from last night's popular sitcom. Trying to keep up on all of this can make you crazy. If you really *must* stay up-to-date this way, just ask your more bleary-eyed colleagues around the water cooler. They'll be happy to fill you in and you won't have to stay up nights, personally getting the scoop from Leno or Letterman.

This kind of schedule adjustment might require a concerted effort to change a long-standing habit. America has become a nation of night owls, so you're probably staying up too late. (I'll discuss the role of sleep in Chapter 13, "Running on Empty.") It can be done, however. Before the 1960s, the concept of staying up late to catch the news and the late-night talk shows was unheard of. Then Steve Allen and Jack Paar became the first in a long line of talk show hosts (the most famous being Johnny Carson) who induced an entire nation to stay up later than it was accustomed to.

Today, Leno and Letterman are battling it out every night, and they're followed by all the "late-late" talk shows that go well into the morning hours. Is it any wonder, then, that so many millions of people drag themselves into the office in the morning? Where is it written that you have to be among the sleep-deprived? Turning in earlier can make a difference in your stress level, and all you'll miss is a couple of jokes.

...Or Staying Until the Cows Have Gone Home

You might not be a morning person—millions of people aren't. If you're not at your best during the early part of the day, you might want to reconsider your departure time from work instead. If you customarily leave between 4:30 and 5:30 in the afternoon, only to fight your way home in that moving parking lot they call a freeway, perhaps it would be better to leave at 6 or 6:30 P.M. after everyone else has taken off. Then, when you actually *do* head for home, you'll have missed the worst of the rush-hour traffic. You might actually manage to get in that extra hour of work and still get home close to your usual time!

Of course, we don't want to confuse the issues. In earlier chapters, I discussed the vital importance of not overworking, and I stressed that you shouldn't stay late. That's still good advice as a general rule. If, however, in your particular instance—based on your job, where you live, with whom you live, your commuting distance, and your mode of transportation—it makes sense for you to work a later shift, by all means go for it. Just don't overload your day with working hours. If you leave an hour later in the evening, go in an hour later as well.

Shake Me, Wake Me

To make sure you have many viable options, here are more ways to shake up your routine and whip distractions so you can work productively with less stress and feel good about yourself and your career.

Find workplace alternatives to your office. When you change your scenery, you open up new vistas and escape interruptions. The anti-stress benefits are immense and immediate. When you do this for certain tasks (especially tasks that require creative thinking), you'll be more productive than ever.

Let your mail sit for a day or two. Postpone tearing through all your mail. We tend to place an immediacy upon things that often is unnecessary. Most communications are not so urgent that you need to attend to them on the very day you receive them. When you're away for a few days and have several days of mail to plow through, often you're more efficient at handling it *because* of the increased volume!

If possible, hold all calls for a day or two. Think of it as if you're on vacation and are unable to be reached for a couple days. Would the world come to an end? Probably not. You don't have to respond immediately to every call. When you hold your calls for a few hours—or for an entire day—you open up a block of time so you can get things done in a way that would be impossible if you were preoccupied with answering calls. You don't want to be totally inaccessible all the time, but you can coach potential callers to adapt to your schedule (see Chapter 7).

Anxiety Antidote

I can proofread much better on the porch of my house than while sitting at my desk. Identify places that are welcome retreats where you can go and work—a library, a park, even a shopping center.

Mind Over Distractions

Even if you can't put an end to the distractions that occur during your day, there are simple mental techniques you can use to diminish their damaging effects. Dr. Wayne Dyer, author of *Your Erroneous Zones*, *Pulling Your Own Strings*, *You'll See It When You Believe It*, and a variety of other self-help books, recalls an instance when he was tranquilly looking out at the scenery, and a gentleman on the next property began using a power mower with a particularly wicked engine noise.

Each time the power mower came close to where Dyer was sitting, he became upset. The noise was disrupting his quiet contemplation. After a while, however, Dyer managed to incorporate the noise of the mower into his environment. It no longer was a distraction, nor did it diminish his feelings of tranquillity.

How did Dyer get to this hallowed state? He accepted that people cutting grass are a normal part of the overall environment and that there's a rhythm and a hum to the power mower, much like that of a gurgling brook or other phenomena of nature. He was able, in other words, to let it slip into the background.

Stress Alert

Realistically speaking, not all background or environmental noise can be rendered benign. Indeed, the decibel level of a particular noise, or of noise in general, can be debilitating.

How can you make this technique work for you? Imagine you're trying to read while on an airplane. Suddenly, someone three rows back starts coughing. If you focus on the cough, you'll find yourself dreading the next time he or she coughs. You'll start *listening* for the cough, *anticipating* it. Sure enough, you won't get any reading done.

If you simply accept that coughs happen, however—even loud, obnoxious, airplane-rattling coughs—you can tune it out and continue to focus your attention on your book. More often than not, the distraction of the cough will diminish, sometimes to the point where you don't even think about it.

Affirm and Win

Tuning out a distraction is one way to go. Using it affirmatively is another. Here's how this technique works: Suppose you're in your office and someone in the office suite upstairs is banging on the wall a couple times every three or four minutes. Obviously, some type of equipment installation or office renovation is going on. How do you take such a potential disruption and turn it to your favor? You can use affirmations to creatively employ potential distractions as triggers to help you concentrate more deeply.

Mentally say to yourself, "With each bang on the wall, I will become even more focused on the task at hand." Thereafter, with each bang on the wall, allow your concentration to get more focused and more intense. This won't happen automatically. At first, each outside disturbance will continue to be annoying. If you stick with the process, however, each successive noise will, miraculously, begin to diminish in amplitude and, seemingly, in frequency.

Once you are adept at this process, you'll reach the point that you don't even hear the external noise. You'll still key into it subconsciously, however, as a signal to tighten your focus.

Calming Concept

Taking control of the noises you tune into isn't as hard as it sounds. Think about people who buy property under the flight path of a major airport. How could they possibly live with planes flying overhead all day long? After a few weeks, however, the noise of the flights overhead becomes part of the overall environment. The noise is no longer disruptive, stress inducing, or even particularly worth noting.

You Gotta Have Zen

With the success of the NBA's Chicago Bulls in the 1990s, the coaching methods and philosophies of Phil Jackson have become of interest to many people (and not just basketball fans). In Jackson's book, *Sacred Hoops*, he discusses his approach to the game and to life in general. Jackson, who has been meditating in the Zen Buddhist fashion for more than 20 years, drew on his meditational experiences when he coached his team:

"Basketball is a game, a journey, a dance. I emphasize to the players that when they work together, good things happen.... [It] requires shifting from one objective to another at lightning speed. To excel, you need to act with a clear mind and be totally focused. The secret is not thinking. This means quieting the endless jabbering of thoughts so that your body can act instinctively."

When Jackson encountered a particularly intense moment, instead of focusing on a mistake or disruption, he focused on *recovering from* the disruption and moving on to the next challenge in the game.

Likewise, your ability to recover from interruptions, distractions, and all the other malarkey that goes on in today's contemporary offices will enable you to get more work done each day, to feel less stress, and to feel better about the whole deal.

Stressbuster

When you focus on what you're trying to accomplish, disruptions simply lose their impact on your productivity. It's only when you let your focus shift to the cause of the disruption that you'll find your productivity slipping.

Relief Is a Maneuver Away

Here are a variety of other short-term maneuvers that can bring relief from office interruptions.

- Take a walk. Whatever is distracting you might be gone by the time you return. If not, perhaps it'll be less of a distraction.
- Turn on a fan, the air-conditioning system, or some office equipment. Its hum can help serve as a noise mask.
- Keep an eye out for distraction-free sanctuaries wherever they might be. This might include the lunchroom after the line closes, the chairs in your building's lobby, or a rooftop overlook.
- Coach others to support you in your quest for quietude. Ask them not to interrupt you at certain times of day, for example.

The Least You Need to Know

- An interruption-management system can reduce your daily disruptions by half or more.
- Multitasking is fine for office equipment, but it's a bad idea for you.
- Consider rescheduling. Maybe you need to get to the office much earlier or stay later.
- Mental methods for reducing distractions can be the most powerful of all.

Chapter 9

The Office Danger Zone: When Stress Leads to Violence

In This Chapter

- The increasing possibility of violence at work
- The dangers of workplace stress
- Dealing with an abusive manager
- Becoming Mr. or Ms. Congeniality

If your work environment is stressful but relatively tolerable, you might be inclined to skip this chapter. It's a good idea however, to skim through it at least once.

This chapter tells you what you need to know if someone you work with, work for, or who works for you is a candidate for workplace violence. I'm assuming that you personally are not prone to violence, regardless of how much stress you experience professionally or personally.

A Rising Tide of Aggression at Work

"Trench Coat Mafia Members Kill 11 Students, One Teacher, and Themselves"

"FBI Arrests Five Teenagers Plotting Mass Murder at School"

"Sociologists Agree That People in This Country Are Just Angrier These Days"

Headlines like these are appearing with increasing frequency, and you might have even witnessed acts of violence at work, at school, or in between. The phenomenon of workplace violence is real. A Centers for Disease Control study reveals that, within a 30-day period, "more than one in three high school boys admitted to carrying a gun, knife, or club." And an article in *Postal Life* magazine poses the question "Are you afraid to come to work?"

Snapping Under Pressure

As the level of violence in society rises, so does the level of violence at work. The National Workplace Resource Center conservatively estimates 1.5 million incidents of workplace violence annually. Nearly 1,000 employees murder their bosses annually. The U.S. Justice Department reports that husbands and boyfriends annually commit 13,000 acts of violence against women in the workplace.

The Society for Human Resources Management surveyed its members about workplace violence and found that one-third of respondents reported that their workplace had experienced a violent incident in the past five years and that the frequency of such incidents is on the rise. Forty-four percent of respondents said that the most recent incident of workplace violence occurred in the past year.

Stress Alert

Since 1990, the volume of information you're expected to process on the job has increased 60-fold over. Put this together with bad bosses, unfair working conditions, and escalating performance demands, and you've got a sure-fire recipe for stress.

Stress, Substance Abuse, and Sabotage

Chemical and substance abuse in one's personal life obviously has ramifications in one's performance and behavior in the workplace. Alcohol and other drugs are associated with 50 percent of spouse abuse cases, 68 percent of manslaughter charges, and 52 percent of rapes.

The workplace is besieged with saboteurs. Deliberate damage to computer hardware and software occurs with alarming regularity. These are not signs of a well-functioning society or harmonious workplaces.

I don't condone violence, not for one second. Yet, I'm beginning to understand it. More people are feeling more stress more often at work. The volume of information, growing responsibilities, and the competition for the time and attention of the typical employee rises beyond anyone's capacity. You already know that the volume of information you encounter is increasing exponentially.

Maladaptive Management

A majority of managers say their jobs are more stressful than a decade ago—no surprise there. Many predict that their jobs will become even more stressful in the next three to four years. By some estimates, at least half of American managers suffer too much stress and are becoming abusive, intolerant, and dictatorial.

If these aren't signs of stress bubbling over the top, what is?

- When General Motors gave a manager in his mid-50s the option of early retirement, he had to think about it carefully. Four of his colleagues in similar situations accepted the offer, but shortly thereafter they killed themselves.
- When JCPenney moved its corporate headquarters from New York to Plano, Texas, many employees were so despondent that the company increased its professional counseling staff from 1 person to 12.
- Mental health experts estimate that as many as 15 percent of executives and managers suffer from depression or critical levels of stress.

Workplace Stress at the Boiling Point

Many organizations don't understand or are in denial about the problems confronting their workforce. Few corporations want to address the reality that their policies and procedures contribute to high stress—high enough to result in workplace violence. Sometimes companies offer programs, but such treatment programs aren't likely to address the needs of seriously stressed or depressed employees.

Your chances of changing your corporate or organizational culture usually are between slim and none. Still, it's best to take a protective posture—arm yourself with some basic facts about workplace violence and some basic tips for what you can do to help yourself and others.

Anxiety Antidote

Keep your cool during hot summer months! June, July, August, and September are the months to really work on your anti-stress techniques because they're the months when most on-the-job violence occurs.

In the Society for Human Resources Management survey, respondents indicated that the motivation for the most recent violent incident was a personality conflict. A majority said they couldn't have identified the assailants' potential for violence, although anger, aggressiveness, and threatening behavior were the most common traits of assailants who could be identified. Other common traits included apparent emotional or mental disorders, loner status, sullen behavior, obsessiveness, extreme quietness, or moroseness.

Following a violent incident in the workplace, many organizations rely on a professional employee-assistance program. Other resources include counseling for employees, training, increased security, more thorough security, reference checks among new hires, and installation of new security systems.

Ticking Time Bombs: Not Just a Postal Problem

The U.S. Postal Service has been gripped by workplace violence for more than a decade. The Postal Service has endured up to 2,000 cases of workplace violence in a year. In his book, *Ticking Bombs: Defusing Violence in the Work Place,* author Michael Mantell says, "Workplace violence has never been a prominent business or social issue until now." Workplace violence has grown and evolved from an "underground problem for business into a substantial hazard, not only for the nineties, but well into the next century."

It's easy to dismiss many incidents as simply another "nut with a gun at work" story, but the problem is far more complex. Murder on the job is the third leading cause of occupational death.

Sabotage at Work

Hopefully, your organization, department, or division has been lucky enough not to experience overt acts of violence such as one individual striking or attacking another. What about acts of subversion? Consider the following questions.

- Has anyone damaged a PC, printer, fax machine, or pager?
- Has anyone tampered with the postage meter?
- Has anyone vandalized a vending machine?
- Are the public phones in and around your grounds inoperable?
- Do electric doors, escalators, or elevators frequently and mysteriously break down?
- Are appliances in your office kitchen in good working order?
- Does the plumbing in your washrooms get backed up often?
- Are any cars in employee parking lots ever vandalized?
- Are any pictures, posters, display windows, bulletin boards, and the like defaced or torn down?
- Do office furnishings break with increasing regularity?
- Is the landscaping outside being vandalized?
- Are objects frequently missing from the waiting room?

If you answered "yes" to any of the preceding questions, this might indicate that subversion is occurring. Because subversion could lead to overt violence, the subversion and anyone suspected of committing it should be reported as quickly as possible.

Firing (And Being Fired Upon)

In some organizations, downsizing continues to be prevalent—not that downsizing itself is the cause for increased violence. Kevin Flynn, Ph.D., a consultant based in Los Angeles, says a key problem with downsizing is that management is often "ill-prepared to deal with the turmoil and anguish of employees. Instead of dealing compassionately with it, they ignore it." Too many employees are hired with the message, "Yes, we value loyalty," only to be let go with the message, "Sorry, things have changed; your services are no longer necessary."

Calming Concept

This concept is not so calming. We're accustomed to thinking that workplace violence is a "postal" kind of thing. Well, it's not. Industries and businesses across the spectrum are reporting violence and sabotage. The reported incidents are just the tip of the iceberg. Countless incidents of violence go unreported every day.

Here's Your Hat—What's Your Hurry?

Professionals who deal with newly unemployed individuals find that approximately 10 percent experience problems, including severe anxiety or depression, sufficient enough to warrant professional help. When weeks and months go by without finding new work, the strain on their family and themselves can lead to undesirable behavior.

In thousands of cases each year, ex-workers show up months after being terminated to seek vengeance on their former boss, supervisor, or someone who they identify as the source of their misfortune.

Defusing the Danger of Departures

If you suspend a worker for breaking rules, will he or she come after you? Maybe. If you need to fire someone for gross incompetence, do you also need to worry about them coming back with a gun? Possibly. Employees who lose their jobs can react with furious anger. More than a few have outwardly destructive outbursts in exit interviews with staff.

In one instance, a supervisor was about to put a problem worker on probation and soon thereafter terminate the employee with no severance pay or benefits forthcoming. A co-worker familiar with the situation told the supervisor to watch out because the employee about to be put on probation had expressed his desire to kill the supervisor should he lose his job.

Stressbuster

An obviously disgruntled employee is a likely candidate for violent reaction to termination. If you're aware of such a possibility, alert your human resources department. Make sure steps are being taken to protect you.

Shaken to his core, the supervisor called his boss, who brought in a specialist in handling workplace violence. In this case, things worked out for the best. The specialist devised a plan in which the employee not only was retained but eventually was rehabilitated. This doesn't usually happen. The supervisor, his boss, and the specialist met with the problem employee and presented the plan in a calm, even-handed manner.

The employee realized the gravity of the situation and agreed to accept counseling as well as additional job training so he could retain his position in the company. The plan worked because the problem employee wasn't dangerous, according to the specialist. He simply was suffering from emotional distress in his domestic life that spilled over to his work life. In such cases, treatment generally is successful.

Responses to Retaliatory Threats

Specialists often advocate that problem employees be dealt with as early as possible, while there's still real potential for improvement. In addition, here are other steps for dealing with problem employees.

- When confronting such an employee, be firm, listen as much as you speak, and visibly show empathy.
- Create a threat-management team. This team might consist of a psychologist, someone from your legal department, someone from human resources, security, labor, and perhaps an outside specialist.
- Devise an organizational policy to let employees know how and where to report threats, violence, and subversive behavior.
- Give supervisors at least an hour's worth of training each month about recognizing trouble signs.
- Instruct supervisors about when and how to refer a problem employee to a specialist.

When violence does occur, the violent party's immediate boss usually didn't recognize the potential threat. Often, co-workers are aware of problems but aren't informed how, when, or to whom to report them.

Proactive Possibilities

Some organizations dispense confidential employee surveys on a regular basis to take the pulse of the organization, a department, or a division. If your organization does this, make sure you have the assistance of an impartial third party who is skilled in dispensing such surveys. Otherwise, you might simply be coaching employees to report what you want to hear as opposed to how the climate really is.

Properly firing someone requires care. Progressive organizations put significant time and attention into the firing process. They recognize that someone who's been laid off or terminated has to be treated with respect and compassion. The longer someone has been with the organization, the more time he or she needs to adjust to the termination.

Organizations that already have invested significantly in their people need to recognize the importance of ensuring that these valuable employees continue to work in an environment in which they feel free to be productive and relaxed.

Anxiety Antidote

If a violent incident occurs in your organization, make sure your employees have a chance to work through the problem with experienced counselors. Without such help, people frequently become less trusting and more defensive. This can seriously disrupt work routines and productivity.

Strategies for Handling an Abusive Manager

Chapter 5 covered how to keep stress under control even when you work for a bad boss. But what about when you work for a boss who borders on psychopathic?

The Monster Masher is a manager who indulges in sexual harassment of the crudest sort—physical and verbal threats and all manner of inhumane acts (despite potential lawsuits!). He (or she) is still a common figure in the workplace. Bosses who engage in such practices can trigger violent behavior in someone who might not otherwise have engaged in it. Employees victimized by such brutal bosses can suffer from anxiety, depression, heart problems, gastrointestinal disorders, headaches, skin rashes, insomnia, and sexual dysfunction.

Obvious offenders such as these are not the only managers—or management techniques—known to trigger workplace violence. Electronic surveillance systems, for example, are used by some organizations to monitor and control employee behavior in ways that cross the boundaries of reason and respect. These actions have driven some employees over the edge into disruptive acts.

What can you do in the face of management abuses?

- If you get overly anxious from working for a harsh boss, remember that, ultimately, you are in control. No one can get to you unless you *let* them.

- Remember that old axiom about "safety in numbers." Be alert for unwarranted behavior from the top and band together with others who are being abused.
- If you're being victimized, take a look at your own workplace relationships. Make sure you're not responding to the situation by victimizing your *own* subordinates.

In his classic book, *Man's Search for Meaning,* Dr. Victor Frankl, a World War II concentration camp survivor, observed that some people, while imprisoned in the camps, died quickly because they could not live in confinement with the harsh treatment from guards, not knowing what would happen next and having no larger purpose in life.

Calming Concepts

One of the most effective ways to decrease your susceptibility to stress from abusive managers is to refuse to adopt a victim's attitude. Instead of submitting to ill-treatment, it's more empowering to educate yourself about the recourses your company has put in place to protect it's employees. Know your rights and know where to assert them without having to get into constant personal confrontations.

Some people, including himself, were able to survive and ultimately flourish. He observed that such people had a larger purpose in life—perhaps there was someone they wanted to see should the camp ever be freed and the war over. Some simply waited until they could get revenge on the guards. Regardless of the treatment he received, Frankl resolved that the guards and the setting would have no effect on how he chose to feel internally, his regard for his fellow prisoners, loved ones he wanted to see again, or his faith in humanity.

You don't have to be a saint, but these are certainly important words to ponder, particularly if you're in a setting in which the potential for workplace violence exists.

R-E-S-P-E-C-T

There are things you can do to be a boss, a co-worker, or a subordinate that others respect *independent* of your situation and the level of stress in your workplace. Having good relations with others can reduce the stress of everyone involved and can keep you from being someone's target. Your behavior can set an example and can diffuse tense situations. Here are some tips to help you be the kind of person others want to be around.

Don't make promises you can't keep. It's better to under-promise and over-deliver than to over-promise and under-deliver. You already know this.

Maintain as cheerful a disposition as you can—even smile at people. They don't have to do anything for you, and you don't have to be seeking anything. A smile is simply a smile.

Be as good a listener as you can. The typical person, when polled, thinks he or she is a good listener. In reality, however, most people aren't. You probably have room for improvement, too.

Treat others in your workplace with respect, regardless of their position. Treat employees who just started with the same respect you show your CEO. After all, the self-worth of an individual can't be determined by rank. People are worthy simply for being human beings.

Look for the best in others. Everyone does something in which you can find approval. Look for the good in others, and they'll look for the good in you.

> **Stressbuster**
>
> To be a better listener, look directly at others when they speak. Don't interrupt. Offer your undivided attention. Nod to show you're paying attention. If the situation warrants it, take notes.

Avoid participating in the rumor mill. Nothing dampens the morale and spirit of an organization faster than spreading stories about other people. Few of these stories are even true. Yes, it's titillating to talk about others, particularly higher-ups in the organization. Ultimately, however, it serves little purpose.

Assume full responsibility for your own mistakes rather than pointing fingers. The truth wins out most of the time, and people know who's responsible when things don't go according to plan. Conversely, seek to give credit to your group when major success is achieved rather than seeking the credit for yourself.

Don't make decisions in anger. Chances are, a decision made in anger won't be a wise one.

There's more you can do to take control of the atmosphere where you work. For one thing, try to remain calm about things people say about you, particularly when they're untrue. Instead of reacting, demonstrate through your actions that such comments are not correct. Let negative comments fall away like water off the proverbial duck's back. Perhaps most importantly, control your emotions. Be known as a person who makes decisions after having first thought them through.

The Least You Need to Know

- Although workplace stress is at dangerous levels, too many companies don't understand the nature of the problems confronting their employees and are loathe to admit it.
- Employees who lose their jobs can react with furious anger. The longer a person has been with the organization, the more time he or she needs to adjust to the change in status.
- Problem employees need to be dealt with as early as possible, while there's still real potential for improved performance.
- Good relations with others can reduce everyone's job-related stress and can keep you from being someone else's target.

Part 3

From the Far Corners of the Globe

Now we'll explore a different but highly significant set of stressors. Don't get bent out of shape over this, but billions more people are going to populate this planet as you age. More news, information, sound bites, and outright drivel than you can imagine will vie for your attention. These developments are likely to exacerbate the stress you already experience.

Oddly enough, some "experts" tell us that the world's population could fit comfortably in the state of Texas. If we used our resources perfectly, they say, the increasing human population would not be a problem. If that's the case, what are we doing so poorly spread out across the globe? Hmmmm .... Could it be that human beings are rather imperfect and make lots of mistakes? I think so. Sure, everyone could fit in Texas. You also could discover a cure for the late-night munchies, but why would you want to?

It doesn't matter what size cyber-surfboard you're riding, an information tidal wave is about to hit—and you thought you'd already seen the worst! Everyone is being bombarded with more data than they can process. More information is generated in 60 seconds than you could take in over the course of the rest of your life—and the true Information Age is only just beginning!

Overpopulation and information overload are not reasons to forsake humanity, but they're definitely external stressors over which no one has much control. In an increasingly crowded and complex world, you need some time out.

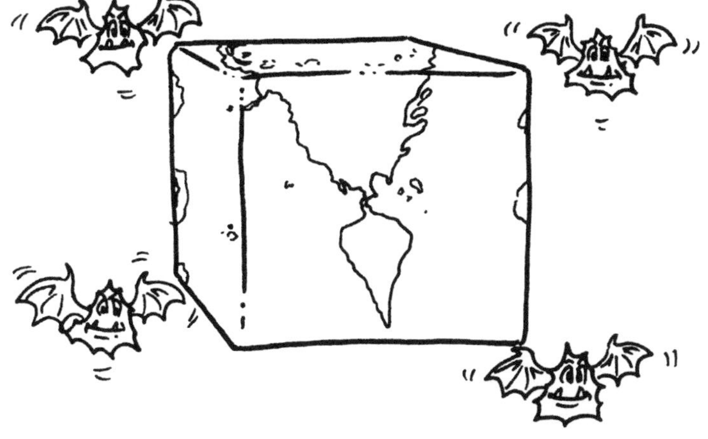

Chapter 10

Overpopulation: Why Don't All These People Just Go Home?

In This Chapter

- Overcrowding of the planet—and your life
- Taking the anthropological view
- The joys of the contrarian lifestyle
- Keeping your cool in adversity
- Advanced strategies for living in an overpopulated world

Could it be that some of the unrelenting stress you experience—getting to work, finding an empty park bench, or simply jockeying for a corner office—can be attributed in part to an increasing world population density? This might sound wild, but in a few minutes you're going to be a believer.

In this chapter, you'll discover the reality of how the ongoing global population increase has infiltrated your daily life and heaps oodles of extra stress on you. It's a tough subject, especially coming on the heels of Chapter 9's treatment of workplace violence, but it's a very real aspect of the stress we all face in today's world. Even though the topic is global in nature, don't despair—there *are* things you can do to minimize the stress it causes.

My, How Crowded It's Getting

In 1960, the Earth's human population was just under 3 billion people. When you juxtapose this fact with a simple geography—there are 58 million square miles of land on the planet—you'll discover that there were about 50 people per square mile. Back then, things seemed pretty spacious.

In 1995, the world's population surpassed 5.8 billion people. In other words, the human population density, on average, now stood at 100 people for every single square mile of land on earth. Feeling crowded yet?

Keep in mind that the land surface of the Earth isn't all habitable. There are huge tracts of tundra, for example, and deep deserts. So the crowding actually is much more intense than the overall population density would imply.

And the crowding has only gotten worse. Four years later, the world's population is approaching 7 billion people! Population densities are approaching the breaking points in many regions of the world.

Stress Alert

The stressful effects of planetary overcrowding range from the subtle—incremental increases in the price of necessary commodities—to the extreme—Manhattan apartments so small that you feel lucky if you've even got a closet. But *all* of them are stressful.

The Uneven Effects of Population Pressure

If you've traveled abroad recently, you might have noticed that some places are a little more crowded than others. According to *Escape Magazine*, the most densely populated places on earth are Macao and Monaco, with 54,782 and 40,666 people per square mile, respectively. At the low end, Greenland has 0.1 person per square mile, and the Western Sahara has 2.2 persons per square mile.

If you reside in America, you'll be pleased to know that the population density in the U.S. is only 73 people per square mile, so we've still got some elbow room to play with. An increasing percentage of the population lives closer to each other, however, namely in urban areas. Escalating global population growth contributes to rapid urbanization, which consumes the valuable arable land needed to sustain communities and exacerbates environmental problems such as deforestation and pollution.

How's Your Overpopulation Savvy?

How aware are you of the rising tide of humans spread out over the world? The following quiz lets you test your knowledge of this important contributor to modern-day stress. Just fill in the blanks and then check the answer key at the end to see how you've scored.

Population Across the Globe

1. The world population increases by the current population of the U.S. every __________.

2. At the current growth rates, another Washington, D.C., appears on earth every _______.

3. At its current pace, U.S. population will increase to ________ by 2050, a year in which may still be around.
4. There are more people living today than have ever _____ and _____.
5. A huge ___ percent of the world's population is now urbanized.
6. In 2025, the urban population will be ___ percent.
7. At present, _____ percent of the U.S. population is urbanized.
8. The U.S. urban population is projected to grow to ___ percent by 2025.

*Answer Key: **1.** 33 months; **2.** 13 days; **3.** 400,000,000; **4.** lived and died; **5.** 45 percent; **6.** 58 percent; **7.** 76 percent; **8.** 85 percent*

It took from the beginning of creation to 1850 A.D. for the world's population to reach its first billion. Those days of relatively wide-open spaces are now long gone. Unquestionably, world population now has an impact on the quality of your life—every day. And every decade, that population is growing by more than a billion people.

A growing number of people believe that, through simple overpopulation, the human species has created an environment that in itself is highly stressful and ultimately destructive. That destruction is wide ranging. It affects society, the economy, and even individuals' health and well-being.

Calming Concept

The world of your parents' childhood (and of your own) is gone. Forever. With each additional person, the population density inexorably increases as literal and figurative space per person decreases. Simply making yourself aware of modern, overcrowded life can go a long way toward reducing your susceptibility to the stress that such a life implies.

On the Ecological Chopping Block

The geometric growth in the human population now permeates and dominates every aspect of this planet—its resources, the environment, and the life of each person. It also results in more of each day being consumed by our efforts to simply maintain our current standards of living. The simple fact is that personal freedom demands personal space. Here are just two examples of why this is so.

- The more than 13 million people of Los Angeles were told by their elected officials that they must give up backyard barbecues and their reliance on individual automobiles.
- In competing for territory and control of resources such as fuels, mineral deposits, seaports, and so on, ethnic hostilities around the world are grabbing more and more headlines. Each winning group leaves the losing group with many people to support but fewer resources to get the job done.

In college, I had an economics professor who defined economics as "the allocation of scarce resources." Only when a society has to manage limited resources is it an "economic" society. Outside the industrialized nations, the population explosion has transformed our world into an economic society only in the last 14 or 18 years, and we don't yet truly understand what impact this will have on global economics. Make no mistake about it, there's a cost for our overuse of resources. As these resources become more scarce, that cost will rise. This is itself a part of the overpopulation problem.

The Vanishing Act

Stress Alert

Two hundred and five Nobel prize winners were polled about the most compelling challenges the world currently faces. Topping the list was population growth. Running a close second? Environmental degradation.

Planetary increases in human population don't necessarily mean mismanagement of resources and increased stress, but that has been the norm. A statement signed by 1,575 scientists from 69 countries was sent to 160 national leaders, as reported by The Union of Concerned Scientists in Washington, D.C. Signers included 99 of the 196 living Nobel laureates at the time as well as senior officers from many of the most prestigious scientific academies in the world.

What were these prestigious scientists and statesmen worried about? Here's the central warning, as contained in the report: "Human beings in the natural world are on a collision course." The signers pointed out that population stress is apparent in the atmosphere, water resources, oceans, soil, tropical and tempered forests, and living species. They lamented that, "Much of this damage is irreversible on a scale of centuries or permanent." They went on to say, "We are fast approaching many of the earth's limits."

What kinds of limits were they talking about?

- Approximately one person in five on the planet has no access to clean drinking water.
- One person in 15 lives in an area defined as water-stressed or water-scarce. By 2025, this number could rise to one in three people.

- Chronic freshwater shortages are appearing in Africa, the Middle East, Northern China, parts of India, Mexico, Brazil, several former Soviet republics, and the western United States.
- Theoretically, humanity has the ability to feed everyone on the planet. In reality, starvation is a way of life and death over vast areas of the planet.
- The Earth has lost 3 percent of its protective stratospheric ozone, resulting in a 6-percent increase in ultraviolet radiation. Greater losses are expected.
- More people imperil many other species. The World Wildlife Federation's endangered species list includes hundreds and hundreds of exotic species with which you are likely unfamiliar as well as tigers, rhinos, and the giant panda.

Making Room for the Future

Some people don't see cause for alarm. They assume nature has a way of making things all balance out. They see war, famine, and pestilence as nature's way of reducing population. There is no war so lethal, however, and no starvation so thorough—even in Somalia or Ethiopia—that can offset the birth of a million new people every four days. No tidal wave, no flood, no hurricane—even in Guatemala and Honduras, despite the thousands who unfortunately perished—has had any significant impact on the unrelenting juggernaut of human population growth.

Who among us would *wish* for tragedy on such a global scale? I, along with the scientists and statesmen who signed that statement, am concerned about the coming generations and the quality of life available to everyone, including you. The key is to find a way to keep population at a replacement level. This means keeping the number of births equal to the number of deaths, popularly known as zero population growth (ZPG).

The Fertility Crescent

The idea of reining in population growth is not a new one. You might even have heard that, in some areas, at least, *fertility* rates are declining. However, the fertility levels in developing countries still average 4.4 children per family. Part of this is due to local cultural rules governing marriage.

Here's an interesting set of statistics. Thirty percent of Latin American women, 40 percent of Asian women, and 50 percent of African women are married by age 18. What does this mean for population growth? According to reports from the World Watch Institute, 40 percent of all 14-year-old girls worldwide get pregnant by the

Tranquillity Terminology

Population density is the ratio of people to the land area on which they live. **Fertility**, in demographics, refers to the probable number of live births likely to occur within a given generation in a given population.

time they reach the age of 20. Because nearly 40 percent of the population of developing countries is under the age of 15, with vast numbers entering their reproductive years, population in these regions is destined to increase for many decades.

Swelling populations across the globe invariably will lead to more strain on the planet and ultimately to more stress on everyone. There is, literally, nowhere to run.

Out of Work? Take a Number

More than 500 million people in developing countries are unemployed or underemployed. Another 30 million are entering the job market each year, with few or no prospects for a job that pays a living wage. Hence, more than a billion jobs will have to be created in less developed countries by 2007 if we want to avoid even greater poverty, misery, and hunger in the world. If the Asian economic crisis of the late 1990s stretches into the new century, this number could rise dramatically.

One political leader in Mexico says that the consequences of not creating at least 15 million jobs in the next 15 years are unthinkable. Mexicans who cannot find jobs will have three options: the United States, the streets, or revolution.

This is true around the globe. Difficult economic conditions, exacerbated by rapid population growth, have prompted millions of rural poor to migrate to cities and millions more—at a rate of 10,000 per day—to cross international borders in search of a better life.

Calming Concept

At its present growth rate, New York, which in 1950 topped the list of the 10 largest cities in the world, is not likely to make the list by the year 2025.

Economist Ben Wattenberg of the American Enterprise Institute, in an all-time shortsighted observation, said in the early 1990s, "Why should we worry? We've gone from one billion to five billion while living standards have gone up exponentially. There's no evidence that population growth diminishes or dilutes development."

I'm here to tell you that he was talking through his hat!

These Boots Are Made for Walking

Famine and poverty are only two signs of the stress caused by overpopulation. Signs of overpopulation show up in other ways all over the globe. Many of these other signs aren't necessarily life threatening, but they *are* worrisome nevertheless. Take, for example, the simple case of *gridlock*.

Tranquillity Terminology

The modern-day phenomenon of **gridlock** occurs when too many cars are traveling the streets. When a traffic light turns red, a few cars try to scoot through, blocking the intersection so the cross traffic can't proceed. Whole cities can be brought to near paralysis when gridlock is severe.

Picture this: The highways in Asia's biggest cities resemble parking lots. In Bangkok, the average speed on the city streets has slowed to a crawl, moving an average of less than six miles per hour when calculated over a full 24-hour time period. Traffic has become so slow that people now sell newspapers, magazines, flowers, soft drinks, and chewing gum to their captive customers—motorists stuck in unmoving lines of cars.

Perhaps we're at the dawn of achieving a sustainable environment. Perhaps we'll get the population under control. However, there's no present-day, reliable indication that this will happen. If we can't manage our resources with a mere five billion people or with seven billion, how can we expect to do it with eight or ten?

On The Home Front

"Ah, but wait!" you say. All this stuff is too far afield to have any real impact on *you*. Is it?

In 1968, the U.S. population was a mere 186 million. Now it's more than 273 million. In other words, we've grown by 50 percent in about a generation. As you learned in the quiz earlier in this chapter, by the middle of the next century, the U.S. population is projected to increase to 400 million people. Just numbers, you say? Try visualizing it another way. This is equivalent of adding 38 new cities, each the size of Los Angeles. And some demographers argue that the 400 million estimate might be low.

Traffic Traumas

Whether you drive a fuel-efficient compact car or a big ol' gas guzzler, keep your eyes open the next time you head out on the highway (and not just to avoid accidents). Do you notice that, whenever you approach a city or town of any size, traffic often slows to a crawl? Remember, it's not just happening in your city or state; it's happening across the U.S.—and across the globe.

The Roots of Road Rage and Other Modern Stress Effects

The saber-toothed tiger is extinct. It isn't a source of stress for humans anymore, but we've got new ones to replace it. Take, for example, the anger and hostility that some people feel towards others when they get behind the wheel. This stress originates from spending endless miles chugging along at five miles per hour. This could be a mirror of the overall feelings that increasing numbers of people are beginning to experience as they're forced to live in a society that is getting too crowded and moving too fast.

You don't need to own a car, however, to feel some of this frustration and stress. How about standing in line at ridiculously slow supermarket checkout counters, doing a slow burn while you notice the cashiers joking with each other and ignoring the customers. Even this low-level source of stress can be debilitating if you endure it frequently or for prolonged periods. Among other things, the repeated release of stress hormones, even in such petty situations, can accelerate the development of clogged arteries.

Standing Out from the Overcrowding

To avoid being stuck in traffic, waiting in line, and scrambling with the masses for goods and services, you need to come up with new strategies. Here are a few to help you get started.

Live closer to your workplace. If you can afford it, few strategies make more sense. Regardless of the metro or suburban area in which you work, undoubtedly there are good neighborhoods a reasonable distance away. When you live closer to your office, you benefit in many, many ways

- Less commuting time.
- Lower gasoline costs.
- Less wear and tear on your car.
- More flexibility in coming and going.

Tranquillity Terminology

A **contrarian** is a person who bases his or her lifestyle on personal choice and taste, not the preferences of the crowd.

Telecommute. If you can work at home as little as one day per week, you cut your week of commuting by 20 percent. The equipment you need to telecommute from home is highly affordable these days. Fast PCs are now available for under $1,000, and good modems are dropping under the $100 price range.

Become a *contrarian*. If everyone vacations on holidays, use those days to work. Take your time off when everyone else is working.

Do more of your shopping by phone, fax, and modem. Rather than fighting for parking spaces at the super mall, order by catalog. Increasingly, catalog vendors offer an 800 number, an 800 fax line, and even 24-hour customer service.

Get more selective about what information you ingest. In a world of seven billion people, there will be increasing numbers of books, articles, movies, plays, commentaries, opinions, and points of view. Unless you actively take steps to limit what you allow to compete for your time and attention, your days will race by faster than you care to live them.

Give yourself a dependable sanctuary. Everyone needs some time for themselves, if only to zone out. In a world that gains more than a million people every four days, this could become harder to do. Undoubtedly, there are places you've already carved out—your rec room, study, backyard, or a favorite vacation spot. The key is to use them and get some of the rest and relaxation you so fervently need.

Calming Concept

For several years, I've been ordering by catalog and now via the Internet. I can sit and think about what I'm doing, whereas in a mall I frequently get jostled, overwhelmed, and unfocused.

Abandon day-to-day tuning in. Instead of seeking to ingest everything the media has to offer, seek summaries of news and information on perhaps a weekly or biweekly basis. As you'll see in Chapters 11, "Cranking out the Factoids," and 12, "Unreality Bites," much of what's presented to you is not news anyway.

The Least You Need to Know

- Growing populations result in loss of individual freedom and an increase in individual stress.
- Become a contrarian—take your time off when everyone else is working.
- Everyone needs to have some time for themselves, if only to zone out.

Chapter 11

Cranking Out the Factoids

In This Chapter

- Information overload
- What *do* you really need to know?
- Setting limits on the information you ingest
- Letting go and loving it!

Although you might not have considered it before, monolithic purveyors of news and information account for much of the stress you feel today. At the same time, too much of the news media—bent on highlighting the latest gore to explore and then piously deplore—offers up a steady diet of unbalanced coverage of the absurd, the titillating, and the sensational. The U.S. government is, unquestionably, the world's largest publisher—by a wide margin. The information it spews out on a daily basis is beyond comprehension. And these are only two of the culprits contributing to our information overload.

Society is beset with news and information suppliers. I could fill a whole book on how too much information adds to your stress level, but I'll be kind. I'll restrict myself to covering the highlights in this chapter.

Social Evolution 101

Right now, you're probably besieged by all kinds of information that's competing for your time and attention—whether you realize it or not. What is the origin of this information buildup? Was it predictable? Can you look to the past to see why there's so much information today? It turns out you can.

An Anthropological Interlude

There have been three great ages of humanity, each based on a particular type of economy and technology. I'd even argue that there's a fourth age about to emerge.

- *The Age of Hunting and Gathering* was the first major human era. In this period, people principally lived by hunting animals and by collecting berries, nuts, roots, and insects. Your ancestors apparently did a pretty good job at this because you're here today.
- *The Age of Agriculture* followed. In this era, many people learned that they didn't have to be nomads, wandering around scrounging for their next meal. Instead, they learned to cultivate the soil, to predict when crops would grow, and to forecast what their yield would be. This was a great leap forward in some respects; it allowed for an understanding of how to work with nature and the seasons. It did have a downside, however, in that it prompted people to have unprecedented numbers of children. After all, in the early days when many children died at birth and all who survived were needed to work the fields, having lots of kids was that age's equivalent of buying insurance.

Calming Concept

It's no coincidence that the Bible and other early texts encourage readers to "be fruitful and multiply." As civilization transformed from the Age of Hunting and Gathering to the Age of Agriculture—around the time most religious texts began to appear—families needed many more children to serve on the farm. Because infant mortality was so high, a couple might have 10 or 12 children to ensure that 4 or 5 would survive. Now, of course, the advice in these texts, if followed, will lead to ever-accelerating human population—something the planet does not need.

- *The Age of Industry* was the third great age. All manner of capital was put together so that consumers, as a class, would be served by producers. Producers learned new ways to provide products through mass-production capabilities. Improved printing and publishing processes were among the key developments of this age, as was the invention of countless new products to compete for the cash of the new consumer class.

The next age that will emerge—but is not here in full swing—is the *Information Age*. (See the following table for a summary of the traits of the four ages.) When this age fully arrives, information will be the single most important commodity available. It will exist to *serve* you, however, and you will not be abused by an *excess* of information. The present, which I call the "pre-Information Age," is really just a precursor. Right now, we haven't yet gotten full control over the information—and information-carrying devices—that will ultimately serve us well. So for now, we live in a time of "overinformation," an idea to which you can probably relate.

I Don't Care How It Works

In the Industrial Age, when everyday people needed to achieve something rather ordinary, did they have to go through a series of motions, read manuals, or become experts at the task? Not at all. The technical expertise was only needed by the people who built the machines and other technologies. Users could live in blissful ignorance. Consider, for example, turning on the lights in your room. Electrical lighting is one of the hallmark inventions of the Industrial Age. To use it, you simply have to know how to flip a switch (or clap your hands, in some cases). To start your car, you turn the key. To take care of other tasks, you push a button, pull a lever, or turn a dial. These are Industrial-Age processes at their best. You don't have to become an electrical engineer or a physicist to function effectively.

The Four Economic Ages of Humankind

Characteristic	Hunting and Gathering Age	Agricultural Age	Industrial Age	Information Age
Principle Goods:	Prey, roots, nuts, and berries	Crops, livestock	Raw materials	Knowledge
Dependent Upon:	Luck, instinct, available game	Timing, weather, location	Capital, labor	System configuration
Knowledge Base:	Oral history, observation	Oral history, almanacs	Training manuals	Overabundance of all data types
Location:	Wilderness; near water and refuge	Rural, on fertile soil	Urban, near labor supply	Anywhere
Lifestyle:	Nomadic	Settled on plots of land	Commuting from home to workplace	Telecommuting
Mobility:	Necessarily mobile	Necessarily stationary	Necessarily mobile	Individual choice
Social Unit:	Tribe, clan	Extended family	Nuclear family	Individual choice
The Elite:	Biggest, strongest, fastest	Most efficient	Capitalists, politicians	Anyone
Success Traits:	Agility, cunning	Strength, stamina	Distribution	Application

Do I Need to Know This?

To function effectively in our contemporary pre-Information Age, you need first to gather the information you need, to go online or open a manual, to make several calls, to consult an expert, or to buy the latest issue of something. Particularly in the workplace, you undertake a series of activities to get the precise information you need.

Your problem frequently is not a lack of information but an *overabundance* of information or too much *general* information.

Calming Concept

Information, *per se,* is not a stressor. It's the expectation—self-imposed or assumed by others—that you're supposed to know *everything* that can make you crazy. All you really need to know is where to go to find the facts you need when you need them.

When the Information Age is *truly* here, you'll instantaneously receive answers to your questions. Before that great age truly arrives, however, you'll be besieged by more information than all previous generations combined. For example, I received a flyer in the mail about a new "superstore" bookseller opening near me. The store will feature more than 150,000 titles; stock more than 2,500 domestic and international newspapers, periodicals, and magazines; and have the capability to order an additional 200,000 titles from national distributors.

The children's section will include 15,000 titles, and the music section will have 25,000 CDs and cassettes. And this is simply one of several outlets for producers and publishers who are probably generating 10 times those numbers of products.

Perilous Publishing

A clear sign came to me that the amount and nature of information our society is generating has gone beyond absurdity. I was flipping through a publisher's catalog. There it was: a book about manhole covers. The description said the book "catalogs an often-ignored yet singular form of urban industrial art and its place in American culture."

A reviewer of the book—how do you find an expert on manhole covers who also can write reviews?—said that it "occupies a rather indeterminate genre category: part history of material culture, part exercise in obsessive photographic cataloging of related objects, part Crypto-Pop artist's book. There's a crisp and even elegant matter-of-factness to their writing and their pictures, a spare functionalist precision."

Information saturation! With books about manhole covers and a legion of books about, say, cats, is it any wonder that at least 3,000 books are published in the U.S. alone every week and at least 2,000 books are published each day worldwide? The real question is, how many of them need to be published in the first place?

Maybe you're one of those special people who have a real need to know about the history of manhole covers. That's the upside of the Information Age. You can find information on any topic under the sun. But for the rest of us, you can see how important it is to become more selective than ever in the type and volume of information with which you're presented.

The Real Reason for Deforestation

The proliferation of books about obscure subjects is one thing. No bookstore chain and no commercial publisher, however, can equal the onslaught of information generated and disseminated by the federal government.

There's a little-known office of the federal government called the Washington National Record Center located in Suitland, Maryland. One of the chief collectors of over-information, the agency maintains 19 rooms that comprise the government's sprawling warehouse. Altogether, more than 8 billion of the federal government's old policy papers, budget projections, meeting minutes, and research reports are housed here.

Eight billion!

Will anyone ever look at this stuff again? Probably not. Can't some of it be destroyed? You bet! And some of it is. But every day new truckloads of boxes arrive at a rate 50 percent faster than the older boxes are destroyed.

Government agencies seem to revel in generating paper and information like it's going out of style—despite the advent of the Internet! The Office of Thrift Supervision has 440 cubic feet of documents relating solely to the Lincoln Federal Savings and Loan scandal of a more decade ago. This would fill 55 four-drawer filing cabinets. The U.S. Department of Justice has 160 cubic feet of paperwork about the Exxon Valdez oil spill. Has more paper been spilled than oil?

Anxiety Antidote

Don't lose sleep over your inability to assimilate all the factoids modern society tosses at you. No one can. Here's a simple truth to keep in mind: When you're hit by too many bits of information at once, it *all* goes past you in one big blur.

"Wait a moment, can't all this stuff be put on disk?" you ask. Theoretically, yes. Even an old 3.5-inch floppy can hold the equivalent of about 240 sheets of paper, so the amount of actual printed documents ought to decline. However, the opposite seems to be occurring.

Federal regulations, and you know there are lots of them, now exceed 200 volumes and number more than 130,000 pages. To give you some perspective, the number of current federal regulations is 16 times greater than it was in 1950 and is 4 times greater than in 1965. In the field of agriculture alone, there are 19 volumes. The environment has 16 volumes.

Now consider the cost. Government regulations impose more than $5 billion upon citizens annually. Spread out over a population of 200 million people over age 16, this translates to $2,500 per person per year and $25,000 per decade. In your life, it shows up in the form of more cumbersome tax forms, higher prices (because retailers must pass on the cost to someone—and it's always you), and a variety of other hidden charges.

Despite noble attempts to streamline the agency, the IRS single-handedly loses more than 2 million pieces of paper annually. I'm still hoping for the day that my tax returns are among them. One day soon, when the majority of returns are filed electronically, we can surmise that your return will be in the far corner of some hard drive that know one will ever find.

Daily Additions to the Overglut

The Library of Congress procures, organizes, and catalogs a minimum of 7,000 new items *every day*. Although the numbers change by the minute, the library's current holdings require more than 500 miles of shelf space and include such gargantuan numbers as 14 million prints, posters, and photographs; 4 million maps; 500,000 reels of film; 3.5 million pieces of music; 39 million pages of personal papers and manuscripts; and, if you can believe it, 5,600 volumes printed before the year 1500.

Despite attempts by each administration to "streamline" government, each year more paper information is generated that weighs us down. The stark reality is that society is being engulfed by too much information, and the preoccupation is catalogued and supported by the government.

Calming Concept

Contrary to semi-popular belief, the Library of Congress does not house every book, English-language book, or American book ever published or even published within a year. It retains only about one third of each year's new American books. Hmm, wonder if they have *Dave Barry Turns 50?*

In any given year, the Smithsonian Institution in Washington adds about one million new items to its collection—despite the fact that they've been in existence for a century and a half. That's 4,000 items a day! Is society that fascinating?

Hold on to your hats. Soon, more information will be generated in one second (yes, one second) than you could ingest in the rest of your life. Humanity has never experienced anything like this, and the effects are incalculable.

Behind from the Start

So what does all this have to do with stress? Think about it! Are you among the millions of people who wake up already feeling behind for the day? It's a socially pervasive phenomenon for people to feel stress upon awakening, even in the absence of direct stimuli, simply because they anticipate another day in which they'll have to take in more information than they can comfortably process.

No one can keep up with the flow of information, you included. Hereafter, you don't need to take it personally.

So Much I Know, So Much More I Don't

Does it seem like the events of the past 20 to 25 years are becoming more difficult to recall? If so, it's because everything has gone by like one big blur. When too many things compete for your time and attention, it's difficult to keep things in context.

During my speeches, I find it's often easier for groups to cite dates in the distant past than to recall something in the last 20 to 25 years. A surprising number of people remember all sorts of obscure facts they must have learned in school, but they can't answer much of anything about today's world.

Try it for yourself.

Did you know when the Vikings landed in Newfoundland?

(It happened around A.D. 1000 to 1002.)

What about the Norman invasion of England?

(It happened in 1066.)

When was the Magna Carta signed?

(For many people, the date 1215 will spring to mind.)

When was it that Columbus sailed the ocean blue?

(I hear you all shouting out "1492!")

Do you recall what year the Pilgrims landed on Plymouth Rock?

(1620)

Stressbuster

Learn to let go of the unimportant things. If your job requires you to stay on top of the latest advances in engineering, don't sweat it if you can't recite the top 10 movies of the past year or name the last three presidents of Botswana. You can always look up such data.

As sophisticated and knowledgeable as you are, how well would you do on a quiz of *current* cultural knowledge? Did you know that Cambodia's principal language is Khmer? Or that Belgium's principal language is Flemish? What about the language of Brazil (Portuguese) or Iran (Persian)? The people of these countries share the planet with us, but most of us have no idea what language they speak.

How about one last quiz question, while we're at it. What do the following place names have in common: Surabeya, Port Alegra, Harbin, Pune, Changdu, Huan, Yangdong, Tiago, Tashkent, and Kanpur?

Stumped? They are all cities of *several million people.* Have you even *heard* of any of them? Their population probably exceeds the population of your city.

If you're feeling bad about how few correct answers you could come up with, don't fret. *Everyone* is being hit with more data than anyone can fathom. So what can you do?

- Be more selective than ever about what you take in.
- Decide what information is truly important to you and don't worry so much about the rest.

Dealing with Minutiae

For me, the anxiety of living in an era of overinformation came into full bloom when I walked into a magazine store containing hundreds of newspapers and magazines. I also felt it when I went into a bookstore with thousands of books, including dozens on the very topics about which I write.

For you, perhaps, something else will trigger the feeling of information overload. Lynn Lively, author of *Managing Information Overload,* observes that many people feel a twinge of discomfort when someone presents important information that they had no clue was coming. The reaction is understandable. You feel as if you're being put on the spot, and there's no time to come up with a well-thought-out response.

Lively offers a variety of responses in the face of being hit with information out of left field.

- "I really hadn't given that much thought."
- "Considering the situation, what do you think is best?"
- "I think Mike in Accounting knows the answer."
- "I appreciate you bringing this to my attention."

- "It's not currently an area of interest to me, although it is interesting."
- "I'm under deadline now and can't give it any attention."

No One Can Know It *All*

Should every U.S. citizen know the dates of the U.S. Civil War (1861 to 1865)? Ideally, yes. It's always good to know about your country's history. If someone came to America within the past half decade, however, and he's been learning English *and* learning how to get along in contemporary American culture, he might not know the dates of the Civil War. The event might not have as much importance to him.

Anxiety Antidote

There is no longer a single body of information that *everyone* can be expected to know. Quite likely, there never was one.

What's the point? Simply this: With all the information coming at you every day, you've got to set reasonable limits to avoid information overload. Certainly, there's no need to take in information because you have some vague feeling that you "ought to." Instead, make your choices based on the criterion of *utility*. That way, you can stop feeling anxious just because you can't respond to all the promotions, discounts, and bonus offers in the mail.

Take in Information that Matters

When you're continually besieged by information, you're likely to feel overwhelmed. This, in turn, leads to feeling overworked and stressed. If you can *eliminate* much of the extraneous information, you won't feel overwhelmed as often, and you won't feel as overworked. So how can you manage this? Here's the biggest tip of all.

> Take control of the spaces in your life because information is stored in spaces—tables, shelves, desks, disks, kitchen counters, dining-room tables, glove compartments, and the back seat of your car to name a few.

Read on for some specific strategies to rationalize the spaces of your life.

Manila Folders: The Key to Sanity

There is an old Chinese saying that works wonders when you're trying to handle voluminous amounts of information—divide and conquer. Here's how it works.

Suppose you're facing a 10-inch pile of information ...

- Group similar items together.
- Eliminate duplicates.

- Put it all into file folders.
- Prioritize the important items in a given file.

Anxiety Antidote

At least half of the chore of dealing with most information is simply dividing it into piles, categorizing it, or putting it into various directories on your hard drive.

As you evaluate any particular item, ask yourself, "Where does this go?" The answer is to use an appropriate file where you can find the material easily. You might need to relabel files, but that's okay. This is *your* system, designed for *you*—never mind what it looks like to others. Relabeling files indicates that you're getting good at filing.

Everyone could benefit from more effective filing and better organization, even students or your spouse at home.

You say you don't have time to get organized? The reality is that you're *already* taking time from other things if you're not organized. At the very least, it takes you longer to find things.

You're also expending mental and emotional energy because you're not organized. Anxiety, worry, and frustration eat into your productivity and your day.

You live in an era that will continue to dump more information than you can respond to. Setting up personal systems to become and remain organized and in control is a solid investment in your career and your long-term well-being.

Tickle Me Elmo: Files by Date

Tranquillity Terminology

A **tickler file** is a time-based organizational tool similar to a pill pack. With each day comes an informational duty and the tickler file makes sure this duty is accomplished.

I highly recommend setting up a file folder for each month of the year and one for each day of the month. This system, called a *tickler file*, has been in practice for years. Create a file for each day from the 1st to the 31st of the month and place it at the front of one of your file drawers. Behind that, have a file for each month of the year.

On the second day of the month, for example, if you receive something you won't need to deal with until the 15th, put it in the file for, say, the 13th (to allow yourself some slack). If anything comes in that you don't need to handle now, put it in your tickler file. This yields immediate benefits. It keeps your desk clear and eliminates a lot of worry about where things go.

As the days and months pass, you continually move files from the front and put them in the back. Once you get this system in place, you'll find that many of the things you file might not need to be acted on later. The benefits of this system are immediate.

The Stress of Excess

Examine your desk, files, and shelves and determine how much you can pare their contents down. I suggest opening your mail over the wastebasket. It's much easier to throw things out with the wastebasket right below you. If you get a magazine or a journal, go through it rapidly and take out the articles or items that look like they'll be of interest. Recycle the rest of the publication.

Stressbuster

There's no need to keep the back issues of most publications—much of the information is now available online. Keep hard copies only of what you need and recycle or dispose of the rest. See if you can use the copier to assemble key facts on a single sheet.

Ditto for books. I receive books from people all the time. I quickly scan the entire book. I read the table of contents and the index and find the pages that contain information of value to me. I photocopy these pages, along with the cover and the publishing information, and I create a dossier of the information from the book that's important to me.

Then (in an act of total charity) I give the book away to an associate, a friend, a library, or wherever.

Later, I don't even keep the dossier. I dictate the key points and have a typist transcribe the tape. I have hundreds of books on my hard disk and can find them easily. There's no accumulation and no pile. With the word-search capability of word processing software, I can find the information I need immediately.

Overload's Gotta Go

From now on, when information crosses your desk, ask yourself some key questions to determine whether to keep and file it, place it in a tickler file, create a dossier, or immediately toss the information.

- Should I have received this?
- What is the issue behind this document?
- Is the information of marginal value? Could I easily skip it and suffer no loss in my career for not retaining it? If so, then let it go!
- Will it matter if I don't handle it?
- What am I saving it for?
- Do I need it? Or do I fear that, if I don't have it, I'll somehow be deficient?
- Does it support what I already know or believe?
- Can I delegate the information in the document?

If you've set up a tickler file, can you file the new information as something to review next month? Most of what crosses your desk doesn't need to linger; it can go elsewhere.

The more in control you are of the information you store, the easier you can retrieve and use it. Information is power, but if you can't find what you retain, it's of no value. It's only of value when you can find it and can combine it with other things.

Tomorrow's Challenge

It's not easy to be part of a pioneer generation, moving into a rapidly changing future. Yet, you can handle it. You have the intelligence and the capability. Every day, for the rest of your life, you are likely to be besieged by more information, not less. When you understand what you're up against, you're in a better position to take control.

The Least You Need to Know

- Information overkill is stressing out nearly everyone; be more selective than you've ever been.
- There's no need to take in information because you feel you ought to or you must.
- You control your space. Hence, you can stay in control of information you encounter by organizing that space.
- It's harmful to ingest too much information at once.
- When information crosses your desk, ask yourself, "Did I need to receive this at all?" Then handle the information accordingly: file it, condense it, or toss it.

Chapter 12

Unreality Bites

In This Chapter

- The reality of unreality in the modern multimedia world
- The media feeding frenzy
- Is it news or infotainment?
- The media's role in increasing your stress

A study years ago by the Louis Harris Organization found that two out of every three adults in the United States "fidget, fuss, take furtive glances in windows and mirrors, and study other people's reactions to the way they look." Harris concluded that a solid majority of Americans are almost "obsessed with their physical appearance." All indications since then—cosmetic sales, cosmetic operations, the rise of the image industry—suggest that this obsession has reached new heights.

What does this mean for your stress levels? Lots! It's bad enough that you have to keep up with the competition in the real world. Thanks to the media, you're also increasingly competing with the air-brushed, professionally scripted, pop-culture icons of TV and the movies. What's the average Jane Doe or John Q. Public to do? Read on.

Mirror, Mirror on the Wall

In the Harris Poll just mentioned, 95 percent of respondents, 19 people out of 20, said they would change their appearance if they could. About half of all men would like to change their weight or waistline. Women, too, are worried about their waistlines, among other things.

"To have others admire one's looks," the Harris study reported, "ranks high on the list of both men and women, especially the young, even if those looks are only superficial and wildly deceiving." Even the most celebrated of Hollywood's sex symbols have undergone considerable cosmetic and surgical alterations to improve their chances of adulation from fans who might otherwise ignore them.

Stress Alert

Trying to live up to the impossible standards set by the media can only do damage to your sense of self-worth.

Even if you're a reasonably attractive single woman, how often do you worry that guys don't call because you don't measure up to their Hollywood fantasy woman? If you're just an average Joe, how often do you wonder whether women give you the cold shoulder because you're just not Brad Pitt?

The wretched truth is this: We're *all* caught trying to live up to the unreal standards set by the media. After spending decades watching how other people supposedly look and live, as depicted on *Charlie's Angels* or *Baywatch*, we've all got a galloping case of discontent with our self-images. *That*, gentle reader, is a form of social stress unknown in previous times.

Pandora's Electronic Box

The impact of television and movies on society is profound, yet it's so intrusive that it is nearly unrecognized. Its electronic "mirror" has made us discontented with ourselves and with others. TV no longer is simply an electronic box in the corner of the living room—it's almost a member of the family.

True, TV characters don't raid your refrigerator (yet) or tie up your bathroom, but they do appear in our homes regularly, and they have a profound influence on the family. We try to walk like them, talk like them, dress like them, smoke like them, and—let's face it—look like them.

The Dark Side of Freedom of Speech

Tens of millions of Americans (and not just "moral majority" types) believe that popular culture, particularly as transmitted by electronic media, is undermining the character of modern society. Regardless of your politics, when 8-year-olds can buy CDs laced with vulgarities and references to rape, incest, murder, and horrible mistreatment of women, you don't have to have a Ph.D. in psychology to recognize that over time, some of it seeps in.

Think about it. Most Americans begin watching television before they can even talk. By age 6, many children have consumed more hours watching TV than they will spend speaking with their fathers *in an entire lifetime*. And what are they watching? The president of the American Medical Association observed that the typical child today sees at least 8,000 murders and 10,000 acts of violence in the media before the seventh grade.

A World Apart

The media's portrayal of life—a portrayal against which many of us have come to measure ourselves—bears little resemblance to real life. According to *Sneak Previews* cohost Michael Medved, the Hollywood perspective on the American family emphasizes novelty-seeking, eccentricity, and nonconformity. It selects as it's "typical" characters single mothers and absent, hostile fathers.

When leading academics and media researchers gathered for a conference about "The Impact of the Media on Children and the Family," one of the organizers was surprised to find so much agreement, especially given the diversity of participants. The group easily reached a consensus opinion. They agreed that the values expressed in much of the mass media, especially with regard to violent and sexually explicit materials, are on a collision course with traditional family values and the protection of children.

Stressbuster

Here's a stress-reducing tip that's inexpensive and easy to do: Turn off your TV and leave it off for 48 hours. You'll be amazed at how much less tense you'll feel when you're free of its noise and its demands.

Separating Fact from Fiction

Among adults, who supposedly can discern fact from fiction, polls show that large numbers of otherwise rational people believe one or more of the following.

- Alien visitors walk among us.
- Aliens helped build the pyramids.
- Homosapiens and dinosaurs appeared on earth at the same time.
- Elvis might still be alive.
- Six million Jews didn't perish in Nazi concentration camps during World War II.
- Wolves attack people in droves.
- The Loch Ness monster lives.
- The Bermuda Triangle swallows up ships and planes.
- JFK's assassination was a conspiracy.

The Myth that Will Not Die

In his 1993 book, *Case Closed*, author Gerald Posner walks the reader through every conceivable detail of the JFK assassination and shows conclusively why it was definitely Lee Harvey Oswald who fired the gun. He even explains how the "magic bullets" could, indeed, have taken the angles they were supposed to. His analysis of the data was so thorough that *U.S. News and World Report* concluded that *Case Closed* would be the last book it would review on the subject of JFK's assassination. Yet the "Who shot JFK?" industry still earns more than $200 million a year with no signs of winding down. The public hunger for even more conspiracy theory books is constantly fed by more TV news magazine investigations, authors, books, and tours.

I don't regard the misinformation surrounding JFK's death lightly. The nature of American society underwent a profound change when nearly an entire generation suspected that a conspiracy, perhaps government-led, might have brought down the leader of the free world in broad daylight. Who knows how much this single event served to increase popular cynicism about government, the press, and even the truth itself?

Calming Concept

Some influential members of the media are not insensitive to their responsibilities. George Lucas, of *Star Wars* fame, said, "It is important that the people who make films have ethics classes, philosophy classes, and history classes. Otherwise, we are witch doctors."

The Price We Pay for "Infotainment"

Consider the distinct possibility that the nature of your life has changed as a result of the misinformation that has glutted society's information channels, passing itself off as "hard news." The JFK assassination myth is only one example of media excess, but it's been a costly one for our society. The fundamentals of what it means to be a citizen in a democracy have eroded since that November day in 1963, for you and for everyone you know, even if you were born after 1963.

Murder and Mayhem on Every Channel

There's a lot of violence on TV, but did you know that violence on television is far more pervasive than in real life by a factor of 1,000 times? 1,000 times! And who are the bad guys these days? Consider this: Characters who are businessmen and -women are twice as likely to represent villains and are three times as likely to commit crimes as characters in other professions. Three out of four programs that show business dealings portray business as dishonest or corrupt. What are trends such as these saying about modern society?

When it comes to judging American media, it's no longer just a few academics or religious watchdog groups who find it lacking in redeeming value. Many countries around the globe are legislating limits as to how much American television they will allow in their countries. Some countries have levied an outright ban on American television programs.

Stress Alert

The National Coalition on Television Violence in Washington, D.C., has undertaken many studies that show a substantial increase in playground violence among otherwise normal children immediately after they watch programs that emphasize combat.

Relaxing in Front of the Tube?

Many people, possibly even you, rely on the tube to wind down at the end of a day. For two decades, however, television viewing has been shown to have the opposite effect. It doesn't help you relax, and it's actually far more likely to *increase* your stress. In their book *Television and the Quality of Life*, authors Mihaly Csikszentmihalyi and Robert Kubey reported the findings of their 13-year study of 1,200 people. They found that most people are more rattled after having watched some prime-time or late-night television and then turning in for bed.

These results are clear. If you've been experiencing a significant level of stress, you are likely to feel worse after having viewed an hour or two of television.

Real Life Versus Entertainment

Entertainment certainly fulfills a necessary function in your life. It can stimulate your thinking. It can be liberating to your soul. It can give you a break from the drudgery or monotony of daily living. Most important, entertainment can free you to explore new ways of thinking, new ideas, and new possibilities. From the dawn of human civilization, people have turned to entertainment for comfort, amusement, and solace.

What happens when the screen—silver or small—makes your own life pale in comparison to the fictional lives it presents? Consider how much time and energy you're willing to spend with your favorite characters on a TV drama or sitcom. Now contrast this with how much time you actually spend with anyone in your community.

Calming Concept

When compared to what you see on the screen, your own life might seem dull, boring, and plastic. Don't be taken in by appearances. Your real life is rich in the potential for satisfaction.

Keep in mind that the quality of your life and the memories you can derive from living it largely depend on what you actively do, not on what you passively ingest while parked in front of the television set.

The Six O'Clock News: If It Bleeds, It Leads

Would you be surprised to learn that most of the news you receive is slanted?

"And that's the way it is ...." This is how legendary newscaster Walter Cronkite used to end his broadcasts. But Mr. Cronkite had it wrong. Indeed, it would be more accurate to say "that's the way a handful of news executives, producers, and writers have decided it would be conveyed to the public." What gets broadcast is, at best, only a subset of a fraction of a sliver of what's actually occurring in the world.

You can't walk 10 paces in an airport without coming into earshot of CNN's airport news monitors blaring away, making everything sound as if it's the latest and the most vital. Television news runs major features that each last 45 seconds or less, followed by titillating television news magazines that don't always check their facts. The print media's not much better. Magazines and newspapers shout out their headlines in huge, urgent letters.

Understandably, it's becoming harder to identify what you need to know out of all the information vying for your attention. Consider the following stories

- U.N. sanctions on Iraq
- Shootings at Columbine High School
- Monica Lewinsky scandal
- World Trade Center bombing
- Clinton impeachment proceedings
- O.J. Simpson civil trial
- Serbian-Albanian conflict
- Russian economic crisis
- Genocide in Rwanda
- Nerve gas attack in Japan
- British au pair trial
- U.S. deployment in the Persian Gulf
- Whitewater investigation
- U.S. embassy bombings in Africa
- FBI shoot-out in Waco

If a friend or a loved one is in the military or was directly involved in something listed here, perhaps one of these stories had a personal impact on you. Otherwise, chances are they were merely interesting stories with little or no impact on your daily life.

You See What You're Shown

Here's a question for you. Why does "news" originate largely in a small handful of "news centers": New York, Los Angeles, London, Paris, Rome, Moscow, Tokyo, and so on? Because that's where the publishers and producers live. They routinely package news according to their preconceptions. Economic vicissitudes, interethnic hostilities, and drug wars are declared to be of "national interest." Floods, crimes, fires, and scandals are packaged as "local."

On the other hand, stories about positive developments in other countries, real scientific breakthroughs, and human triumphs don't fall into either category, so often they are simply "not news."

On the local level, few reporters actually have an in-depth understanding of what they're covering. Many are assigned beats for which they have no experience; many stories are covered by whomever the station can dispatch. When one assignment is completed, the story is aired, and tomorrow they'll do it all again. Each night, the stories might feature different names and faces, but they'll all be covered for the same reason—to fill those 22 minutes of a normal nightly broadcast.

Stress Alert

Your local television news has become a cesspool that portrays in living color—usually blood red—all sorts of personal tragedies, mayhem, and tabloid violence. It seems as if journalists, or perhaps their editors, revel in creating what some call "dramatic tension." The rest of us might simply call it exploitation for the sake of ratings.

If you received a constant barrage of positive stories starting from your infancy, your life would be different. Even award-winning local news teams don't do much better. At best, they might engage in a three- or five-day feature that will run three to four minutes each night. Their focus is almost always the same—human misery in it's many forms. Even when they take on a positive topic, it's not enough to offset the unrelenting negativity of the rest of the nightly newscast. Why is this?

"News" or Snooze?

To answer this question, we have to get back to basics and discover just what, exactly, *is* news? "News" is a derivative of the word "new," but conventional newscasts seem to be a never-ending rehash of the same-old, same-old. Here are some news items that I don't consider new.

- Ethnic clashes that have been going on for thousands of years aren't news. There would have to be a breakthrough for it to be news.
- Exposés of political corruption or government blundering have been going on for years. They're not news unless the story comes up with something unexpected—like the successful prosecution of the participants.
- Unsubstantiated allegations against politicians or celebrities are definitely *not* news.
- Last night's warehouse fire, daily inner-city crime, and the plight of the homeless are all undesirable situations, but reports of their occurrence are not news.

It's not that these events don't merit concern—they do. Let's not, however, lump them in with news. Real news would be reports of *new* developments, such as

- Ways that some ethnic groups have made substantial progress in resolving their differences.
- New forms of cooperation or instances of political integrity.
- In-depth analysis of good deeds, service, and sacrifice on the part of public figures.
- Innovative strategies communities are exploring to reduce the incidence of fire, crime, and homelessness.

Now, *these* would be news.

But we never get *these* stories. Instead, night after night you see, hear, and read about the tired old scandals and negatives. This can't help but distort your view of society—and perhaps diminish your opinion of humanity.

Crying in the Wilderness

Some years ago, news anchor Dan Rather blasted his fellow news broadcasters at the annual Radio and Television News Directors Association convention. Rather delivered a scathing attack on current trends in the news industry, claiming it was more concerned with dead bodies, mayhem, and terror than with giving viewers any semblance of balance in reporting.

Unfortunately, Rather's stand was not a popular one. It was largely ignored and was quickly forgotten.

Calming Concept

Well, this might not make you feel calmer. More than a quarter century ago, the now-revered Edward R. Murrow blistered the Radio and Television News Directors Association about the then-current state of affairs in the news industry. By comparison, however, newsroom standards in Morrow's time were far superior to today's standards.

Speak Up, Speak Out

If you'd like to express your views in writing because you're concerned about television content or programming, here are some key addresses.

ABC Entertainment President
2040 Avenue of the Stars
Los Angeles, CA 90067

CBS Audience Services
524 West 57th Street
New York, NY 10019

NBC Entertainment President
3000 W. Alameda
Burbank, CA 91523

Public Broadcasting Service
1320 Braddock Place
Alexandria, VA 22314

Federal Communications Commission
Complaints & Investigations
Branch Enforcement Division
2025 M Street, NW Room 8210
Washington, DC 20554

News You Can't Use: Tabloids

You've seen them often enough. The bold headlines shout to you as you stand in line at your supermarket checkout counter. You can't help but notice the tabloids. In the 1960s, they obsessed about Richard Burton and Elizabeth Taylor. In the '70s, they provided lurid tales of life inside the Nixon White House. In the '80s, they gave you all the dirt on Burt Reynolds and Loni Anderson that you could take. And in the '90s, at least for the past couple years, Bill Clinton and Monica Lewinsky dominated the covers. If attacks on the well-known or the well-to-do aren't enough for you, there also are stories about miracle diets, militia taking over Nevada, alien visitors, the "I spotted Elvis" crowd, chain saw massacres, and little-known facts about the Pope.

Quaint as it might now seem, the tabloids once were quite distinct from what was known as the "legitimate press." It's hard to tell them apart today.

Stress Alert

I routinely ask checkout-aisle cashiers why they carry publications with such lurid headlines in full view of children and other gentle creatures. Of course, none of them actually knows. One responded that the tabloids probably pay a lot of money to be placed in such a prominent position.

Stressbuster

When you see an item in print about a company or an individual with whom you compete, don't let it get you down. Consider instead how it got there. The odds are good that it's just another public relations success story and, thus, not worthy of causing you stress.

But Is it News You Can Use?

Sadly, although the sheer volume of news sources has increased, the reliability of the information they report is increasingly suspect. Do you doubt this? See for yourself. Get a copy of your local newspaper and flip to the business, outlook, lifestyle, or health section. Every edition carries an interview with or a feature on some executive or entrepreneur. If you read carefully, however, you'll discover that the majority of these stories are placed by public relations firms who have been paid by the person whom the story is about.

Many of the features and profiles you see are part of a coordinated public relations effort undertaken and funded by the company or individual. Publishers, particularly magazine publishers, know that executives and entrepreneurs in their community want to be written about and have the funds to commission an article. It's might be good business to let them do so—but it's definitely *not* news.

Solicitation Everywhere

Click here! Sign up today! Subscribe now! Free trial demo!

You've seen the endless parade of articles about how important it is to be wired to the rest of the world via cell phones and pagers. Do these messages seem to have a familiar ring? They should. They mirror what happened 20 years ago when the PC was introduced.

PC vendors advertised heavily on television. One showed a Charlie Chaplin–type figure who sat down at a keyboard. With the greatest of ease, and hardly cracking a software manual, he effortlessly and efficiently ran a business. The trouble with these ads was that it took another three to five years before even progressive businesses had a majority of their employees working with a PC.

In the years ahead, you will be flooded with as many articles about personal-communication technology as you saw about PCs in the early 1980s or about AIDS during 1986 and 1987. Articles about communication technology will begin to diminish just when it becomes more important, just as there were fewer articles about AIDS when it started to have a major impact in the early 1990s.

In the early years of any new technology, oversaturation of the market is normal. Lots of people leap onto the bandwagon without carefully assessing just how (or even *if*) the new technology will help them meet their goals. If the communication technology available today readily enhances your position in the minds of the people you serve, by all means proceed with it. If you're unsure, it's wiser to proceed at a more moderate pace.

Calming Concept

If the strategic and personal advantages you can acquire by being wired are crucial to your business or your life, chances are you're already online. If you're not, it's probably time to cautiously begin looking at the possibilities. The days when you can function effectively without computers are fast coming to an end.

Mass Communication Insanity!

From now on, forsake using the media as the decision-maker of what merits your time and attention. Instead, make profound personal choices about where you'll seek information and advice. Strive for objectivity despite the unreality all around you. Don't let reporters, journalists, and the industry vendors who influence them add undue stress to your life or make you feel inadequate. Don't let them set your agenda or your timetables. They're not qualified.

Here are some quick tips to reduce media intrusion into your life.

- Watch only one news program per day.
- If you read the paper, don't watch the TV news.
- Limit your viewing to one or two hours of entertainment TV per week. Spend your new free time exercising to eliminate stress.
- After you cut your TV viewing to three or four total hours per week, stop your cable subscription to save money.
- Check out movies for free from your library. This will limit your selection and will offer more nonviolent choices.

The Least You Need to Know

- If you're experiencing stress, you are likely to feel worse after having viewed an hour or two of television.
- Become more discriminating about your attention to news, information, and entertainment.
- At least 75 percent of all the optional features and profile pieces (not "hard" or late-breaking news) in smaller local newspapers and magazines have been "placed" by agents representing those parties featured.
- Don't let reporters, journalists, and the industry vendors who influence them add undue stress to your life.

Part 4

Empower Thyself

External factors, such as population density and the ceaseless output of the news and information industry, have a combined stressful effect that is staggering. When you add our constant exposure to unreal expectations regarding our looks, performance, and abilities, you're looking at a high probability for burnout. Still, as you learned in Chapter 1, "Stress: A Very Old Phenomenon," most stress is self-induced. It can't get at you unless you invite or allow it into your life. This section examines three critical areas in which the stress you experience is clearly self-induced.

- *Getting too little sleep*
- *Not conditioning your personal environment*
- *Not completing what you start*

You probably already know about getting too little sleep from an experiential standpoint—odds are you're an expert in the field. Not conditioning your personal environment and not achieving completions might represent unfamiliar terminology, but they'll become clear soon enough.

Are you fatigued this very minute? If you can muster the energy, go right to Chapter 13, "Running on Empty." If you're among the handful of people who are well rested and fit, perhaps you need to work a few 12-hour days, get as little sleep as you can, and then tackle it. Either way, you'll understand firsthand what I mean.

Chapter 13

Running on Empty

In This Chapter

- Taxing times—a society of thoroughly tired people
- Identifying the link between sleep and stress
- Determining how much sleep you need
- Giving it a rest (your body, that is)

You didn't get enough sleep last night, and you're not getting enough sleep in general. You're not alone. All around you, other people are showing symptoms of fatigue as well. Undoubtedly, you've probably heard or said one of the following

> "I'm so tired! How will I make it through the work week? Sometimes it's a miracle I don't get in a car accident on the way home."

> "I've got no energy left. When I put in a decent day's work, there's not much left by the end of the day. My family and friends haven't seen the real me for ages."

These statements might sound like simple words of fatigue, but they're much more than that. In this chapter, you'll learn about fatigue and its relationship to stress.

Sleepwalking Through Life

Would you believe that

- During the 20th century, Americans' average sleep time per night dropped by 20 percent from the previous century.

- Americans have added 158 hours to their yearly working and commuting time since 1969.
- Fatigued employees cause business to lose as much as $1,000 per employee in lost productivity.
- Doctors' offices are flooded with people wondering why they feel exhausted.

Believe it all.

The Pervasiveness of Fatigue in Modern Life

The medical community—doctors, nurses, administrators—used to be among the most likely to experience fatigue. Now the exhaustion has spread to all parts of society. And with that exhaustion comes stress as well as illness.

How many people suffer from *insomnia*? No one knows for sure, but estimates range between 36 and 62 million people in the United States alone. Second- and third-shift workers are particularly prone to insomnia, as are older adults. Women seem to be more susceptible than men. If you're like most stressed-out adults, you've probably endured mild insomnia—a few sleepless nights—brought on by your stress.

Tranquillity Terminology

Insomnia is a sleep disorder characterized by the inability to fall asleep at appropriate times. In another sleep disorder, called **narcolepsy**, the individual is struck by sudden, unexpected attacks of deep sleep without warning.

Sleep Disorders Abound

Somewhere between 250,000 and 300,000 people are affected by *narcolepsy*, a malfunction of the central nervous system. Narcolepsy causes daytime sleepiness including sudden, temporary losses of muscle control and brief paralysis when falling asleep or waking. This can be dangerous. Narcoleptic sleep attacks occur without warning and can occur while you're driving, operating dangerous equipment, or simply in the middle of a conversation.

Another fatigue-inducing affliction, *sleep apnea*, causes a person to stop breathing during sleep, usually because of some type of obstruction. In most cases, the person is aroused from sleep by an automatic breathing reflex, so he or she might end up getting very little sleep at all.

Not Enough Coffee in the World

In a survey of 1,000 adults commissioned by the Better Sleep Council, one in three respondents admitted that sleeplessness affected their work. Here are some of the survey's other observations about sleep.

- Men are twice as likely as woman to confess to dozing at their desks on company time.
- Nearly one out of two people believe that long work hours keep them from getting all the sleep they need (which, as I'll discuss, is not true).
- Approximately one in five people who call in sick or are tardy for work say they didn't sleep well the night before.
- One out of three adults say they are not well-rested when they wake up for work.

Stress Alert

Stress can cause a lack of sleep, and a lack of sleep can contribute to stress. It's a pretty vicious circle!

Not New But Certainly Notable

Exhaustion, whether yours or that of the people who report to you, is nothing new, but it's also nothing to take lightly. George Washington knew this. It has been reported that he used to retreat for days if not weeks on end to get precious rest and to restore his faculties during his presidency.

But *why* is sleep so important? Simple! Sleeplessness is potentially dangerous. Without enough sleep, you're more prone to accidents, faulty judgment, and error. You're also more susceptible to illness because your body's own immune system can become compromised.

Remember, you respond to stressful situations by working in a higher gear. Your heart pumps blood faster, your muscles contract, and your blood thickens. Even though you're not facing woolly mammoths or saber-toothed tigers like your prehistoric ancestors did, you *are* confronting the modern-day equivalent. In our hectic, work-a-day world, your engine is revving for eight, maybe ten hours straight. Maybe even longer. Maybe all the time.

Even when you arrive home, you're still exposed to stress. As you learned in Chapter 3, there are potentially more stressors at home than in the office. The net result is that you don't sleep as many hours as your body needs. Even if you do manage to drop off into dreamland, you don't get very good sleep. As a result

- You're being worn down.
- Your immune system is weakened.
- You're much more susceptible to illness.

Growing evidence suggests that getting too little sleep on a consistent basis can undermine your entire being—impacting your entire life to your detriment. Any illness you contract, if combined with too little sleep, will be more severe.

Warning: Get into Bed Now

So often throughout the day you feel tired, but how do you know when the tiredness is bordering on danger? These are some of the many signs.

> **Stressbuster**
>
> A little going-to-bed ritual sometimes can help bring on sleepiness. Try getting into the habit of brewing a cup of herbal tea—chamomile is particularly good at bedtime. Keep any bedtime noshing light—a full stomach can make it hard to get to sleep.

Your fatigue is prolonged. Getting several nights of extra sleep in a row or sleeping for an entire weekend doesn't seem to put a dent in your feeling of fatigue. Perhaps worse, you feel as if you'll never catch up.

You experience indigestion or lack of appetite. You normally look forward to meals, but when highly fatigued, you have trouble swallowing. Maybe you're eating less.

You experience a loss of sex drive. This isn't as obvious as you might think. Loss of your libido can occur gradually. Your partner will notice.

You have trouble getting to sleep, if not outright insomnia. During the night, you find yourself waking more often. To exacerbate the situation, you spend the rest of the night worrying that you're not getting good sleep.

You're tired in the morning even after a full night's sleep. Realistically, there's little reason for this. If by 9:30 or 10 A.M. you can hardly keep your head up, it's time to take heed.

You don't feel in control. In many ways, this is the most insidious of the signs. You doze at inopportune moments, such as in an important meeting or when driving. (This will be discussed further later in the chapter.)

Knocking on Danger's Door

Why wait until your lack of sleep hits the danger level? Here are some early-warning indicators that you're not getting enough sleep.

- Your eyes are red.
- You avoid tasks that involve adding up numbers.
- In situations with others, you simply go through the motions.
- You don't want to handle any phone calls if you can help it.
- You watch the clock frequently throughout the day, hoping time will go by more quickly.

Your Needs, Not Theirs

Some high-achiever types often feel they can shortchange sleep without penalty. Some believe that, by working longer or harder and perhaps getting less sleep, the potential payoffs can be larger.

These people might knowingly take less sleep as part of a calculated plot to become prosperous younger or sooner.

Hmm .... The most successful people I know tend to have regular, sufficient sleep patterns. Whether they retire early or late, they get ample sleep daily and weekly to keep themselves vibrant and moving forward.

Anxiety Antidote

We all have our own unique sleep needs. As long as you're getting adequate rest, don't worry that others claim to need less. You get no extra points in life for coming in first in the sleeplessness sweepstakes!

When you read about some ultra-high achiever who only sleeps an average of four or five hours a night, stop and consider that

- Your need for sleep differs from others. Don't compare yourself.
- Unless a longitudinal study of their sleep patterns has been done, no one knows the long-term effects of their sleep habits. Maybe such people will develop acute disorders.

Many who claim to get by on less sleep actually do not. (These probably are the same people who claim they don't watch much television.)

Neither the Time nor the Place

Too many transportation mishaps today are the direct result of someone being fatigued at the wheel. Frankly, my dear, you're a danger to yourself and others when you try to function with consistently too little sleep.

Although it is not common knowledge, vast numbers of people are subject to episodes of *microsleep*, in which the body tries to compensate for insufficient sleep. School bus drivers with 40 children on board might be engaging in microsleep. Train conductors responsible for hundreds of passengers might engage in microsleep. Nuclear plant engineers whose behavior can affect millions of people for years to come might be engaging in microsleep. The potential dangers are obvious.

Tranquillity Terminology

Microsleep is a five- to ten-second episode in which your brain is effectively asleep but you're still physically up and about.

Estimates from the National Highway Transportation Safety Administration reveal that, each year, at least 1,500 deaths and 32,000 injuries can be attributed to vehicle crashes associated with driver drowsiness, as illustrated in the following table.

Dreaming and Driving: Auto Accidents in Which Drowsiness, Fatigue, and Sleeping at the Wheel Was a Factor

Year	Crashes	Injuries	Deaths
1990	57,000	40,000	1,596
1991	59,000	45,000	1,579
1992	50,000	33,000	1,440
1993	43,000	32,000	1,557
1994	36,254		
1995	37,241		
1996	37,494		
1997	37,280		

Source: Fatal Accident Reporting System of the NHTSA. Note that information on Injuries and Deaths for 1994–1997 is not yet published.

What's scary is that the incidence of drowsy-driver crashes might be *highly* understated. Because many drowsy-driver crashes only involve the driver, many go unreported. Or, in the case of a fatal accident, many accidents are misclassified.

Even if your car is equipped with an advanced driver-warning system that potentially can reduce the overall number of drowsy-driver accidents, it's no excuse for you to ever get behind the wheel *if you even suspect* that your level of fatigue will impair your driving ability. The act of driving in itself is *not* sleep inducing. If you weren't sleepy to begin with, you wouldn't nod off while driving.

In any case, driving and fatigue don't mix. If you can't do much about completely overcoming your fatigue right now, consider doing the following.

- Using public transportation as often as possible
- Becoming part of a ride-share system and at least being well rested when it's your turn to drive
- Avoiding any long trips (the probability of a mishap increases markedly)
- Taking a taxi, a bike, or walking for shorter trips

Between Us Girls

According to the National Commission on Sleep Disorders Research and several other groups, women often have a more difficult time getting good sleep than men. Particularly among women who work outside the home and raise children, the effects can be pronounced.

Calming Concept

We're all accustomed to the idea that a person needs eight hours of sleep each night, but many of us can't manage that amount. If this sounds like you, try scheduling a nap during the day. After all, cats are great nappers. Have you ever seen a stressed-out, exhausted cat?

Up to half of any given group of working women routinely experience a sudden awakening in the wee hours of the night. Here are some of the many reasons why women might have sleep-related problems.

- Women usually spend more hours on domestic tasks in addition to occupations outside the home.
- Society's expectations regarding their appearance prompts them to spend more time getting dressed, groomed, and so on, hence potentially less time for sleep.
- Traditionally, women have had lower incomes, which means they must work longer or harder to earn the same amount as men. Thus, many have a difficult time meeting household expenses and are prone to fatigue.
- Many women are involved in their children's education such as attending PTA meetings, participating in school events, reading to the child at night, and so on. (This is not to slight men—your section is coming up.)

As increasing numbers of women find themselves assuming full responsibility for supporting a household (the number of single mothers has increased dramatically in the last two decades), they might find their role as sole caretakers of the emotional and spiritual well-being of family members to be increasingly stressful. This means the new pressures arising from their household responsibilities might ultimately have a negative impact on the amount and quality of their sleep. The Women's Bureau of the U.S. Department of Labor notes the following sleep-disrupting statistics.

- Sixty-three percent of women with children work outside the home.
- Fifty percent of working women return to work within a year of having a baby. An additional 30 percent return to work after more than a year.
- Ninety percent of elderly parents needing care are cared for directly by their families. Sixty-seven percent of the primary-care givers are working women.

More and more women who work don't have time to advance their careers because of dual home and family responsibilities. By some estimates, women still do about

80 percent of all work associated with housekeeping and raising children. By the time they get to bed, women are all but exhausted. You'd think that would be a scenario for deep sleep, but the more wired and agitated you are mentally throughout the day, the less likely you are to sleep through the entire night.

However, women aren't the only people with tremendous demands on their days that in turn impact their nights.

Stressbuster

Remember that there's a difference between *exhaustion* and *physical tiredness.* Working out or engaging in strenuous physical activity early in the evening actually can help you get a better night's sleep. In fact, many sleep experts recommend a regular regimen of physical exercise in the evening to alleviate problems with insomnia.

It's a Man's World? It Doesn't Feel Like It!

Since the early 1990s if not earlier, an increasing percentage of men have found themselves to be candidates for exhaustion. After all, trying to be a good father, a responsive husband, a champion breadwinner, an enlightened manager, an on-call handyman, and a pillar of the community takes its toll. Consider, too, these little bonus tasks.

- Men do most of the driving on family-related trips, particularly long trips.
- Men spend more time working around the yard and on other physically strenuous tasks.
- Men spend more time working on family finances and, in particular, income taxes.
- Men are more likely to be Little League coaches; officers of social, civic, and charitable organizations; volunteer fire fighters; or part of the National Guard.

These observations could lead a person to the notion that men have it pretty tough. Life spans bear this out. The gap in life expectancy between men and women in America today is an astounding seven years. Lest you believe this is attributed to the "genetic superiority" of females, guess again. In 1920, the gap between the expected life spans of men and women was only one year. In certain regions and at certain times, men routinely outlive women.

Many men face increasing responsibilities at work, and far more men face potential health hazards on the job than women. *Hazardous occupations are virtually male domains.*

So the consensus is that many factors contribute to the feelings of fatigue on the part of both sexes.

Alternating Your Required Performance Levels

Let's pretend that you are the president of the United States. You have foreign dignitaries coming to a lavish dinner at the White House. You're going to get up and say a few words and dance with the First Lady (or First Gentlemen, as the case may be). You're going to be charming, magnanimous, and witty.

Night falls, the guests arrive, and the affair comes off without a hitch. You are dashing and the center of attention, a suitable symbol for all that's right with the Western world.

The Natural Ebb and Flow of Intensity

No one, however, can maintain this level of performance consistently. Most days, even as president, you drop back to a lower level of operation. You sign executive orders, handle important phone calls, and meet with your staff, but you don't have to be "beaming."

Now let's return to the reality of your everyday life. In whatever your occupation, you alternate between periods of performance and recovery. You're not hibernating during recovery; you're just regrouping your physical and mental resources and replenishing your spirit and emotions for the times when you might be called upon to "perform."

Calming Concept!

Deep REM sleep enables you to more fully engage in conceptual, first-time, and breakthrough thinking. If you have to learn a new routine, new instructions, or new equipment, the amount and quality of REM sleep you get the night before will decidedly impact your abilities.

Regular, sufficient sleep enables your body to recover from the stresses and strains you experience during the day. Although recovery also comes as a result of being mentally and physically relaxed, getting deep sleep is critical for the challenging tasks you face daily.

A Bedtime Rx

Wouldn't you know it? You're most likely to resist allowing yourself a recovery period of good sleep precisely when you're *most in need of it.* If you're among the multitudes at war with themselves when it comes to getting the sleep you need, perhaps these suggestions for restructuring your sleeping environment will help.

- Have you checked your mattress lately? A bad mattress engages your muscles all night as if you're *working* all night.
- Particularly in the summer, make sure the air in your bedroom is cool and fresh. You're better off sleeping in a slightly chilled room with an additional blanket than in a warmer one with fewer blankets.
- Make sure you have a bed sufficiently large enough to allow you and your partner freedom of movement. If you're afraid of clunking into one another, you'll restrict your movements and, unknowingly, diminish the quality of your sleep.
- Turn off the ringer on your phone. If an answering machine is attached, also switch the appropriate lever to silent. As I pointed out in Chapter 7, too many people sleep with their heads by the phone because they have an aged loved one far away or because they worry about the one call that might haul them out of bed at 3 A.M. Realistically, you can't do much at 3 A.M. anyway. You'd be better off getting umpteen years of sound sleep.
- Keep your room dark or wear a night blindfold.
- Buy a snore-control device if a sleep partner keeps you awake or simply to improve the quality of your own sleep.

Set the Stage for Slumber

Getting good sleep, like many things in life, is a habit. If it's been months or years since you've engaged in the habit of regular, sufficient, sound sleep, you've got an unfamiliar but pleasant task ahead of you. Here are a few ideas for redeveloping the personal habit of getting good sleep every night.

Anxiety Antidote

If you're waking up in the middle of the night and can't go back to sleep, get out of bed, leave the room, and read for awhile. Lying there obsessing about your sleeplessness will just increase your frustration.

- Although exercising in the evening can help you get better sleep, avoid too hard a workout, particularly just before retiring. It might keep you too keyed up.
- Nix caffeine at least six hours before retiring and nix alcohol altogether if you're interested in getting good sleep that night. Alcohol, in particular, disrupts sleep. You might fall asleep quickly, but invariably you'll arise too early. Then you'll likely have trouble getting back to sleep.

- If the spirit moves you, drink a glass of milk before you sleep. It can help.
- Go to sleep when you're tired, not because the clock happens to say a particular time.
- Let others around you know when you need quiet because you are going to sleep.

On Unfamiliar Turf

What about when you're traveling for work or on vacation and you'll be staying in a hotel room? What happens to all your careful plans to get good sleep then?

- Specifically ask for a room where you'll have peace and quiet. Explain that you have a huge presentation to deliver in the morning and that sleep is crucial. This might prompt them to give you a room in a quiet section of the hotel.
- Ask for a room without an adjoining door to another room, where the couple from hell will likely be staying.
- Investigate getting ear plugs. They can reduce about 70 percent of the sounds you might hear from your external environment. You also could buy a sound screen, which creates a blanket of "white noise" sound around you to drone out the effects of the more obtrusive sounds outside your door. Here are some key contacts.

  Noise Filter
  Cabot Safety Corporation
  5457 West 79th Street
  Indianapolis, IN 46268

  Sound Screen and Sleep Mate
  Marpac Corporation
  P.O. Box 3098
  Wilmington, NC 28406-0098

- Try a midday siesta. Does napping sound good to you? You might wonder what napping during the day does to your ability to sleep soundly during the night. If you take a nap between the hours of 1 and 3 P.M., you'll be fine. Your body temperature takes a natural dip at this time, allowing you to nod off quickly. If you nap for less than 20 minutes, you don't incur REM sleep and can wake from your nap refreshed and alert.

Stressbuster

To be fully effective, a nap needs to be long enough to include one cycle of deep sleep. This usually takes about 3 hours. So-called cat naps—about 15 minutes long—can offer quick refreshment, but they can't replace a good night's sleep.

Refreshed and Invigorated

Getting good, sound sleep gives you the recovery time you need from the stress you experience during the day, keeps you sharp and alert, and perhaps even can restore your sex life. Here are some signs that you're getting the sleep you need.

- You spring out of bed upon awakening.
- Your voice is clear and strong.
- You experience no fatigue during the morning.
- You have enough energy to have a life after the workday.
- You find yourself whistling or humming.
- You actually have the energy to be nice to people.
- You think to yourself that your boss or spouse is not so bad after all.
- You have sex on your mind.

It might take a few weeks or even months, but you *can* get back into the groove when it comes to having good sleep!

The Least You Need to Know

- Lack of sleep is endemic in our society and is both the result of and a contributor to stress.
- You need to proactively ensure the probability of sound sleep for the whole night.
- Don't compare the amount of sleep you need to the amount others need. Your needs are unique.
- Sleep provides a crucial opportunity for your mind and body to recover from the day's stresses.
- If you're going to nap, the best time for most people is between 1 and 3 P.M.

Chapter 14

Creating a Peaceful Kingdom

In This Chapter

- Making your home your castle
- Slamming the door on door-to-door solicitors and other uninvited guests
- Hanging up on unwanted callers
- Winning the space race

Have you come to feel that you can never get a moment of peace at home? Is the television or radio always blaring, the dog always barking, and so on? Are you feeling besieged by door-to-door solicitors and telephone marketers? Are the spaces of your home cluttered, uncomfortable, and not conducive to unwinding?

It is not your imagination. It *is* getting hard to defend your turf from outside noise, information, interruptions, distractions, solicitors, and other disturbances—not to mention all that self-generated clutter. Your home *can* be your castle once again, and this chapter will tell you how to make it so.

Raising the Drawbridge—A New Trend

If you've ever traveled the intercoastal highway in Florida, you've seen the hundreds of luxury condominiums that line the road. Virtually every community is sealed off from the main street. A fence or a gate surrounds the property, and there's a guard house with at least one guard on duty (and often two). These guards stop all visitors, ask them who they will be visiting, and obtain clearance for the visitors. Residents have their own gate pass, sticker, or another identifying insignia that enables them to breeze right through. Somewhere near the entrance, usually prominently posted, is a sign that reads "No Soliciting."

Privacy is Possible—At a Premium

Although it might seem like such communities are obsessed with the notion of privacy, consider that the residents usually are elderly people. Yes, they want privacy, but they also fear crime and are willing to pay for the protection. Increasingly, people are taking drastic steps to secure their privacy and security by moving to places that enable them to keep others from "invading their space." The phenomenon is so common that there's even a name for it—*enclaving.*

Tranquillity Terminology

Enclaving is the term used to describe the rapid growth of closed communities in American societies. Walled off from the rest of the world, they are closed to all but residents and their guests.

The Invaders Are at the Gates

Some days, the idea of living in an enclave community seems perfectly reasonable. I live smack-dab in the middle of semirural North Carolina in the posh town of Chapel Hill, an ultra-liberal bastion where no crime is too heinous to be forgiven. Every so often (too often, in my opinion), people come to the door offering everything from magazine subscriptions to opportunities to make donations to the police officers' benevolent fund to scout cookies to tree-cutting services.

On occasion, I've been "greeted" by members of various religious sects who smile so intently that I fear their mouths are locked in the position (and who I must assume actually believe they're going to convert someone today), people campaigning for political office, telephone-repair people who never seem to get the job done right, people with a cause, people without a cause, and a host of others. It sometimes feels as if making sure your home and other spaces remain private refuges requires that you take specific measures. I am happy to report that none are arduous.

Invasion by Other Means

A ring at my door, now and then, from someone selling something is not particularly stress inducing in itself—far from it. However, when you add in the phone calls from people selling newspaper subscriptions, brokerage services, and long-distance services or seeking charitable contributions, survey information, and who knows what else, the situation can easily intensify.

Throw in all the junk mail you get, not to mention faxes and e-mail if you have a PC, and you soon have the makings of an *unconditioned personal environment.* In other words, anyone or anything is likely to beg for your attention at any time.

Home Sweet (and Stressful) Home

Recall the observation from Chapter 3 about how the direction of stress has changed—it now flows from home to office instead of vice versa—and you begin to understand why it becomes increasingly important to reclaim your castle.

It's not just family demands and obligations that contribute to your stress at home. Noise and clutter are major problems, too. If you've lived at your current residence for any length of time, you undoubtedly have begun to accumulate things. The closets that looked so big when you first moved in probably seem undersized now, given everything you've acquired that needs to be stored in them. You're probably thinking that you could use more shelves. Kitchen cabinets seem woefully inadequate; the linen closet is too small.

> **Tranquillity Terminology**
>
> The term **unconditioned personal environment** refers to a home in which there are no protections in place to keep unwanted intrusions and distractions from interrupting your peace and quiet.

In short, your place is looking like cluttersville. Plus, the TV is probably on a bit too often, stereos or CD players might be blaring out music you don't want to hear, and people on the radio might be jabbering away, saying nothing, for hours on end.

Merely keeping your home clutter free and at the level of quiet you desire does not necessarily guarantee a happy home life. Certainly, there are relationship issues of greater magnitude. Having a *conditioned* personal environment, however, certainly can't hurt. To help you reclaim your castle, this chapter discusses five issues starting with the most intrusive—solicitors and other uninvited guests—and working down to the least intrusive—self-generated clutter and noise.

Beating Back the Invaders

You could take your cue from the luxury condominium communities in Florida and post a sign that says "No Soliciting." This will fend off about 90 percent of the uninvited door-to-door salespeople who could knock on your door.

Sometimes people use a security-system sign for the dual purpose of providing security and keeping away solicitors. You've seen the signs. They say things like

> "Premises secured by XYZ systems."

or

> "Warning, alarm will sound if you XYZ."

Calming Concept

Nowhere is it written that you must answer every knock at the door or ring of the phone. These are only signals. You have every right to ignore them when they come at inconvenient times.

This won't solve your problem entirely, however. Some groups—certain religious groups, collectors for charities, political campaigners, and the like—ignore such postings with regularity. My friend Don, who lives in Great Falls, Virginia, has a strategically placed sticker that says "Premises secured by Smith and Wesson." This might be a little excessive, however, especially in today's everybody's-got-a-gun culture.

Uh, Not Right Now

What about neighbors and other acquaintances who stop by at inopportune moments? Especially for those of us who work from home, this can become a real problem. People who would never just drop in to visit you at a business office during working hours often have no compunction in interrupting your work at home. You want to protect your work schedule, but you don't want to offend your friends—what can you do? Courtesy mixed with firmness is the rule.

> "I'd invite you to come in, but I'm updating my tax log now, and I don't want to lose my place."
>
> "Nice to see you. Can I take a rain check? This is the evening I promised Bill I would complete the XYZ."
>
> "I'd love to chat, but now is not a good time. I'm in the middle of a work project. I'm generally free about 3 P.M. if you'd like to stop by later."
>
> "Glad you stopped by. As it turns out, I'm expecting a phone call from XYZ. Perhaps we could get together another time."

You also have the option of not responding to a knock at the door or the ring of the bell. If your car is in the garage and not clearly visible, this strategy offends no one. If your car is visible or if it's obvious someone is home by the lights or sounds in the house, it's still your option not to answer the door. Some friends, however, might look for an explanation later on.

Isn't Our Time Our Own Anymore?

Alarmingly, the pervasive notion has gripped society that you and I, like good little soldiers, must respond to the beck and specifically the call of others. Not so. This probably is a holdover from colonial days when people didn't have phones or fax machines, received but one letter per month, and had a different orientation toward visitors.

In centuries past, a visitor meant a relatively rare chance to interact with humanity. Visitors brought news and even entertainment. In times when you couldn't switch on a radio, channel surf, cruise the Internet, or get on the phone and chat, a real, live, in-your-face visitor gave you a chance to reconnect with the outside world. You only have to watch movies such as *Little Women, The Age of Innocence*, or *Sense and Sensibility* to see this phenomenon at play.

That was then, however, and this is now. Today, with the information overload that characterizes our age, it's *escape* from distractions we seek and sanctuary from the interruptions and disturbances that pervade modern life. Home is where we expect to find that sanctuary.

Anxiety Antidote

Don't worry that taking charge of your environment will leave you isolated. Reasonable people—your friends are reasonable, aren't they?—will understand.

Was There Something You Needed?

Unexpected surprises happen. If, out of the blue, someone pops over and you have to be "on" (see Chapter 13,) at a moment's notice—let alone bathed, dressed, and otherwise presentable—this disruption in your evening is likely to have its effect.

Remember the 1968 movie *Rosemary's Baby*? There's a memorable scene in which Mia Farrow as Rosemary is curled up on her couch about to dive into a big, thick book. There's a knock at the door. It's Minnie, her elderly neighbor, played by the irrepressible Ruth Gordon. Unbeknownst to Rosemary, Minnie is a broom-carrying officer of the local witches coven.

Minnie barges in and sits down on the couch. Then she takes out her knitting. All of a sudden, Rosemary's evening is disrupted. She's forced to play the gracious host and participate in meaningless conversation. Her plans for a relaxing and restful evening are killed.

That's the point, unless you take control, at which you can easily find yourself at the mercy of uninvited intruders (and giving birth to Satan's spawn!). Your free time is no longer your own.

Stress Alert

If you're not taking phone calls for part of the day, turn down the ringer on your phone. Many people find it more stressful to let the phone keep ringing than to put up with the interruption of taking the call.

Let's Be Reasonable

But how do you take control? You want to avoid sending the message that you *never* want anyone to call or drop by because, soon enough, that's what will happen—no one will. There are ways, however, to convey when it's a good time to visit and when it isn't.

- If you can keep your front door open without concern in your community (and there are fewer and fewer of these communities every year), you can use this as a signal that a quick chat or drop-in visit would be welcomed.
- If you're actually on your front or back porch or are working in the yard, this is another sign people will take to mean that you're available for a visit. Of course, this is a problem if you want to enjoy your outdoor activities without interruptions from others.

When an unexpected but otherwise highly welcome visitor appears—someone you like and want to see, but the timing is inconvenient—you have various options at your disposal:

- Invite your visitor in but preface the invitation with, "I only have a few minutes, and then I have to get ready for XYZ."
- Tell your visitor, "Um, I was just about to take a nap, but why don't you come in for a few minutes? I apologize if I seem a little tired. I've just been running around so much." That way, if they had intended to stay for 30 minutes, you've effectively conveyed that 10 would be more like it.
- Step out and meet with them on the front steps, the walkway, or the porch. This tells them that you're glad to see them but that you're not going to let them in on this particular visit. This also gives you the opportunity to head back in when the time is right. At least a good 10 minutes is polite; a little longer is generous.
- Turn the tables. Announce some important task you were going to tackle at that moment, but ask if you can drop by their house when it's convenient for you.

Phone Solicitations: Have You Had Yours Today?

A few unwanted calls a day are enough to make you want to get an unlisted number. More than one out of five homes in America already have done this. If you make the switch to an unlisted number, you can count on 20 to 40 fewer solicitations per year.

You can always distribute your number to the people you want to have it. If an unlisted phone number is too drastic for you, or if you already have one but it's not keeping the unwanted callers away, here are a few more strategies.

- Resistance is futile. Get an answering machine. This enables you to screen calls. There's no reason you have to disrupt dinner to listen to someone's pitch about newspaper subscriptions, financial services, or the latest poll the person is taking.
- When confronted by a telephone solicitor, be polite but firm. My typical response is, "I'm sorry, but I'm not interested," and then I hang up. The law is on your side here. They're supposed to cease and desist in 10 seconds.
- Turn the tables. Jerry Seinfeld's response to unsolicited calls was, "I'll tell you what, why don't you give me your home phone number, and I'll call you back tomorrow night while *you're* having dinner."
- If someone asks whether the man or woman of the house is in, you could say, "No, and I don't know when they will be returning."
- Inform the telemarketer that you no longer want to receive solicitation calls regarding the organization she or he is representing.

Calming Concept

You do have rights! The Telemarketing and Consumer Fraud and Abuse Prevention Act provides that you need not be forced to endure unwanted calls. If you inform telemarketers that you want your name taken off their list, they are prohibited from calling you back.

You *Do* Have Options

Here's something worth dwelling on. Telemarketers who keep calling a consumer who has requested *not* to be called are in violation of Federal Trade Commission (FTC) regulations and are risking a $10,000 civil penalty.

There are exceptions to this situation, however, such as when the telemarketer has implemented "Do not call" procedures, but the consumer is called in error. Shucks! If a telemarketer is shown to be committing a great many errors, the FTC can determine that the telemarketer's procedures are inadequate and, once again, can impose a fine. If there's a low instance of errors, it might not be a rule violation.

Feel Free to Complain

If you have a complaint against a telemarketer or want to air any other grievances, the FTC is the place to seek relief. Send your written information to the address below.

Office of the Director
Bureau of Consumer Protection
Federal Trade Commission
6th & Pennsylvania Avenue, NW
Washington, DC 20580

To obtain a complete copy of the telemarketing sales rules to which all telemarketers must adhere, write to the following address.

The Direct Marketing Association
1120 Avenue of the Americas
New York, NY 10036-6700

Anxiety Antidote

Keep a trashcan by your door so that when you walk in with the mail, you can toss the unwanted materials before they make it to your desk or counter.

Junk Mail 101

The Direct Marketing Association (the national association of junk mailers) tells its members that consumers whose data might be rented, sold, or exchanged for direct-marketing purposes periodically should be informed of this possibility. It also tells them that list compilers should suppress names from lists when requested by the individual. The problem is that, even when direct marketers provide such information, you're unlikely to read it. After all, it looks just like the junk mail you're already tossing, unopened, into the trash.

Get Off the Junk Mail List!

Here is a strategy for reducing—even eliminating—junk mail. All you need to do is send your name, address, phone number, and request to receive less junk mail to the following address.

DMA Mail Preference Service
P.O. Box 9014
Farmingdale, NY 11735-9014

If you have a problem with a particular direct-mail company, send your name, address, and phone number; the company's name, address, and phone number; copies of any canceled checks, order forms, or other documents; and a letter summarizing the facts of the complaint to the following.

Mail Order Action Line
Direct Marketing Association
1101 17th Street NW, Suite 705
Washington, DC 20036-4704

Supposedly, the Mail Order Action Line refers the letter to the company on the consumer's behalf and asks that the company resolve the matter. Most complaints, the DMA alleges, are resolved within 30 days.

Advanced Anti-Junk Mail Strategies

After you've written to the DMA Mail Preference Service, your junk mail should be drastically reduced. In many cases, you'll stop getting any at all. If you still have trouble, however, here are some additional, little-known tips you can use to make sure the offending parties get your message:

- If an item comes to you by first-class mail (currently 33 cents or more for letters and 20 cents or more for postcards), you can simply write "Refused" on the outside of the envelope and put it back in your mailbox with the flag up. Your postal carrier will return it to the sender at no cost to you.
- "Presorted" first-class mailings can be handled just like regular first-class mail. Write "Refused" on the outside of the envelope, and again, the postal carrier will return it at no cost to you.
- If you receive mail at the true bulk rates (less than 26 cents per item), you can't refuse the mail. In this case, you'll have to throw it out yourself or pay to have it returned.

Stressbuster

If it strikes your fancy, get yourself a big red rubber stamp that shouts out "Refused" in huge, unmistakable letters.

Mercifully, much of your junk mail uses the two first-class rates. This means you are only seconds away from having it zipped back to the offending party.

The Space Race

The disruptiveness of outside intruders—in person, by phone, or through the mail—is obvious. But they aren't the only way you can lose control of your home environment. A more insidious cause of your feelings of being besieged comes from within—the clutter that you allow to build up in your home. One of the easiest ways to control your space is to pay homage to what I call the replacement principle. Simply put, the replacement principle requires that, before you acquire a new item, you must dispose of something of the same type.

The Replacement Principle in Action

Let's say you've accumulated a collection of videos over the years. Some are copies of your favorite movies; others are presidential speeches, impeachment hearings, sports contests, the Olympics, or maybe—ooh boy!—an hour-long Jane Pauley/Stone Philips special feature.

Because 60 percent of what people videotape is never viewed more than once, out of every 25 tapes you have, on average, you'll never even play 15 of them again.

Should you throw away 15 of your videotapes? That would be unnecessarily wasteful. Instead, when you tape a program, copy over one of your existing tapes. When you want to tape a second or third program, find a second or third video to tape over. As long as you keep your collection at whatever you deem to be a reasonable number, you'll be able to

- Not spend another dime on a new, blank videotape.
- Keep in control of the spaces in your life.
- Demonstrate to yourself that you are capable of restraint.
- Be a positive example to others in your household who are becoming overrun by their own "collections."

Tranquillity Terminology

Think of the **replacement principle** as "zero population growth" for clutter. Simply put, it means that for every new acquisition, you must discard, recycle, or donate to charity an item you already own of similar type.

I developed this *replacement principle* to deal with my own household's escalating level of clutter. When my little girl was 3 years old, her coloring book collection alone totaled 18 books. When she wanted a new one, she had some tough decisions to make. Which of her old favorites would have to go? Would it be *Pinocchio, Smokey the Bear, Sesame Street,* or *Mother Goose*? I can say with pride, it was surprising to see how quickly she grasped the concept and made intelligent choices even then.

I haven't won a parent-of-the-year award for teaching her this, but the principle spread into other categories in her life. She no longer needed to have 18 of these things, 14 of those, 26 of that, and so forth. She realized that a reasonable number of cassette tapes, toys, and dolls was more than enough.

What do we do with the replaced items? Every year in late December, we go to the Ronald McDonald House and give any items in excellent condition to less fortunate children. Goodwill, the Salvation Army, and various causes around town also are regular haunts. I only wish that, as a child, such practices had been instilled in me.

Tossing the Garbage While It's Still Fresh

Replacing things isn't enough in many instances. Sometimes you have to make a retain/toss decision. This is not easy for many people. After all, tossing can be permanent. Still, to be the master of your castle, you have to acknowledge on occasion that you, like everyone else, hold on to too much.

Deciding between retaining, recycling, and tossing things sometimes can be difficult. The following table breaks down some common choices and suggests the criteria you might use when making such decisions.

Retain, Toss, or Be at a Loss

Item	Feel Free to Toss or Recycle If ...	Feel Free to Retain If ...
Business cards, assorted notes	You have many cards and never call anyone, you can't recall the person, goods, or services.	You have a card holder to store it in, or you are sure you'll use it.
Paper, files, documents	It's old, outdated, uninformative; it's been transferred to disk; you no longer need it to cover your derriere.	It's your duty to retain; you refer to it often; it has future value; it comforts you.
Reports, magazines	They're old, outdated, and taking up space; you never refer to them.	They're vital to your career or well-being; you refer to them at least once in awhile; there'll be a quiz on the contents.
Books, guides, directories	You've copied, scanned or made notes on the pages of interest and removed them to a file; they're outdated copies and you've got the updated version.	It's part of your life's collections; you refer to it monthly; it has sentimental value.
CDs, cassettes, videos, and A/V	You never play it; it's been played so often the quality has deteriorated badly.	You play it; you like it; you couldn't bear to not have it in your collection; it's your keepsake.
Outdated office equipment	You've got a more efficient replacement; you don't use it anymore.	It still serves a specific purpose; it adds to the decor, or it can be overhauled and made useful again.
Mementos, memorabilia	It no longer holds meaning; you have many similar items; you no longer have room to keep it.	It still evokes strong memories; you will hand it down someday; it looks good on display.
Gifts, cards, presents	You never use it; you don't want it; the giver won't know or mind if you toss it.	You use it often; you're glad you have it; you're saving it for some special reason.

You alone must walk through the shadows of the valley of your junk. If you don't muster the will to toss all the stuff you are hanging on to, who will? Unless you have a vociferous spouse, you must be the self-appointed standard-bearer of clean hallways, closets with excess capacity, and bureau drawers that still can hold more.

The Disruption-Free Home: Truly a Castle

When you've freed yourself from intrusions and disruptions on the home front, you'll have gone a long way toward reducing the stress in your life. You'll have at least this one place where you can relax and enjoy life at the pace that suits you best. You can recharge your batteries before striding out and taking on the challenges of life once again.

The Least You Need to Know

- An increasing percentage of people choose unlisted phone numbers—maybe you need one, too.
- A simple sign that says "No Soliciting" can work wonders.
- Just because people drop by doesn't mean you have to entertain them. Make it clear when you will and won't receive visitors.
- Be polite but firm when fielding unsolicited phone calls or visitors.
- Replace some items and toss others when your collections begin to overrun your home.

Chapter 15

Finishing What You Start

In This Chapter

- What? Me worry?
- Incompletion and stress: a paralyzing pair
- Identifying the unfinished business in your life
- Coming up complete

If you want to manage stress ineffectively, try worrying. Worrying occupies your mind, sometimes to a great extent, chews up your time, and accomplishes nothing. It's like a tire spinning in the mud while the car goes nowhere.

If you spend a lot of time worrying, you're wasting everyone's time, most of all your own. You're also potentially impeding any positive action you could be taking to achieve your desired goals. Fruitless worrying inhibits achieving "completeness"—coming to terms with an element of the past or the present so you're able to move on with your life. In this chapter, you'll learn more about the concept of completeness and how to make it an active principle in your life.

The Futility of Worrying

In the book *Emotional Intelligence*, author Daniel Goleman makes a stunning observation. He says some people erroneously believe that, if they devote a certain amount of time or of themselves to worrying about something or someone, they've somehow paid cosmic "dues." Certainly, appropriate concern in specific instances might be justified or even necessary. Outright worrying, however, doesn't help the cause or the person over whom they're worrying.

Likewise, worrying doesn't make the worrier any more (or less) noble or altruistic. Worrying simply occupies a person's mind. Equally insidious, it often immobilizes you both mentally and emotionally not to mention physically.

Tranquillity Terminology

Achieving **completion** means being able to close out a project, a problem, or an emotional response that belongs in the past. This frees you to move on to new challenges. **Incompletions** are worries and emotional reactions that you carry with you long after they've lost their utility or appropriateness. They are inherently stress inducing.

Worries Equal Incompletions

Worries—short- or long-term, nagging, or otherwise—contribute to stress. They contribute to what I call a lack of *completions*. If you consider what you worry about in the course of a day, a month, or a year, they invariably are issues, no matter how big or small, that are *incomplete*. It is the incompleteness that is likely to be the most difficult aspect of the situation for you to handle.

The Paralyzing Problem of Unchecked Incompletions

What if an aging loved one is gravely ill? If you're like most people, you'll find yourself worrying for weeks or months about whether he or she will make it. But how constructive is this worry? It cannot make your loved one well, but it *can* render you less able to help him or her in a time of need by keeping you up nights so you're too tired to help provide care or comfort.

The fact of the illness is already here—worrying won't make it go away. Achieving completeness in this case means accepting this fact and moving on to dealing with things you still *can* control: finding appropriate medical care, perhaps, or making your loved one more comfortable during the illness.

Calming Concept

"Don't cry over spilled milk" is an old saying we've all heard. It's just another way of saying "Let go of your incompletions." The spill has already occurred—crying or worrying won't change that fact. It surely won't get the mess wiped up, either!

Workaday Incompletions Abound

It's not just in dire situations that incompletions threaten your ability to cope. Let's say you are a solo entrepreneur, and several clients have been slow to pay your invoices. The mortgage on your home is, as always, due on the first of the month. This is a mere eight days away, but your clients are unmoved by that fact. It's beginning to look like you are not going to be able to make your mortgage payment on time.

Should you worry about the money you're owed? Perhaps. But worrying won't get the mortgage paid. You're better off *accepting* the fact that some clients simply don't pay on time and dealing with it. How? You can become more proactive about collecting your accounts receivable, or you can prune from your client list the chronic slow- or nonpayers.

Some people carry their incompletions even further. In the preceding example, such people would continue to worry even *after* they receive the past-due money and make this month's mortgage payment on time. After all, they reason, "It might happen again!" Again, this is an unproductive kind of worry. It's far better for you to take the steps necessary to insulate yourself from such eventualities by streamlining your accounting practices and by checking out your clients for reliability. You gain com-pletion about your current finances, and you productively move on to a better billing situation.

Of course, it's only human to still be riled about the nonpayment. Being upset, however, accomplishes little. In fact, it contributes to your stress level.

Inanimate Contributors to Incompletion

You don't need a slow-paying client to fill your work and home life with incompletions. The objects in your environment can be just as troublesome.

Take a look around you! Mentally survey your office, your home, and your life. Equipment that you bought and haven't used, projects that you started but haven't finished, and personal relationships that are a little frayed at the edges—incompletions all—also are potential topics for worry or stress. Fortunately, you have the capability to deal with the incompletions that surround you.

Anxiety Antidote

Once a situation is largely (if not entirely) resolved, it's difficult to drum up any more worry about it unless you actively expend effort to do so. Let it go, but *do* be careful not to go looking for new issues to fill the now vacant "worry gap."

Incomplete and Doomed

A psychologist I know believes that every incompletion you let build up around you is a stepping stone to a major heart attack. Certainly, people who are chronic worriers are statistically more susceptible to illness and even major disease. Why run the risk?

Signs of Incompletion Everywhere You Look

Is your desk buried under mounting piles of paper and periodicals? Is the kitchen counter (or the dining room table) adrift in unopened junk mail? (See Chapter 14 for more information about this problem.) Are your bookshelves and CD collection all in a jumble? Clutter like this is a highly visible form of incompletion. Incompletions, however, come in many other forms as well.

- Files left undone
- Drawers open
- Items purchased but not used
- Plans made but not executed

In both your professional or personal life, the list of possible incompletions is endless.

The Five-Minute Rule

One way to get complete about a situation over which you've been worrying is to say to yourself, "I'm going to give myself five minutes to fret over this, and then I'm going to move on." This works enough of the time to be worthwhile. In essence, you are *getting complete about your excessive concern* over an issue.

Learn It! Get It Done! Move On!

A direct relationship exists between the speed at which your life unfolds and the potential for incompletions. Look around your office. There are copiers, PCs, pagers, fax machines, modems, laser printers, answering machines, cell phones, calculators, dictating equipment, electronic postage meters, scanners, paper shredders, and a variety of other equipment. How many of these tools do you fully know how to operate? How many come with thick instruction books that lie around gathering dust and taking up space? All of these are incompletions.

Stressbuster

Concern about specific issues can be valid, justified, even totally appropriate. Eliminating *excessive* concern, however, not only can brighten your day, it can reduce your stress substantially.

In Chapter 6, you learned that, regardless of your industry or profession, expectations about your performance are at an all-time high. Bosses, co-workers, and customers, in particular, expect a speedy, accurate, and *complete* response. Worrying about meeting these expectations inhibits your ability to fulfill them—and gives rise to *more* incompletions.

Meanwhile, in an environment where you can both send and receive messages in a millisecond, the potential for incompletions increases daily. How many e-mail messages that you've received in the last several weeks are sitting in your various in-baskets, but you haven't taken any action on them?

Excess e-mail or snail mail, too much equipment or software instruction manuals, or a pile of stuff accumulating in the corner of your office—they all represent incompletions. And one incompletion leads to another.

And another.

And yet another.

Stress Alert

Don't let worrying about incompletions become *another* form of incompletion in your life. Merely having many incompletions in your career or life is not, in itself, debilitating. It's when they build to overwhelming levels that they can paralyze you.

One Stress-Inducer Among Many

When you add a rising tide of incompletions to a physical state of continual stress and fatigue (see Chapter 13), the situation begins to feed on itself. One task merges into the next and so on. You never get true mental relief from the tasks before you. You face a seemingly unending series of incompletions that perceptually make your hours run into days, your days run into weeks, your weeks run into months, your months run into years, your years run into decades. Gosh! No, make that double gosh!

Never fear! There *is* a way to get complete about the mounting incompletions in your life—and you're to learn how, right now.

The Inevitability of Completion

A fundamental concept to grasp on your path to mastering completions is understanding that, ultimately, *everything* reaches completion one way or another. Every single pile in your office will, one way or the other, cease to exist in time. Your piles will diminish either because you've acted on them, because an earthquake occurs and the building collapses, or because you move on, are replaced, or die and someone takes over your office.

Your printer toner cartridge will run dry after making so many copies. From a time perspective, the light bulbs in your fixtures will burn out in 700 to 800 hours, just as your car's water pump will give out in about $3^1/_2$ years. Jupiter will complete a revolution around the sun in 11.9 years, and a tortoise on the Galapagos Islands will draw its last breath after about 100 years.

The third millennium will end in about 1,000 years. Cro-Magnon man lasted about 30,000 years; Neanderthal man lasted perhaps two to three times as long. Dinosaurs ruled the earth for a couple hundred million years, but they're about as complete as you can get now. The sun's remaining life is about five billion years, and then it'll be gone. Even humankind will come to a completion at some point.

Calming Concept

Completion is the state you're always instinctively trying to attain—why else would it be so stressful to face a pile of tasks as yet unfinished? When you can fully embrace this fact, you'll find yourself actively seeking the hidden incompletions of your life and finding creative strategies to reduce or eliminate them.

Getting Complete, Now and Again

In many respects, you already are a master of achieving completion. When you wake each morning, you have completed sleep for that night. When a big report is ready and you turn it in to the boss, that's a completion. The goal is to learn how to make these completions occur when and as you need them. If you gain nothing from this book but guidance about using completions, you will have benefited greatly.

Completion Is Therapeutic

Whether your completions are large or small, they provide a mental and emotional break. They help you feel better. Simply putting away the dishes or taking out the garbage is a completion that yields benefits. You can continually gain completions in every area of your life. You can achieve them on multiyear projects or on activities that last only a few seconds.

Specifically, to achieve more completions

- Break down tasks to subtasks.
- Acknowledge yourself using positive terminology (mentally and silently) after finishing each subtask.
- Move on to what's next.
- Keep seeking completions.
- Keep acknowledging your accomplishments to yourself.

Going All the Way—to Completion

Let's take the example of Megan to make the concept a little more clear. Megan was a systems consultant to several organizations. To complete each engagement, she had to prepare and deliver a final report for each of her clients.

For a long time, Megan felt it was enough to write, proof, and e-mail the entire report to the client by the due date. The problem was, Megan would then spend several days or weeks tidying up after the project, usually while she was trying to get going on a new client's requests. This project-overlap situation was the direct result of not having achieved a timely completion.

Once Megan came to recognize the power of completions, however, she took control of the situation. She devised a new work routine in which she

- Built proofing and formatting her report into her schedule.
- Updated her files.
- Completed project logs.
- Calculated cost data.
- Prepared invoices.
- Streamlined her working notes file.

She began to view all aspects of the engagement as a unit and thus strove to finish up all related activities involved with the delivery of the final report. By the time she transmitted the report, Megan was clear—mentally, physically, and emotionally. She felt good about her accomplishment and had high energy to start whatever came next.

Saying Goodbye: The Ultimate Completion

On February 17, 1977, my father passed away suddenly. He experienced his first and last heart attack that Thursday morning in Hartford, Connecticut—my birthplace. At that time, I was a management consultant in Vernon, Connecticut. I had last seen him on Monday of the same week.

I learned then that the sudden death of loved ones, particularly when you didn't get a chance to talk to them again, is doubly upsetting because:

1. You have lost someone dear.
2. It is more difficult to get complete.

Anxiety Antidote

Gaining completion when you've lost a loved one does not mean forgetting about them. In fact, it can mean that you honor their memory more appropriately because you're memories are positive, satisfying, and *complete*.

The stress of such a situation can be deep and long-lasting. For some, the recovery process can take years. In sharing this part of my life with you, perhaps I can help you to learn, as I did, how to move beyond such a loss with grace.

Learning of Loss

My brother called me at 9:30 A.M. "Father's stopped breathing. It doesn't look good. I've called the ambulance, and they're taking him to Mount Sinai Hospital." I raced from my office in Vernon with dread. Hoping against hope, I sped into Hartford and pulled over as the very ambulance carrying my father passed me. Thirty seconds later, I trailed him into the emergency ward. My life would change forever.

Minutes after hearing the doctor's cushioned blow, I asked one of the nurses if I could be with my father. Somehow, years before I even knew about completions, I had to see my father one last time, "talk" to him, and tell him everything would be all right.

Working Through to Completion

I faced the physical shell of what had been to me a force larger than life. My father "stared" blankly at the ceiling. It was as if a switch, a life switch, had simply been turned off. Yet his massive frame was everything it had been.

I grieved for all the simple earthly pleasures he would never experience again. Then and there, I told him of the deep sorrow I had for the experiences he would never realize—grandchildren, retirement, travel. I had no regrets about our relationship, but it took me months to begin to get complete about his sudden passing.

Stressbuster

To help achieve completion when dealing with the loss of a loved one, pick up Allan Klein's touching and insightful book, *The Courage to Laugh: Humor, Hope, and Healing in the Face of Death and Dying* (Tarcher, 1998).

When Time Allows...

My mother's death, 14 years later, occurred during circumstances that gave me time to reach completion somewhat more easily. My mother's health was rapidly deteriorating, so we (her children) knew we might soon lose her. One Monday in February she entered the hospital, and we knew she would not be exiting.

Still, we had several opportunities to visit her on the tenth floor of Hartford Hospital. We were able to reflect on our times and relationships. Other people came to pay their respects. When I left her hospital room one Wednesday morning, I sensed it was the last time I would see her on this earthly plane. Her death wasn't as sorrowful as I thought it would be.

Knowingly or unknowingly, the time we spent with my mother during her last days enabled each of us to achieve completeness about her passing.

Today, 22 years after my father's departure, I still wish I could have one last time to be with him, as I did with my mother when her time came. I still wish I'd had the chance to talk to him of the past we'd shared and reach a more fully developed sense of completion.

When someone you love dies suddenly, spend some time alone with their "physical body," and

- Talk to them as if they were still alive.
- Tell them how you feel.
- Feel their energy still present.
- Leave after you compose yourself.

Completions Despite Complexity

Continually achieving completions in your life—no matter what their magnitude—is fundamental to your sense of well-being. This is so even if you have to seek completions in the face of stressful situations that seem beyond your control.

The Best-Laid Plans of Mice and Men...

A common career-related stressful situation is being late for a business engagement when you're out of town. No matter what you do or how carefully you work out your schedule, when your work involves business travel, there are many opportunities for things to get out of your control.

Airport delays, equipment failures, missed connections, the airlines' habit of overbooking flights, lost luggage, and lost rental-car reservations all can make a hash of your best-laid plans for arriving at your appointment with grace and on time.

The opportunity for stress is extreme. After all, you're coping with all the frustrations of watching your plans unravel beyond your control. You're also worrying about arriving late at your engagement and what this might mean for your business and your career.

Making Completions Where You Can

What can you do to take the disruption, frustration, and stress of such a situation and turn them into completions? Let your thoughts unfold as follows

> "OK, I'm going to be late. I accept that."
>
> "There are a dozen things I could have done differently, such as depart the night before, but all other scenarios are simply moot at this point."
>
> "I am taking every constructive step I can to offset this disruption in my schedule and my plans."

Now it's time to recite an affirming litany—one in which you literally say "goodbye" to the stressors and insecurities this nightmare of a trip has introduced in you. You say to yourself:

"I feel complete about my career."

"I feel complete about the plane ride."

"I feel complete about my capabilities."

Finally, upon your arrival at the site of your business engagement, reinforce your sense of completion about all that's gone before and prepare yourself to face your client with grace and ease. To do this, narrate to yourself (silently, of course) the condition in which you choose to appear. You are, in effect, willing yourself into a state of calmness. (See Chapter 18, "What You See Is What You Get," for an idea of why this works.)

"I choose to feel relaxed."

"I am walking purposefully but not hurriedly into the building."

"I am walking purposefully to the elevator."

"I am entering the room with poise and confidence."

"I am greeting the client."

"I am assuring him that I am ready to go."

"I am starting the session with energy."

The Constructive Side of Completions

Once you actually arrive and begin your work, you'll find you've achieved completion *at each stage* of a trip that otherwise would have been highly stressful. You'll have taken a situation that might have caused you trouble and stress and used it instead to make yourself stronger.

You've just been confronted with—and successfully overcome—a series of practical problems associated with business travel, right? As you're working your way through your completions, you're in a position to note where and how such events can be avoided in the future. Here are but a few.

Anxiety Antidote

When you're in a stressful situation over which you have no control, stop a moment. Take a deep breath. Acknowledge that you've done your best. Turn your mind to how to salvage the situation instead of fuming about what's already happened.

- Book to arrive the day before your engagement is scheduled.
- Have backup plans should your original arrangements fall through at the last minute.
- Make certain you always keep your necessities (presentation materials, for example, and basics such as ID, room reservations, and so on) in your carry-on luggage so it can't be lost.

Completion in the Face of Overload

What if you face a daily deluge of information? (Since you've read Chapter 11, you know this to be true.) You have options! What can you do, for example, when much of the information you take in originates from the Internet or other sources?

Before allowing yourself to be overwhelmed with mounds of new information, take steps *in advance* to eliminate what is not useful to you.

Stressbuster

What you can't find, you can't complete. This is why improving your organizational skills is key. But don't stress yourself out by trying to retool your computer and paper files all at once. A 10-minute stint setting up one file drawer or creating a subdirectory each day will have you all sorted in no time.

- Create a default download directory on your hard drive or the network and specify this directory in the "preferences" section of your favorite Internet software. This way, you'll always know where to find freshly downloaded files instead of having to search throughout your computer system.
- Create directories into which you'll transfer important files from your default download directory—after you confirm their long-term usefulness.
- Download *only* the information you truly need to have in your possession. Files you might use only occasionally need not clutter up your hard drive. You can bookmark their addresses and leave the information on the Internet.
- Because you'll be saving Internet addresses for future reference, create a computer file for storing and organizing them as well.

As you can see, getting complete sometimes takes preparation. Once you begin seeking completion, however, the payoffs are so tremendous that you won't avoid the preparation. Yes, you're already inundated with rules, guidelines, and checklists. Seeking completion, however, isn't a bunch of rules—*it's a way of being.*

Other People's Completions

Up to now, this discussion of completions might have made it seem like they're very personal things. In other words, you seek completions to events that you subjectively find worrying, stressful, or overwhelming. There's another class of completions as well—those required by the people around you.

Suppose, for example, you're in a business in which you distribute goods to customers, and they set high performance standards for your work. Sometimes, no matter how well your system is functioning, things are bound to go awry.

Completion-thinking helps you (and potentially others) deal with this moment, the next, and the next. When your customers are counting on you for timely delivery (which will provide them with their completion), but something is temporarily out of your control, the best you can do for both you and them is to get *mutually* complete about the situation. In other words, the moment you're aware of any problems, inform the customer. This takes the pressure off both of you and allows both of you to get complete.

- You get a new delivery deadline reflecting the new conditions (a completion for you).
- Your client has a realistic expectation of the revised delivery schedule (a completion for the client).

We all know people who, when due to arrive at 6 P.M., call at 6 P.M. to say they will be 30 minutes late. They think that, as long as they call by 6 P.M., they've temporarily met their responsibilities. They haven't. If you are expected at a certain time and you know you cannot make it, the onus is on you to be complete about your lateness and to let the other party know as soon as possible.

If it's 5:40 P.M. and you know you are not going to make it by 6 P.M., call at 5:40 P.M. This lets the other party readjust and get complete about the fact that you will not be meeting at 6 P.M.

End Run Your Procrastination

Anxiety Antidote

One woman always procrastinated about writing—whether it was a letter to a friend or a report for top management. Her solution? She decided to merely begin writing without worrying about how well she was doing or even if she had started at the beginning.

Procrastination is the antithesis of completion. I do not condone procrastination, but I understand why it happens. The more things you have competing for your time and attention, the more stressors will impact you during the day, and the greater the probability that you are going to put off some things.

When you begin to have piles and piles of minor tasks, they all begin to loom larger in your consciousness, and you feel incomplete. As a result, your stress level goes up.

Watch out. If the lack of completions is chronic, such as when there are piles all over your desk and all the other flat surfaces in your life, you might be approaching the danger level discussed at the beginning of this chapter. Certainly, such a situation suggests that your life and career have reached points of immobility on several fronts. This immobility translates itself into procrastination.

How do you break through procrastination and achieve completion?

- Line up all the project materials the night before with the intention of starting tomorrow. Then sleep on it.

- Develop a clear vision of how you'll feel after you achieve completion.
- Seek three to five small tasks you can initiate quickly and easily. The momentum from handling these might prompt you to stay on track.
- Promise yourself that you'll only work on an activity for five minutes. Thereafter, you might not want to stop.
- Find a partner to help you get started and stay with it until you are fully immersed in the project.

Focusing on One Thing at a Time

Bouncing from one project to another can be somewhat psychologically satisfying. After all, you can say to the world, "Look at me. Look how busy I am." Or "Look at how important I am. I've got these multiple demands on my time."

Such appearances are deceiving. Sure, when you're juggling a dozen balls at once you get the ego strokes of looking like a go-go entrepreneur, but you also get chronic stress and worry that you'll drop one or more of them. To get back to that sweet mindset in which you're able to tackle one thing at a time, try some of these tips.

- Identify which tasks you can complete entirely on your own versus those that require the input of others. Schedule accordingly. If you know you cannot meet with your colleague John until Tuesday, complete all the tasks you can do on your own on Monday.
- Define for yourself—mentally or on paper—the precise steps you need to take to successfully complete the tasks ahead of you, one task at a time.
- Allow yourself quiet time throughout the day. Set aside 5-, 10-, or 15-minute breaks when you can close your eyes and let some of the tension wind down. Take some deep breaths. Let your forehead, neck, and shoulders relax.
- Get complete about where you are right now and what you have accomplished. As you saw earlier, getting complete about the present energizes you for tackling what's next.

9/10ths and You're Done

Not all tasks you encounter require 100-percent effort on your part for you to achieve completion! Allow me to explain.

A study showed that many projects originally submitted within a company were 90 to 95 percent "correct." When such projects were returned to the project managers for finalization, it took them another 50 percent of the original project time to accomplish that last 5 to 10 percent of the task.

The last 5 to 10 percent often is the most stressful part of any project as you try to get every "i" dotted and "t" crossed. It stands to reason, then, that in cases where "almost" is as good as "perfect," eliminating the stress and time of finalizing the last 5 to 10 percent could be a very good thing.

Calming Concept

For getting complete, it helps to have a well-developed ability to prioritize. This is not just a case of ranking tasks in numerical order, however. To be truly useful, prioritizing means knowing which deadlines must be met when, which tasks will take longer than others, and how the individual tasks are interrelated.

Don't get me wrong. Some projects demand 100-percent precision. You wouldn't want your surgeon to skip the last 10 percent of your surgery, after all. But many other projects and tasks don't require this precision, so don't stress yourself out by working on them to perfection unless you're specifically asked to. Examples of tasks that do not need to be 100-percent perfect are

- Internal project notes.
- Memos between staffs.
- Rough prototypes.
- Draft reports.
- Research on inconsequential items.

The goal is to save your energy for the tasks that really *need* it and to avoid diffusing it in a senseless quest for perfection when a less intense application of your time and attention would do just fine.

The Least You Need to Know

- New technology, increased expectations, and change in general all potentially contribute to more incompletions in your life.
- The more incompletions in your life, the more stress tends to accumulate.
- Completions are mental partitions between tasks, activities, or even thoughts.
- The art of doing one thing at a time enhances your ability to achieve completions.
- Many tasks you face don't require 100-percent "correctness." You're only wasting your energy if you hold on to unreasonable expectations of perfection in completing them.

Part 5

When Stress Comes, Tell It to Back Off

It's potentially stressful to be a part of society, no matter what you do, where you live, or where you go. It's a challenge these days for anyone seeking to live with a minimum of stress—a challenge certainly worth the effort. Part 5 contains six chapters that address a variety of techniques you can use when stressors pop up. You'll be glad to know that none requires significant physical exertion.

Chapter 16, "Mastering Your Environment," discusses how to reduce stress levels and recharge your batteries by knowing how and when to pause throughout the day. Some of the best times and places to pause will surprise you. Chapter 17, "The Isle of Tranquillity," introduces a variety of techniques people use to successfully stay in control of stress.

Chapter 18, "What You See Is What You Get," focuses on, well, how to focus on what you want through imagery and visualization. Chapter 19, "Take a Breather," explores the rewarding world of deep breathing, meditation, and the common act of getting some fresh air.

Chapter 20, "Potions, Massage, Bubbles, and Beads," delves into the world of stress-reducing vitamins and food supplements, aromatherapy (what you smell affects how you feel), bath beads, and massage. Chapter 21, "Can We Talk?," covers the stress-reducing benefits of prayer and spirituality, positive self-talk, and communicating with others.

Chapter 16

Mastering Your Environment

In This Chapter

- The strategic pause that refreshes
- Recharging to regain control
- How making haste can waste you
- Taking control of your immediate environment

It's a simple truth but one that's frequently overlooked: Mastering your immediate environment can do wonders for your ability to keep stress in check. We've already talked about how some areas of your physical environment can be made less stressful, but that's only the beginning. What about the *human* elements in your environment? There's you, of course, and mastering your personal reactions and interactions with the world at large can be an important way to reduce stress. That's the subject this chapter explores.

Learning from a True Professional: The Strategy of the Pause

Here's a tale from my youth that illustrates the power of strategically taking charge of the moment.

> In my late twenties, I moved to Washington, D.C. During my third week in town, I was at a party talking with three women when someone asked us if we would like tickets to see *The Westside Waltz*, starring Katharine

Hepburn, playing at the Kennedy Center. I barely knew any of the women but what the heck; the four of us took immediate advantage of the offer.

I recall the details of the evening vividly: If you had been there you would, too. We found our seats—and they were good ones—with about eight minutes to spare. It was a thrill to be at the Kennedy Center for the first time, with free tickets, seeing Katharine Hepburn, and yet I had barely moved to town. We were in the balcony, dead center, about two rows back. From our vantage point we could look down on nearly the entire theatre; we felt like kings and queens—I played the king part.

Some time during the second act, while Miss Hepburn (it was never "Ms." with Miss Hepburn) was delivering a line, a man in the fourth row center stage took a flash picture of her. This, of course, is forbidden in the Kennedy Center and during theatrical plays in general.

The actors and the audience froze—the flash seemed to linger for more than the customary split second. Miss Hepburn stopped in her tracks and for a few seconds seemed to be in a trance. Then she broke out of character, walked the few paces to the front of the stage, and peered intensely at the perpetrator.

"How rude! How utterly rude," she said in a voice and tone that the offender, let alone I and probably everyone else in the hall, will never forget. I was so embarrassed, *I* wanted to disappear, and I hadn't even done anything! Imagine how the guy felt who had snapped the picture. In a few more seconds, ushers came racing down and asked the man to surrender his camera, which he did without protest.

Seizing the Moment, Successfully

When Miss Hepburn stepped out of character to confront the photographer, she *seized the moment*. She did so successfully—within seconds of her remark, she returned to her position on stage and, in a magical metamorphosis that took place before our eyes, became her character once again. She picked up her lines right where she left off. It was as if the incident had never occurred. The rest of the play continued without a hitch. Everyone in the audience, however, was aware that something more than mere drama had occurred.

The Secrets of Miss Hepburn's Success

Many years passed before I understood the phenomenon in its full context. Katharine Hepburn was the master of her environment, certainly on stage, and no boorish, unauthorized, amateur photographer would have the temerity to "invade" her space like that.

Yet, there's more going on here. Hecklers, rude people in the audience, and the popping of unauthorized flash bulbs are all stressors that can break the stride of an actor on stage. In this circumstance, Miss Hepburn was able to keep her stress in check. She did so, responding directly to the offending source and airing her views on the matter, however dramatic, and then by moving past it. Her consummate skill as an actor allowed her to vent on the spot and then carry on without damaging her performance or the run of the play.

An incident such as this makes it easy to see why Katharine Hepburn—and other actors of her caliber—has endured so long and so prominently on the stage and screen. This is, after all, an ultra-competitive profession that offers little mercy. You are only as good as your last performance, and your next performance might *be* your last. A strong mastery of your actions and interactions with the public and the audience is vital.

Actors aren't the only people helped by this mastery. Each of us needs to act with control. This, in turn, helps reduce the feeling that we're experiencing stress.

Mastering the Moment

In the tale of Miss Hepburn's performance, where is the key to her mastery? The crucial clue is in the moment when she stopped, mid-line, and seemed to go into a trance. What she did at that moment was take a *strategic pause,* during which she rapidly assessed the situation, evaluated her possible responses to it, and chose the one that seemed best to her. She dealt with an acute stressor as it arose.

Tranquillity Terminology

A **strategic pause** is one in which you take a moment or two to breathe deeply, to reflect on your situation, and to gather yourself to take the best next step in whatever you are doing.

Making Moment-Mastery Work

Why might Miss Hepburn have chosen to handle the offending photographer the way she did? What might she have been thinking during her strategic pause? She might have thought something like the following.

Would the offender have tried it again?

Would others have attempted it?

Would she have been as sharp in portraying her character for the rest of the performance?

Would the others in the play have been as sharp?

Would she feel that she had compromised herself for allowing the perpetrator to soil her art?

Making Mastery Your Goal

You don't have the time available in your life to read enough books, take enough courses, attend enough seminars, or make enough observations that will tell you how to function effectively each time you encounter another stressor in a world filled with them. The goal, then, is to learn the principle strategy to accomplish your goal of reducing your stress. The primary means of keeping your level of stress in check is to become, to the degree that you can, the master of your immediate environment.

The Steps to Becoming a Master

How do you begin to achieve mastery? First you need to cultivate the ability to take the strategic pause, even if it's only fleeting. It allows you to assess where you are and to take the most appropriate action to maintain control. The pause might last merely seconds, as in the Hepburn example, or it might last several minutes.

Anxiety Antidote

At the end of the day, take a few minutes to sit quietly and allow the tribulations of the workday to dissipate before resuming your family role. With this pause, you'll become calm, relaxed, and able to be the spouse or parent you know you can be.

This might sound like it goes directly against the grain of modern life. All around you, you're encouraged to speed up—read more, take in more, do more. Sometimes, however, the best response to a situation is *not* to proceed rapidly. If you take a strategic pause, you give yourself a chance to do the following:

- Breathe deeply (and perhaps take a sip of water)
- Compose yourself
- Collect your thoughts
- Determine the best way to creatively address the situation

Unfortunately, in many work environments, motion and activity are still probably valued more than thought and reflection. Sometimes, however, the most important thing to do when confronted with an issue is to simply sit and think. I saw a clever book title once that encapsulates my observation: *Don't Just Do Something, Sit There.*

Is It All Worth It?

Several years ago, a *Time* magazine editorial lauded a senior writer who died of a massive heart attack. They described him as a bright personality, a first-rate intellect, and a consummate professional. The editorial-page obituary said that this fellow did an extraordinary number of things extraordinarily well. He vigorously filled his post and also wrote extensively about politics, social issues, the media, and books. In addition, he frequently appeared on TV panels and was ready to express provocative but well-thought-out opinions. The article also talked of his wide circle of friends, comprised of people from all social levels and walks of life.

Fatal Success

The article, in attempting to praise this fellow, had some telling points for all of us who want to live productively and well. For one thing, it said that this fellow rarely did *fewer than two things at once* (italics mine). He read his mail while discussing story ideas. When he went to lunch with a co-worker, he often took a book to read. Apparently, he never turned down an assignment, and he attacked the most mundane task as if heaven and earth depended on it. The piece concluded by observing that he had a forthcoming book in which he decried that it was plainly evident that some individuals are better than others—more intelligent, industrious, hard-working, inquisitive, productive, and harder to replace. He was 44.

Zounds! Don't the good people at this magazine understand that cramming everything into your life at hyperspeed can lead to an early death? I wrote to *Time* following this commentary, although I didn't expect them to answer, and they did not.

Pointing to the Better Way

Given the pace at which the senior writer had lived, I have to ask myself a few questions: Where was the time for reflection in his life? When did he pause? When did he ever reset his body clock? I understand that he was a notable individual, but to praise him publicly for doing two things at once and in the same breath recount that he died of "a massive heart attack at 44" *drips* with irony.

The deceased was the antithesis of someone who masters his environment. Rather, he allowed all the assignments, all the intellectual queries, all his interests, *anything* that appeared on his personal radar screen *to master him.*

Alleviating the Feeling of Powerlessness

If mastering your environment is akin to maintaining control, here's an example of how a person can dissect a situation and at least formulate a strategy to alleviate the feeling of *lack* of control—or *powerlessness.*

Data from national moving companies indicates that, when an employee of a company is transferred, the employee's spouse experiences more stress than the employee. This is understandable for many reasons. The employee

- Knows something about what he or she will be doing in the new job.
- Probably has visited the new city.
- Perhaps had a hand in selecting the new locale.
- May be receiving a promotion or a raise that positively reinforces the move.
- Will know some people in advance.
- Has been mentally gearing up for the move.

On the other hand, the spouse

- Might not have visited the city.
- Might not know anyone one in advance.
- Might be mentally resisting the move.

The Pause that Refreshes

The employee knows something about what he or she is getting into and, therefore, has some sense of control over the situation. The spouse, on the other hand, feels like he or she is stepping into the unknown with no control over what's happening. How can the spouse gain some control over the new personal environment? It can be done. Here are just a few steps the spouse might take.

Stressbuster

Got a problem? Write it down. Then list the steps it will take to solve the problem. It's good practice. After a while, you'll be able to do this kind of analysis automatically without the need for pencil and paper.

- Plan a weekend (or longer) visit to the new location to look around in an unhurried manner.
- Learn about the local schools and colleges, places of worship, community groups, and so on.
- Subscribe (before the move) to the local newspaper and any weekly or monthly local or regional publications to get a sense of the new community well in advance of the actual move.
- Contact the Chamber of Commerce, the Welcome Wagon, the Visitors and Convention Bureau, and so on. Request a list of businesses, family-support services, maps, and other readily available literature.
- Contact the state office of tourism and request information about resorts, beaches, mountains, lakes, streams, and hiking paths.

If you pause and think things through, the answers sometimes are self-evident. The important point is to give yourself the time to strategically pause and to let the proper course of action emerge, no matter what situation is confronting you.

Control from Within

Learning to use the strategic pause is like learning any other skill—you need to practice a set of techniques you can use to improve your ability to pause, collect your thoughts, reduce your level of stress, and move on with relative grace and ease. Here are some techniques that work.

- Close your eyes for as little as 60 seconds and visualize a pleasurable scene. It could be a waterfall, a favorite hiking trail, a mountaintop view, the shoreline, a campfire, or simply the image of a loved one.
- Slip on your headphones and listen to a piece of music you like—with your eyes closed. When you concentrate on music you enjoy, giving it your undivided attention, time begins to expand. A 3- or 4-minute song seems to last 10 minutes.
- For several minutes, close your eyes and simply explore your immediate environment by touch only. Sure, you already know how these things feel when you touch them, but pretend your sense of touch is the only vehicle you have for understanding your environment. You'll discover whole new worlds of texture you never noticed before. When you open your eyes again, the world will look a little different, and things will be a little less intense.
- Exercise your sense of smell. Concentrate on the smells in your environment. (It helps to close your eyes for this one, too.) Focus on isolating and identifying all the different smells. If you work in an office environment, close your eyes and concentrate. Do you smell the uncapped magic marker on the desk? The flowers in the vase on the bookcase? The fresh pencil shavings in the sharpener? How about your cup of coffee? When have you ever stopped and actually smelled the coffee?
- At lunch (or at any meal, for that matter) focus on the taste of the food as you eat. Savor the flavors. (We'll discuss this further in a moment.)
- Play with Rover. Interacting with pets actually enables you to reset your internal clock. Doctors and other health-care workers have long been aware of the calming effects pets can have on patients, and scientific studies are beginning to prove them right.

Anxiety Antidote

Want to learn more about the techniques of tuning in to your senses more fully? Pick up a copy of Richard Pellegrino's *The Complete Idiot's Guide to Improving Your IQ*. It's got lots of exercises that will help you improve your sense awareness.

Recharging—Whenever and Wherever You Can

There are plenty of times each day when you can stop and get a second, third, or even fourth wind by taking a strategic pause. All too often, however, your internal motor is revving a little too high, and you miss the opportunity. Think about the last time you stood in a slow-moving bank line. That could have been a prime moment for a strategic pause. But did you use it? Or did you fidget and fret because you wanted to be out of there? If so, you added to the stresses of the day when you could have reduced them.

Next time you find yourself in a line that's moving too slowly, use the opportunity to

- Take some deep breaths.
- Straighten your back.
- Envision a pleasant scene.
- Focus on what you have accomplished so far today. (Chapter 15 discusses completions in more detail.)

A bank line is merely one place where you can recharge and de-stress. There are many, many others, as you'll soon see.

Use That Gentle Rolling Motion

When you're riding as a passenger—in a plane, train, bus, or cab—you have no need to worry about your safety. After all, you're leaving the driving to someone else. This gives you a wonderful opportunity to pause and reflect.

If you're a white-knuckle passenger, always keeping an eye on the road, you're adding to your stress. Keep this fact in mind: Statistically speaking, the chances of your demise while you're a passenger in a vehicle—any vehicle—are slim indeed. Use the opportunity of being a passenger to your best advantage. The longer the ride, the longer you get to pause.

Stress Alert

Gulping down a fast food lunch at your desk is not stress-inducing, it's downright unhealthy. Done often enough, it can cause chronic indigestion and contribute to the development of an ulcer!

Give Us This Day, Our Daily Bread

You don't have to wolf down your food. No matter what meal you're eating, stop and reflect how great it is that you are about to eat. Think about how the food is going to taste before you actually taste it. Many people recite a prayer (see Chapter 21, "Can We Talk?") for the "bounty which we are about to receive." If that works for you, splendid. Then, when the food arrives, enjoy each bite. Notice the various tastes and textures. You'll find your internal engine revving a little slower and your stress level dropping.

Who's Making Love

Shhhh .... Don't tell anyone, but sex is a great way to take that pause. If you're in a loving relationship, making love provides a wonderful opportunity to momentarily dwell on where you are in life.

The Sporting Life

Have you observed that the best free-throw shooters in basketball take an extra couple seconds before releasing their shot? Similarly, the best hitters in baseball stare into the field, get firmly set, and then look at the pitcher. In all sports, there's an advantage in taking a strategic pause to maintain a higher level of personal control.

In the Midst of Conflict

When you're getting chewed out—at work or anyplace else—your best choice most likely is to simply *take a brief pause*. If you do, you are in a better position to defuse inflammatory situations.

Fortunately, much of the anger other people direct at you is self-correcting. That is, later they will apologize for overstepping their boundaries or for blowing their stack. This is especially true if you refrain from responding in kind and simply meet the anger with a quiet demeanor. When you pause and rather matter-of-factly reflect on the situation, you have a much better chance of responding in a way that is helpful to both parties.

A compelling scene in the movie *Crimson Tide* has Gene Hackman smack Denzel Washington on the jaw twice. It is a dramatic moment in which their differences about whether to launch a nuclear missile towards Russia come to a head. Part of the drama is that Washington's character is much younger, bigger, and more physically fit than Hackman's, and it would be no sweat for him to take Hackman out with one punch.

Understandably, Washington would be justified in striking back. After both blows, however, he simply puts his hand to his jaw as if to survey the damage and to relieve some of the pain. Then he looks back at his attacker with an almost curious detachment.

Washington is pausing and reflecting on an issue of importance to humankind. There are three minutes left to make the decision whether to launch the missile. The men are awaiting crucial information that will affect the decision. Washington is pausing and reflecting on an issue of importance to humankind—an issue that, to his mind, greatly outweighs the momentary pain and discomfort of being struck.

Calming Concept

When a boss or spouse is angered and you are the cause, you can gain insights into their concerns and issues by pausing. You won't have this chance if you simply jump into the fray.

Four Walls and a Ceiling: Mastering Your Space

Mastering the strategic pause gives you a sense of control in your interactions with others. Becoming a master of your environment can improve your mastery of yourself in other ways, and it certainly improves your ability to control stress.

In her book, *The Power of Place: How Our Surroundings Shape Our Thoughts, Emotions, and Actions*, Winifred Gallagher says that the reason "we work so hard to keep our surroundings predictable is that we rely on them to help us move smoothly from role to role throughout the day." Moreover, your thoughts, feelings, and actions are shaped to a great extent by your surroundings. The right furnishings, enough space, and the proper tools make a considerable difference in both your productivity and your frame of mind.

The Asians call this skill *feng shui*—the power of arranging your surroundings to achieve harmony and prosperity. At the corporate level, this might involve designing a landscape around a building in a specific way to nurture employees as they enter or exit. It also might mean constructing two waterfalls at the entrance, as Motorola did in its office in Phoenix, so employees will be impacted in favorable ways.

What steps can you take to begin to exert mastery over your environment? You have many options. Here are just a few to get you started.

- Set up your desk for the way you actually work (see Chapter 7).
- Minimize disruptions. Let people know when it's best to call, best to visit, and best to leave you alone (see Chapter 8).
- Create a quiet environment. Employ a room divider or sound barrier, if needed, or a white noise machine (see Chapter 14).
- Find alternative quiet locations (see Chapter 8).
- Control the room's atmosphere. Make sure you have the right temperature and the right lighting.
- Have amenities on hand. These might include tissues, light snacks, a bottle of water, or breath mints.

> **Tranquillity Terminology**
>
> The Asian concept of **feng shui** refers to the power of your surroundings in achieving harmony and prosperity. It incorporates skills in decorating and landscaping to provide a nurturing environment for the people who use the space.

These ideas simply require you to pause, reflect on your work situation, and then take action. You might have heard the joke about the construction worker who opens his lunchbox at noon every day and complains that it's always a bologna sandwich. After several days of this, a co-worker asks, "Why don't you ask your wife to make you something else?" The first fellow replies, "What do you mean? I make my own lunch."

And so it is with your office and other environments. Even though your basic workspace is designed and assigned by others, you have the ability to modify it and to create your own personal environment within the space allotted to you.

Getting It Right

When I was in high school, my mother redecorated our upstairs bathroom with snazzy wallpaper, a new shower curtain, pictures on the wall, and some flower arrangements—even a bowl of those multicolored, circular, aromatic mini-soaps that no one uses. I didn't understand why she went to all that trouble. After all, it was only a bathroom.

In retrospect, I understand her redecorating perfectly. She was conditioning an environment in which she knew she would spend at least 30 minutes of every day of her life. She was simply ahead of her time. Today, designer bathrooms are all the rage in the homes of the well-to-do.

Begin with the Basics

What do you see the moment you walk into your house? Is it simply a hallway with a coat rack, a side table, a closet door half open, and a well-worn rug? When company's coming, you no doubt make an effort to spruce it up some. But don't you deserve some of that same consideration? After all, you walk in that door every day, sometimes a couple of times a day, all year-round!

Anxiety Antidote

Becoming the master of your environment improves your productivity while reducing the stress that may come from living or working in impersonal or unpleasant surroundings.

With a little imagination and hardly any expense, you can convert your first view upon returning home into something more pleasant, upbeat, and—need I say it—inspiring! Paint costs very little and so do runners. A simple portrait or a silk flower arrangement won't even set you back $25. A new, improved light fixture or higher-wattage bulbs can immeasurably brighten that cavern.

Moving on Throughout the House

What is your view when you enter your bedroom? Is your supposed sanctuary cluttered with more furniture than you need or use? Are any shelves, tables, or night stands strewn with clutter? How about the decor? Has it been the same since 1993? Do you even notice?

What about when you step into your kitchen, living room, or den? How about the hallways in your home? How about shelving and storage areas? How about your garage? Walk around your home and all the other spaces of your life to actively rearrange and better manage your "view" points. Here are some of the questions you may ask yourself.

- If you work at home, how about the moment you walk in your office?
- How is the view from your office?
- How about the entrance to your home?
- How about the environments of those living with you?

The fundamental question is this: Do you control the spaces of your life? Or do they control you? Are you the master of your environment? You can be.

The Least You Need to Know

- Take a deep breath and collect your thoughts—the strategic pause—as often as you need to throughout the day.
- Anytime you need an immediate "time-out," give yourself one by visualizing a pleasurable scene.
- Your thoughts, feelings, and actions are shaped by your surroundings.
- Mastery of your personal environment will enable you to become more productive, and you will experience less stress.

Chapter 17

The Isle of Tranquillity

In This Chapter

- De-stressing the drug-free way
- Popular techniques worth a try
- You, too, can relax in minutes

Sometimes simply taking a few minutes out of a hectic day and assessing the situation (see Chapter 16) can spell the difference between frenzy and tranquillity. If you've been experiencing severe stress, it also might mean the difference between a long life and an early exit. The strategic pause, however, is not the only possible weapon you can add to your anti-stress arsenal.

Throughout the ages, people have engaged in all manners of behavior to become more calm and to reduce stress. In this chapter, I am going to summarize what has been consistently shown to work well for people—what is safe and what you can practice with confidence. In the six chapters that follow, I'll elaborate on many of the methods summarized in this chapter.

Of Dubious Value—Or Even Dangerous

Before getting started on a summary of the best stress-reduction techniques, let's look at a few common ones that you're better off avoiding.

Bio Dots and Stress Cards Yield Bogus Results

Have you ever encountered stress control cards or biofeedback cards? They are about the size and shape of a credit card. Don't bother with them. Variations in your skin's temperature render them highly misleading.

Stress Alert

Relying on chemical substances to keep yourself cool is risky at best. You take the chance of getting short-term relief at the cost of long-term dependency. That's *not* the most productive way to go!

Just Saying No

Since humankind first wrote on cave walls, people have used all sorts of substances to achieve certain effects—among them, the reduction of stress (see Chapter 27, "De-Stressing for the Long Haul"). I'm not knocking these substances—some of them probably live up to their mystique. What I *am* saying is that, for many people—perhaps most of us—there is no need to take drugs. There are many other ways to effectively reduce stress, and drugs are just not required.

When I say "drugs," I'm not simply talking about illegal substances or anti-stress or mood-altering medications. Alcohol and nicotine are drugs as well. Many people rely on a glass or two of wine each day to relax, and a flurry of recent reports from medical researchers confirm that this can have therapeutic value. Who am I to argue with medical researchers? I'm concerned, however, about the long-term effects of having, say, two glasses of wine 365 days a year for 10 or 20 years. My point is that you have many other options—options that don't carry the possibility of liver damage.

What about cigarettes or cigars? Even today, many people still smoke to relieve tension. This definitely is not your best choice in stress-reducing behaviors—not with all the evidence linking smoking with cancer.

In the end, you're better off avoiding these artificial so-called stress-relieving techniques. Read on for better ways to get the job done.

Tried and True

Hundreds of techniques for reducing stress are safe and are not habit-forming. All are easy to implement, and many are likely to be very familiar to you. Some, such as visualization and guided imagery (see the following section and Chapter 18, "What You See Is What You Get"), might be entirely new concepts. In every case, you can implement the strategies easily, even naturally, into your everyday routine.

As you read, keep in mind that not every technique will strike your fancy. This is okay—you can just skip the corresponding chapter. There should be plenty of techniques that fit your lifestyle and that work for you. You just need to stay with them and, ultimately, you can exercise control in ways you've always wanted.

Warming Up to Serenity

The simple application of heat can do wonders to relieve stress—no matter what form the heat takes. Hot tubs, for example, can be wonderfully relaxing. For some people, however, elevating the body's temperature for longer than 20 minutes can do more harm than good. Pregnant women and anyone with a history of heart disease should be especially careful when choosing this means of winding down.

Electric heating pads are another way to reduce tension, especially if your stress is showing up in the form of tight muscles. Heating pads have been popular for several decades for this very purpose. They and other similar devices, however, have been shown to emit electromagnetic waves that could be harmful to cell reproduction. Short-term use is probably okay, but avoid prolonged, continual application of heat in this manner.

Finally, don't forget that old stand-by, a hot shower. Water running in an intense stream—preferably with a hand-held shower head so you can direct the flow—can quickly take the tightness out of your neck and shoulder muscles.

Imagery and Visualization

I've already referred to visualization throughout this book in a loose and generalized sense of the term. You engage in some forms of visualization all the time. Daydreaming, imagination, certain kinds of memories—these are all examples of visualization. Visualization also refers to more directed and guided kinds of imagining that can be directly employed as a stress-reduction technique. The examples and suggestions I offer here are designed to get you to focus on positive, pleasant scenes—to take an active role in converting your everyday reveries into powerful allies in your quest to reduce stress.

Anxiety Antidote

Whenever you visualize a pleasant scene, you also reset your internal stress-o-meter. It's like taking a self-proclaimed "time out." It gives you a refreshing moment, a miniature mind-vacation that leaves you better able to cope with the problems at hand.

Visualization, also called imaging, is a simple process in which you conjure up a mental image of something that conveys happiness, warmth, or peaceful feelings. You might, for example, remember a meadow or a farm from your childhood, a waterfall, a picnic site, a scene from a movie, a favorite cousin, or a lover. By focusing on the image for even as little as a minute or two, you can achieve a drop in pulse rate, heart rate, and even blood pressure. With guided imagery, you summon imaginary scenes as well, but in this instance, you have someone to help you achieve the mental pictures and emotional states you seek. Chapter 18 thoroughly explores these techniques.

Keep in mind that you can use visualization to reduce tension in several different ways. You can, of course, use it to cool yourself out after a negative experience or confrontation. But you also can use it to sail more easily through things that haven't occurred yet—to reduce anticipation anxiety and to improve your future performance.

Breathing, Meditation, and Getting Fresh

A growing body of evidence suggests that panic disorders are, in part, respiration disorders. In other words, the onset of panic is often due to improper breathing on the part of the victim.

Improper breathing?

Yes, indeed!

Doctors have observed that panic patients frequently practice chest breathing, which uses more muscles and energy to draw shallower and less efficient breaths. When an individual is breathing improperly to begin with, then finds himself (or herself) faced with a difficult or frightening situation, this inefficient breathing can quickly turn to *hyperventilation.*

Tranquillity Terminology

Hyperventilation is a condition in which a person begins to take faster and ever more shallow breaths. At a certain point, the breathing becomes so inefficient that the victim is pulling inadequate amounts of oxygen into the lungs and might even pass out.

Because breathing is something we do unconsciously, we tend to take it for granted and underestimate it's importance to our well-being. Beyond keeping you alive, it is fundamental to your ability to function optimally and to maintain a feeling of ease and control.

There really is a right way and a wrong way to breathe. Chest breathing will keep you alive, but it doesn't relieve stress—in fact, it can cause it. The right way to breathe is from the diaphragm, and diaphragmatic breathing is easy to learn.

Once you learn how to do it, you'll be amazed at the difference it makes. Phil Jackson, legendary former coach of the Chicago Bulls, has said that when he feels anxious or out of control, especially during an intense moment in a game, it is because he is shortchanging his breathing in some way. When he focuses on his breath and gets it back to a normal rhythm, he more readily regains control. If you can breathe fresh air, oh my, what a treat it is. Fresh air is literally a godsend. Fresh air can help you achieve measurably lower levels of stress and oxygenate among other benefits.

Meditation

Meditationis another stress-reduction technique that, like proper breathing and visualization, can have big payoffs with just a little practice. It is a way of focusing on deeper thoughts and feelings. Master meditators merely need to focus on the ebb and flow of their own breath to achieve a meditational state. If you meditate often, over time you can get to the point where you don't respond so intensely to potential external stressors. Chapter 19, "Take a Breather," expounds upon the benefits of breathing and meditation.

Calming Concept

"Laugh and the world laughs with you, cry and you cry alone." The use of humor has long been recognized as a stress reducer. The ability to laugh at yourself and your situation can spell the difference between overcoming obstacles and being overcome by them.

Supplementary Speaking

Many natural substances can help you feel calm and serene. Vitamins and food supplements such as St. John's Wort, ginseng, and ginkgo have won themselves a strong following among millions of Americans—and others around the world—for their ability to promote calmness, vitality, and clear thinking.

Good nutrition goes a long way to help you cope with stress. When you're already at less than your best due to a poor diet, it's hard to summon the concentration and the strength to handle difficult challenges at work or at home. It's hard to guarantee yourself a completely balanced diet, so vitamin and mineral supplements can be an important addition to your anti-stress repertoire. Turn to Chapter 20, "Potions, Massage, Bubbles, and Beads," for more on this subject.

The Touch of Tranquillity

Touch does much to reduce stress. This explains why massage can have such a positive effect on you. A certified massage therapist can do wonders, working on the outside of your body to soothe and heal the inside. At the end of a particularly stressful day, there's nothing like it.

Even an untrained amateur—such as your spouse or significant other—can massage you into a condition of relaxation. A trained masseuse can take you much farther into healing, however, because he or she knows how to get at toxic buildups in your lymphatic system and is skilled in one or more massage techniques including bipolar, deep muscle, and Swedish massage. (This subject also gets more detailed treatment in Chapter 20.)

Stressbuster

Chlorophyll is one aroma that helps many people reduce stress and feel more energetic—it's the scent of spring. You don't have to wait until the calendar rolls around to April, however, to surround yourself with green potted plants at home and at the office.

Get a Whiff of This!

Do you remember, during your last trip to the mall, when you got a strong whiff of the chocolate chip cookies baking just around the corner? Or how about a whiff of pizza as the dough was rising in your favorite pizzeria? These smells stimulate your olfactory sensors and help take your mind in the opposite direction of whatever was concerning it.

Today there's strong interest in the way particular scents can accomplish specific, stress-relieving goals. Aromatherapy is the result of this interest, and it is now being widely used as a safe and effective method for altering moods. Once again, Chapter 20 is the place to get the scoop on this anti-stress technique.

Prayer, Spirituality, Self-Talk, and Conversation

Prayer and other forms of reflection or contemplation about concepts and beliefs beyond this mundane world have been an effective method of soothing the soul since time immemorial. For some people, the payoff comes simply from sitting still and being quiet. Many feel a direct connection with their faith, which in itself can be calming and comforting.

People who attend a place of worship every week find that praying with others provides a sense of community—both social and spiritual. If you haven't prayed in a while, you might consider rediscovering it's benefits. In addition to the religious aspects, the stress reduction can be magnificent. Even if you never attend a formal prayer service, informal prayer by your bedside, in a comfortable chair, or somewhere in nature can work just as well. This can help you take a more spiritual (and hence less materialistic) view of the world, your life, and those around you.

The benefits of private contemplation are not limited to prayer. By letting positive, self-boosting statements into your internal dialogue—a technique known as self-talk—you can enhance your personal development, experience less stress, and feel far better about yourself.

When you find yourself facing problems you can't resolve on your own, it might be helpful to talk them out with a sympathetic person. The mere act of talking to someone else about issues confronting you can reduce stress, and it certainly is more effective than mentally stewing over things alone. What's more, depending to whom you're speaking, it can be the single most effective stress reducer in your arsenal. All these topics are covered in much more detail in Chapter 21, "Can We Talk?"

Let's Get Physical

Physical exercise is a great mood elevator—no matter what form it takes. It gets the blood moving, elevates your mood, and energizes your body and your spirit. There are many different types of exercise to choose from. Here are just a few examples.

- **Taking the show on the road.** Whether you're into power walking, jogging, or anything in between, a regular on-the-road regimen is easy to start no matter where you live. Just beware of safety issues. Wear appropriate clothing—especially if you're on public streets after dark. You don't want to get fit only to get hit by a car!
- **Eastern wisdom goes West.** Yoga is the granddaddy of exercise from the East. The idea is to awaken the mind, strengthen the body, and rekindle the spirit—creating a union between mind and body. The masters tell us that 10 to 15 minutes each day of basic yoga exercises can enable you to feel more relaxed at work, improve your concentration, give you a healthy appetite, sleep more soundly, and even improve your sex life.
- **Striking a divine balance.** T'ai Chi Ch'uan, or T'ai Chi as it's more popularly called, is designed to help people gain a more even temperament and a more tranquil mind. T'ai Chi is a martial art as well as a philosophy that, in one way or another, attempts to explain everything in the universe. At its base are the concepts of yin and yang, two complementary forces that exist in both the material and spiritual state. Their complementary nature is best illustrated by the idea that yin is understood, in part, as the internal, dark, feminine, receptive essence or principle, and yang is understood as the external, light, masculine, dynamic counterpart.

  Properly practiced, T'ai Chi enables you to concentrate better on routine tasks, to make decisions more effectively, and to maintain an alert mind for longer periods of time. As an exercise, it resembles a classical dance form, although it actually is more like a drill. It is designed to balance the muscles and joints through movement, deep breathing, and manipulation of the diaphragm. These movements impact the central nervous system, which regulates the efficient operation of the organs within your body.

Anxiety Antidote

The health benefits of yoga are well documented—even hospitals are including it as part of their rehabilitation programs for heart patients. It's been shown to reduce chest pain and even to help clear arterial blockages!

The wisdom of the ages, from East and West, indicates that your physical state affects your mental state. For more information about all your options in the field of exercise as a stress-relieving tool, turn to Chapters 22, "Let's Get Physical: Yoga and Exercise," and 23, "Peace of Mind Through T'ai Chi."

The Least You Need to Know

- Taking a few minutes out of a hectic day to pause and reflect can spell the difference between frenzy and tranquillity.
- Simply talking to a trusted listener about issues confronting you can help reduce stress.
- You need to stick with the stress-reduction technique of your choice for it to pay off.
- Adult education programs in guided imagery, progressive relaxation, visualization, and meditation abound.

Chapter 18

What You See Is What You Get

In This Chapter

- Visualizing your way to less stress
- How guided imagery works
- Becoming your own guide
- Is virtual reality in your future?

What you see is what you get when it comes to managing stress. If you can maintain a strong focus on relaxing images in your mind, your body will respond in kind. You can experience a decrease in blood pressure, a lower heart rate, and greater muscle relaxation, all for the price of a daydream. Does this sound like something you might want to do a little each day and throughout your life? You bet it does! In this chapter, you'll learn how it's done.

Altered States Yield Less Stress

John C. Lilly, M.D., a pioneer in the exploration of altered states of consciousness and relaxation, experimented with *sensory deprivation* and its effects on stress. Lilly's research subjects entered flotation tanks designed to minimize the effects of sound, light, gravity, and temperature. They experienced drops in blood pressure, reduction in muscle tension, and decreases in other signs of stress. The process achieved notoriety in the early 1980s movie, *Altered States*.

Tranquillity Terminology

Sensory deprivation is a technique in which the various senses (sight, sound, touch, taste, and so on) are masked so the subject can focus more completely on his or her inner state.

Lilly's original studies were somewhat controversial at the time, but Peter Suedfeld, Ph.D., a psychologist at the University of British Columbia, confirmed Lilly's findings with his own experiments and found that even "brief exposure to sensory deprivation is one of the surest ways to induce deep relaxation."

The opportunities for you to immerse yourself in a flotation tank are, shall we say, limited. Nevertheless, you still can engage in a limited form of sensory deprivation to induce your own form of deep relaxation. Among the easiest ways to initiate this process is through the techniques of visualization and guided imagery.

Picture This

You're busy. People are asking a lot of you. Sometimes, it seems as if you have no place to hide. Can you scurry off to a quiet place somewhere, even if only for a few minutes each day? If so, you can engage in a rewarding, relaxing technique that can help keep your stress levels low, can give you more energy, and can help induce a more positive outlook more of the time.

Oh Say, Can You See

Visualization is the ability to close your eyes and conjure up relaxing scenes drawn from your past, present, or a desired future. You might think of a moment from your childhood, time with a loved one, a favorable experience, something you anticipate experiencing, or simply a feeling you've had that was distinct and vivid.

Calming Concept

Your brain is a highly creative organ that can recall almost everything it has ever experienced in full sensory detail. Through visualization, you can tap into that creativity to reconstruct a soothing image that feels, sounds, and even smells like the real thing.

Follow the Leader

Guided imagery is similar to visualization, but it uses an external source to guide you along. This guide can be a person, or you can use a cassette tape (even one you make yourself) that talks you through the steps of the visualization process. Whatever the external source, you can employ it to help you achieve the "altered state" more readily.

Visualization Basics

You begin visualization (or guided imagery) with an exercise in "progressive relaxation." This is a stress-reduction technique that involves sequentially tensing each muscle group of your body and then letting go. You generally start at the feet and work your way up the body to the head until each muscle group has been fully relaxed.

Setting the Scene

With both visualization and guided imagery, you next focus on a scene or perhaps a smell, a touch, or a sound—anything that's comforting and relaxing. If you have trouble coming up with an image, here are some suggestions.

- A hug from your mother
- The smell of chocolate chip cookies baking in the oven
- The feel of the upholstery on your new couches
- The sound of chimes dangling in the wind
- The smell of salty sea air
- The "A" at the top of your term paper
- A refrain from your favorite song

If you can bring any of these stimulating images to mind—and everyone can—you're on your way to a host of mental and physical benefits.

Imagine the Benefits!

Visualization and guided imagery have been known to strengthen your immune system, believe it or not, and to help you deepen your breathing, decrease muscle pain, and even lessen the potential side effects of medications.

Dr. Michael Samuels, author of *Healing With the Mind's Eye*, says that imagery is so powerful "you don't have to believe it works. If the image is held in the mind, whether you believe it or not, the physiology works." This seems almost too good to be true, but it is.

Your Mind's in a World of Its Own

Your brain is connected chemically with each cell in your body. Because of human physiological mechanisms—tens of thousands of years information—the body can't tell whether the vision you hold is real or fantasy. Frankly, it doesn't care. If you imagine a horrific train crash, you can actually "scare your heart into wild beating," says Dr. Samuels.

> **Anxiety Antidote**
>
> Some people suggest closing your eyes and placing your hand on your chest, cheek, or forehead while visualizing a pleasant scene because it helps connect your body with the image you conjure up.

Conversely, if you imagine a pleasant spring day with birds chirping, a babbling brook, and bright sunshine, the muscles in the walls of your blood vessels will relax. You'll actually increase your blood flow, achieve improved circulation, and potentially feel more vital and more energetic.

Now get this … Samuels says that when you conjure up the right mental scenes, you achieve a state of consciousness in which time itself actually flows differently!

Daydream Believer

Before you dismiss all this as too difficult to do, consider this: Visualization is a close relation to daydreaming. When you elect to direct your daydreams and decide what to focus on, you're engaging in visualization.

Making Visualization Work for You

Athletes have long recognized that visualization techniques can help them improve future performance. Basketball players have found that, by visualizing themselves stepping up to the line and making the basket over and over, they can increase their actual foul-shot percentage in game situations.

If you watched any part of the 1998 baseball season, or saw any of the film highlights related to the season, undoubtedly you saw Cardinal Mark McGwire hit a home run or two on his way to 70. St. Louis Cardinal fans, as well as baseball fans everywhere, got countless opportunities to see Mark McGwire practice visualization in the on-deck circle before he came up to bat.

Seeing It Can Make It So

As McGwire approached and then surpassed the single-season home-run record formerly held by Roger Maris, cameras caught him approaching the on-deck circle, closing his eyes, and with a slight nod of his head, going through the motions of visualizing favorable outcomes.

Then, at the unheard of pace of one home run in fewer than every eight at-bats, he would step up to the plate and make it happen!

I can guess that in his mind he saw the pitcher wind up and deliver the ball.

- He saw himself uncoil the bat and swing it around lightning fast.
- He saw the bat strike the ball right on the button.
- He saw the ball take off at a ferocious speed, much faster than the pitcher had thrown it, and at a high trajectory.
- He saw the ball clear the home run fence, be it 380 feet, 410 feet, or 425 feet.
- He saw the ball land somewhere deep in the stands, and a happy fan catch it.
- He saw himself trotting around the bases, waving to the crowd.
- He saw himself stepping on home plate, high-fiving the other runners.
- He saw himself walk back to the dugout, with 50,000 fans screaming.
- He saw his teammates rise to greet him.
- He saw his son jump for joy.
- He saw the box score for the next day listing yet another home run.

A Hop, Skip, and a Jump

Olympic performers also make use of visualization to improve their performance when they step into the competitive arena. As far back as the early 1970s, Dick Fosbury revolutionized the world of high-jumping by leaping over the bar backwards. He attributes the success of this innovative jumping style to visualization:

> I began to develop my new style during a high school competition when my body seemed to react to the challenge of the bar. I became charged by the desire and will to achieve success. Then I developed a thorough process in order to repeat a successful jump: I would psych myself up; create a picture; *feel* a successful jump—the perfect jump; and develop a positive attitude to make the jump. My success came from the visualization and imaging process.

Years later, fellow high jumper and Olympic gold medalist Dwight Stones also used visualization and imaging to achieve similar success. Jackie Joyner-Kersee, perhaps the greatest female athlete ever, also devotes part of her training regimen to visualization, in which she mentally conditions herself to have superior physical workouts. These same techniques used by McGwire, Fosbury, Stones, and Joyner-Kersee can help you diminish any type of stress you experience.

So Why Does It Work?

Visualization is a form of mental practice. You repeatedly perform a certain task or activity in your mind until you achieve perfection. Because your brain makes no distinction between what it imagines and what it actually experiences, each of these "rehearsals" helps the visualizer learn how to properly engage in the activity. The trick is to make your visualization as detailed as possible so it closely approximates the actual activity you're trying to perfect.

Practice Makes Perfect

During each visualization, you have the opportunity to run through each of the elements in slow motion. Think of it as your personal, internal VCR—complete with freeze-frame, pause, and slow-motion controls. You can imagine yourself performing a task, rewind, and then replay areas you feel need improvement. This way, you form a strong mental blueprint for the activity, event, or behavior.

Stressbuster

If you fear presentations or confronting your boss about an issue, first visualize yourself successfully handling the situation. In so doing, you will increase the probability of success.

Upgrading Your Tapes

Miraculously, as you get better at what you're attempting to do, the "tape" on file in your brain improves as well. Hence, repeated use of visualization actually can help you achieve increasingly improved performance.

In addition, you can use visualization to de-stress situations you would normally find intimidating. By using repeated visualizations, you can make yourself more familiar with the situation and can guide yourself into a state of greater confidence and control. When you're done, normally stressful events or activities become far less anxiety-producing.

I Work, Therefore I Visualize

Let's run through a series of work-related situations and then a couple of personal situations to see how visualization and guided imagery can help you dramatically decrease your stress.

Lend Me Your Ears

Suppose you have to speak to 12 people in your department on a weekly basis. You never enjoy this. You feel as if everyone is staring at you, hanging on your every word. What if you slip up? What if you perspire too much? What if you blank out and completely lose your train of thought? They might laugh. You might be regarded as inept. You might be fired!

If you face giving presentations with fear and trepidation; if the mere thought of speaking in front of others makes your blood pressure rise, your heart beat faster, and your sweat glands open up; if the mere thought of giving a presentation stresses you out to the max; rest assured it *doesn't have to be that way*. What can you do before giving a presentation to have a better experience? Hmmm .... Let's see.

Wow, I'm Going to Be Dynamite

Before you're scheduled to speak, find a quiet place where you won't be disturbed. Sit comfortably, close your eyes, and visualize a relaxing image. After you've held that pleasant vision for a minute or two, gradually shift your focus to your workplace.

Take some strong, deep breaths and imagine you've had all the time you need to prepare a speech. Your notes are in order. They make perfect sense, and you've reviewed them frequently. You're so on top of what you're going to present that you almost don't need notes at all, but you're going to bring them anyway.

See Me, Hear Me

Envision yourself standing before the group. You take your place with confidence. You breathe at a normal rate. My goodness, you even feel good in front of the group. You feel peppy, cheerful, and ready to lead. You remember that each person in the group is just that—an individual person. Whether there are 12 people attending or 2 or 212, you're speaking to individuals.

Envision yourself speaking, and listen to the sound of your voice. It's clear, sharp, and melodious. You glide over your words with ease. You enunciate with distinction. You pause to allow your listeners to collect their thoughts. You spend time looking at each person in the room, acknowledging each individual's presence.

You handle questions and concerns with aplomb. If any discussion ensues, you're easily able to recall facts, figures, and points of logic. The words roll off your tongue. Visualize yourself feeling that it's good to have these kinds of opportunities to present to the group. It's good to air your views. It's a privilege to be able to influence and impact others. You look forward to the opportunity.

Be Happy, Don't Worry

You might have noticed that many of the elements in the preceding example are *feeling* oriented. Many athletes report that their visualizations don't necessarily focus on winning but rather on the experience of engaging in the activity. Running down the football field, swinging the golf club, or taking the jump shot is the key. When they feel good engaging in the activity, improved performance naturally falls into place.

Likewise, when you can visualize yourself in front of the group and feeling good, you'll no longer worry about whether people are intently focusing on you. You don't have to be concerned that you're going to leave out some key point.

Anxiety Antidote

If you're feeling good in front of a group in your visualization, you increase the probability that you'll feel good in front of a group in reality. You'll also increase the probability that you'll be effective.

You *can* get to the point where giving a presentation is not a stress-inducing event. It's no big deal.

Good Practice When Time Is Short

From a practical standpoint, you often have a limited time in which to prepare for a presentation. Undoubtedly, you also have other tasks that demand your time and attention. In such cases, visualization becomes a highly efficient tool for increasing your performance. After all, if you're giving a 15-minute presentation, you don't need to visualize all 15 minutes of the presentation. Two, three, or four minutes might work just as well. In other words, you can tailor your visualization to your specific needs.

What other stressful situations at work can benefit from visualization?

A semi-hostile boss, co-worker, or staff person. Believe it or not, you can visualize your way to more pleasant interactions with difficult colleagues. No, you're not going to change the other person, but by visualizing a better relationship, you'll alter your own behaviors toward that person. He or she will most likely respond more positively in return.

- You can envision greeting the other person cordially, listening to what he or she says (even if it's not entirely to your liking), and responding without anger, defensiveness, or hostility.
- You can envision engaging in chitchat, something you never would have considered doing with this person previously.
- You can envision parting cordially, looking forward to (or at least not dreading) the next encounter, and eventually having a fairly decent level of repartee with this person.

Completing a large assignment. If you're good at the small stuff but find yourself continually racing the clock when it comes to big jobs, put visualization to work for you. Chances are, you get behind because you procrastinate. What visualizations can help you address this problem?

- Each day, envision yourself completing the smaller, constituent tasks that lead to total project success. You feel good about what you're able to accomplish each day.
- You see yourself beginning easily.
- You see yourself more readily focusing on the task at hand and ignoring or simply not allowing distractions.
- You see yourself doing brilliant work, drawing on all your faculties.
- You see yourself assembling the resources you need, whether they're manpower, cash, or equipment.

In your visualization, you feel good about starting, engaging in, and completing tasks allocated for that day that contribute to the overall project. Heck, you feel good about taking on some extra elements on any given day so you can even get somewhat ahead of schedule. Rather than leaving work defeated and drained, you see yourself ending your day feeling complete and energized.

Overcoming environmental impediments. Perhaps you feel stressed because you can't do your best in your work environment as it's presently configured. There are too many distractions, too many intrusions, and too many items competing for your time and attention. Visualize how you'd like your workplace to be and engender some pleasant images in your mind.

- You see yourself able to maintain higher levels of concentration all day long.
- You see yourself rearranging your office or workspace so you can be more productive.
- You envision the predictable faxes, pages, e-mails, and other forms of correspondence that call you away from the task at hand for what they are—mere forms of communication. Some request immediate and strenuous effort. Most do not.
- You see yourself as a resilient, highly competent, creative, productive person who is more than equal to the challenge.

The Visionary at Home

Let's say you chronically have too much month at the end of your money. When you find yourself continually coming up short each month and not knowing where you're going to find the money to pay some of your bills, begin visualizing.

- You see yourself calmly, even cheerfully, writing checks for the products and services that make your life richer.
- You see yourself spontaneously finding ways to lower your expenses.
- You see yourself being more prosperous in the workplace. The digits in your savings account start to increase.
- You have enough to initiate your retirement account.
- You invest in a 401k, SEP, or Keogh plan.
- You're able to put a down payment on the house you've always dreamed of owning.

Most of our society's extremely successful people first had dreams—visualizations—of what their life could and would look like. They had clear notions of a luxury car, a boat on the lake, their child going to medical school, or taking a cruise around the world. The visualization made their goal more real. It provided some tangibility.

Could We All Get Along, Here?

Suppose your home life has become stressful because you simply can't see eye-to-eye with your spouse, one of your children, or someone else in your relationship cosmos. Sit down and quietly contemplate visions of having a harmonious relationship with that person.

- See yourself talking, listening, and reaching higher levels of understanding.
- See yourself anticipating their needs and concerns and becoming a more responsive partner, father, son, or whatever.
- See yourself smiling, even laughing, about situations that used to be intense. Keep taking good, deep breaths.
- See yourself always saying the right thing as opposed to flying off the handle and saying something you might later regret.
- See yourself becoming more diplomatic, a better listener, more understanding, and more empathetic.

Hey, it could happen to you!

Calming Concept

Here's a variation on visualization: Before he became a *best-selling* writer, the co-author of *Chicken Soup for the Soul*, Mark Victor Hansen, took a copy of the *New York Times* best-seller list and, using the same font and point size, pasted the words "*Chicken Soup for the Soul* by Mark Victor Hanson and Jack Canfield" in the #1 position for nonfiction books. He put the altered best-seller list on his wall where he could see it everyday and draw dynamic energy from it.

When Visualizing on Your Own Is Rough

Some people find it difficult to practice visualization on their own. They can't find a quiet place, have difficulty inducing the preliminary state of relaxation, or even have trouble coming up with an image that works for them. If this sounds like you, guided imagery might be just the ticket. You can find practitioners who'll lead you through the process by checking out local adult-education courses, the YMCA, community colleges, new age instruction, or perhaps classes at your health club.

In such classes, an instructor or teacher will lead you through the process using a series of suggestions. The instructor's guidance acts as a memory prompt. He or she asks questions that help you embellish your basic visualization with the rich texture of sensory details. When you've had enough practice visualizing with the aid of a guide, you might discover that you're now capable of achieving the same state on your own.

The Split Screen of the Mind

Robert Fritz, author of the best-selling book *The Path of Least Resistance*, suggests a unique form of visualization. In his technique, you use what can best be described as "split-screen viewing." The bottom part of the screen is how things are now: stressful, anxiety provoking, and undesirable. At the top of the screen, you envision how you would like the situation to be. Get a clear view of this. Fritz calls this *structural tension*, and thousands of his students have found this to be a powerful form of visualization.

By envisioning both your current state and your desired state, the inherent structural tension of having these competing visualizations "on-screen" at the same time helps move you in the direction of your desired state. I've used this method for years, and it works as well as anything available.

Tranquillity Terminology

Structural tension is the energy that arises from confronting two opposing visualizations of the same circumstance—one of how it is at present, one of how you seek to change it.

Anxiety Antidote

The benefits of any visualization technique are enhanced by the relaxation techniques that accompany the process. The simple fact that you're taking time out to relax and reflect for a while is inherently stress relieving.

Roll the Audio Tape, Please

If you don't want to attend courses or you simply find it more convenient to engage in guided imagery in the comfort of your own home, you can experience guided imagery via cassette. Such programs usually range anywhere from 15 to 45 minutes or more per side. Most health-food stores today carry such cassettes, as do many bookstores and superstores.

In Your Master's Own Voice

You might consider creating your own tape to serve as your visualization guide. After all, who knows better than you the words, phrases, and key images that will best help you achieve your goal. Here's how to do it.

- Prepare a script of what you'd like to envision, how you'd like to feel, and what you want to achieve.

- Read the script in a calm, soothing voice. Leave pauses after each suggestion so that, when you're listening to the tape, you'll have time to mentally engage in the activity suggested.

Anxiety Antidote

For a jump-start in creating your own imagery scripts, pick up *Rituals of Healing: Using Imagery for Health and Wellness*, by Jeanne Achterberg, Ph.D., et al. (Bantam, 1994).

Your tape need not be long or elaborate. Making 8 to 12 suggestions to yourself, spaced out over several minutes, can be highly effective.

The more often you engage in the guided imagery and visualization, the faster you can achieve results. If you play your self-recorded tape once in the morning, once during the day, and once in the evening, you'll have a bigger and faster payoff than if you play it once a day or only a few times a week.

Ensuring No Distractions

Remember Dr. Lilly's sensory-deprivation tanks? Reducing distractions while you're engaging in visualization and guided imagery enhances the effect of the sessions. Current technology has made many devices available that can help screen out background sounds—and they're a lot less unwieldy than Dr. Lilly's tanks. The Sharper Image company at **www.sharperimage.com** offers the Ultimate Sound Soother. This product enables you to dial up a variety of restful environmental sounds such as the gurgling waters of a brook, the soft patter of rain, or the restful summer sounds of a countryside at night. These sounds can help block out more distressing or discordant sounds in your normal environment.

Other devices available from a variety of vendors include light dimmers and telephone mufflers. Neither is necessary for visualization and guided imagery sessions, but they might help. If your goal is to reduce stress in an efficient, enjoyable manner, it makes sense to take control of your immediate environment.

For low-tech readers, there's always the old standbys. Earplugs and eye shades can help you minimize external distractions.

Progressive Relaxation, in Detail

The process known as progressive relaxation, also called the stress inventory, is a way of listening to your body to see where your stresses lie and then purging yourself of them. You perform an abbreviated version of this technique whenever you relax before visualization, but the long form can be extremely effective. It starts with closing your eyes and taking a deep breath. With your eyes closed, turn inward and focus on various parts of your body.

Bottoms Up!

As you focus your attention on your toes, notice whether you feel any tension there. While taking deep breaths, attend to your physical sensations. With each exhalation, imagine tension flowing out of and away from your body.

Moving on Up to the Big Time

Move on to the next place on your body in slow, careful increments: from toes to foot, from foot to ankles, from ankles to calves, and so on. At every muscle group, repeat the process you used when relaxing your toes. Getting all the way to the top of your head can take quite a while.

Sometimes you'll doze off before you get to your head, but that's fine because it means you've reached a relaxed state. Otherwise, you can simply remain alert but relaxed for a time, move on to visualization, or get up and reintroduce yourself to the world.

Instructing Your Body the Biofeedback Way

Biofeedback is a technique that teaches people to become aware of their involuntary bodily functions and to employ a conscious mental effort to control them. It has been used to help people control their blood pressure, body temperature, and heart rate. It also has been used in the treatment of migraine headaches, anxiety disorders, gastrointestinal illnesses, and back, neck, and jaw pain.

Get Wired

Suppose you have a stress-related headache. In biofeedback, you're first given an electromyograph (EMG) that indicates when tension in various parts of your body is occurring.

The biofeedback equipment responds to contracted (tense) muscles by emitting a tone. As the muscle relaxes, the tone decreases in volume and intensity. You, as the subject, learn to make the tone decrease by relaxing the muscle group under examination. In essence, you're training yourself to refine your conscious focus so you can relax the tensed muscle or muscle group at will.

Stressbuster

In the stress inventory, when you identify an area of tension and associate it with your exhalation, you're really retraining your brain to help specific parts of your body relax more readily.

Like, Get Normal

Once you've successfully manipulated the tones of the biofeedback equipment, your tension has been alleviated. The effects of biofeedback are cumulative. After repeated sessions, your relaxed state can last for days at a time.

The biofeedback you generate does not actually *cure* your stress-induced headache. Rather, it teaches you to function effectively despite the headache by eliminating its symptom—the pain. In essence, you get to detach yourself from the stressor. Once trained, biofeedback subjects can practice on their own without sophisticated equipment and, hence, can accelerate their progress.

All By Myself

As subjects learn how to become more calm and relaxed, they become more aware of all the sensations in their body including breathing and heart rate. As their bodily awareness increases, they find it easier to stay relaxed—even during the normal stresses of everyday life.

Virtual Reality

An innovative way to visualize is emerging, called computer-generated virtual reality. It's already helping phobics vanquish some of their imagined fears. As a stress reducer, it's potential is vast.

Walk the Plank

Psychologists from the Kaiser Permanente Medical Group experimented with a virtual-reality program that allowed acrophobics—people who suffer from a fear of heights—to "walk" through a three dimensional, computer-generated landscape. The landscape featured a narrow plank crossing high above a street and a bridge hundreds of feet over water. The virtual-reality equipment—an electronic headset and visor—allows a subject to insert him- or herself directly into the scene with such a sense of immediacy that it feels *real.* The sensation can be so vivid that subjects have been known to respond with panic at first.

Can I Do It Again?

In the Kaiser Permanente experiments, the subjects' heart rates and blood pressure increased as they neared and then walked onto the "virtual" plank and bridge, but they were encouraged by the therapist to move only when they felt comfortable.

After a single 40-minute session, 90 percent of the subjects were able to transfer their "virtual" experience into the real world and withstand a real 15-story ride in a glass elevator. Compare this success with what's normally achieved by conventional treatments using anti-anxiety medication and a gradual exposure to heights. The conventional approach usually requires six to seven sessions to be effective.

If people with severe disorders can be helped using this method, chances are good that, someday soon, you'll be able to use a similar process to diminish stressors on demand. For now, the various tools and techniques at your disposal are more than sufficient to help you vanquish your stress.

The Least You Need to Know

- Visualization and guided imagery are two of the easiest and most powerful forms of stress reduction you can employ.
- You can employ visualization specifically to improve your relations with others, to become less flustered by potential distractions, and to meet challenging deadlines.
- The more often you engage in visualization and guided imagery, the greater your progress.
- Taking a stress inventory can help you quickly identify and bring relief to areas of your body in need.
- Technology such as virtual reality will soon enable you to make rapid progress in managing stress as well as meeting other challenges.

Chapter 19

Take a Breather

In This Chapter

- The breath of life
- Making the mind tranquil
- Concentrating on nothing
- Getting a whiff of the best

To breathe is to live. So… how's your life? If you find yourself racing to work, racing down hallways, racing to lunch, racing back home, racing through your weekends, and racing through your life, when do you have the chance to breathe?

In our go-go society, it's easy to understand why we're all breathless these days. In this chapter, you'll learn about the benefits of proper breathing and how to do it. You'll also learn how to use breathing techniques to achieve the stress-busting benefits of meditation.

Catching Your Breath

The topic of proper breathing has heated up in recent years. A slew of books with such titles as *Breathe Better, Feel Better*; *Breathe to Live*; *Conscious Breathing*; *The Breathing Book*; *Deep Breathing*; and so on offer techniques for the millions of dysfunctional breathers in today's society. In addition, instructions for breathing—sometimes coupled with meditation and yoga classes—are available everywhere from YMCAs to adult-education courses and from health and fitness clubs to international-training centers. You can pay from $10 to $1,000 or more just to make sure you're drawing a nice, deep breath.

> **Tranquillity Terminology**
>
> "Shallow breathing" is the popular term for **chest breathing**—powering the action of your lungs from high up in your chest. **Diaphragmatic breathing**, on the other hand, is deep breathing that originates lower in your body at the diaphragm.

Most people simply don't know how to breathe efficiently. They don't realize that the shallow breaths they draw are caused by *chest breathing*. What they should be doing instead is *diaphragmatic breathing*.

Imagine there's a balloon in your stomach. As you inhale, you fill up the balloon. As you exhale, you deflate the balloon. Inhale, exhale. There's no need to rush. This is diaphragmatic breathing—the kind you want to learn how to do all the time.

What Kind of Breather Are You?

Learning to breathe properly is not complicated. In fact, you were once a master at it. From the time you were born until you first started experiencing any kind of anxiety, you were a natural-born diaphragmatic breather.

You still can experience it naturally today. All you need to do is lie on your back. Diaphragmatic breathing is automatic in this position. While lying down, place one or both hands over your stomach near your navel and then take a few breaths. You'll notice an up and down motion.

Compare this to the way you normally breathe. Stand up and place one hand on your stomach, the other on your chest. Breathe naturally. You'll notice that the hand on your chest moves more than the one on your stomach—that's proof positive that you're chest breathing.

If deep breathing is so natural and so much better for us, why do most of us breath improperly? It's a simple matter of physiology. When you're excited, tense, or in a hurry, you tend to raise your shoulders and expand your chest. This shift in posture makes these parts of your body the driving forces behind your breathing.

The Paradox of Chest Breathing

With as much as a quarter of the U.S. population thoroughly invested in chest breathing and with potentially equal numbers in other societies, what's the big deal? If you've been chest breathing for the last 15 years and you're otherwise in good health, you might find it difficult to buy the argument that the way you breathe is dysfunctional. Your lungs are in your chest and that's where you're drawing in air, so why mess with a good thing, right?

Wrong.

It's true that you can get all the air you need to survive by chest breathing, but some benefits can be gained only through the deeper breathing you do from your diaphragm. By engaging in diaphragmatic breathing, you decrease your rate of ventilation and actually fortify your body's ability to respond to stress. We'll get into the mechanics a little later in this chapter.

Don't be Fooled by False Claims

Some New Age gurus make extravagant claims in support of proper breathing. They say that, when you breathe from your chest, the oxygen molecules in the upper lungs don't diffuse into the blood vessels efficiently because most of these vessels are found in the lower lobes. The implication is that countless organs and muscles in your body, waiting to be oxygenated, have to do without and then end up underperforming.

To overcompensate, according to this theory, chest breathers need to breathe more often. This supposedly causes you to exhale carbon dioxide too rapidly, upsetting the balance of acid and alkaline in the blood, known as the pH factor. Eventually, the gurus allege, you can develop a chronic state of low-grade hyperventilation. This can lead to a host of minor but nagging disorders.

Stress Alert

If you're wearing pants too small or your belt is too tight, you might be disrupting your ability to breathe properly. By simply wearing looser clothing or loosening your belt, you can increase the amount of air you inhale by at least 20 percent.

And Now a Word from the Medical Establishment

Most of these New Age claims are based on shaky physiology. Whether you're a diaphragmatic breather or a chest breather, your blood is normally about 99-percent saturated with oxygen. When you're at rest, you only need about 25 percent of your available oxygen to function properly. Most of the rest is sent back to the heart unused. You are in no danger of suffocating, and your organs are not facing any imminent threat of oxygen starvation.

Deep breathing is far superior to chest breathing for one important purpose: It naturally reduces the physical damage associated with stress!

Calming Concept

At the Spa Bar, which claims to be the first of its kind in North America, you can slip a plastic tube up your nose and inhale 99-percent pure oxygen, scented if you want, for $10 to $20. Patrons claim they feel more energetic, more relaxed, and more alert after a visit, although the bar makes no medicinal claims. Pulmonary specialists say there's no advantage to such activity, although it is harmless.

How so? Deep, rhythmic breathing has a calming effect in and of itself. Short, shallow, rapid breaths, on the other hand, actually can exacerbate your stress responses.

Taking Over the Controls

Recall some of the symptoms of stress we discussed in the first few chapters. When you feel anxious or tense, your body prepares for fight or flight. Your blood pressure increases to transport fuel in the form of oxygen and glucose to the muscles. Your heart rate speeds up. You start breathing faster so you're better able to expel the carbon dioxide generated when you metabolize fuel.

Anxiety Antidote

In an era in which perhaps as many as 85 percent of all patient visits to doctors are stress related, learning to reduce or head off stress entirely by using one of the most fundamental of human activities—breathing—is a physiological bargain.

As it turns out, you don't have much control over how fast your heart beats, how much glucose you release, or the level of your blood pressure (unless, of course, you engage in the biofeedback techniques discussed in Chapter 18). Your breathing, however, is both a voluntary and involuntary function. You do it all day long throughout your life, even when you're not thinking about it. By regulating your breathing, you can exercise a degree of control over all the other involuntary bodily functions.

In other words, take a long, deep breath when you encounter a situation that you think is going to be stressful. You actually can help convert your body to a more normal (nonstressed) condition.

Harvey Wichman, Ph.D., of Claremont McKenna College says, "When you give all your attention to managing your breathing, you stop thinking the thoughts that produced the arousal in the first place." Hence, breathing is the near-perfect foil to potentially stressful situations.

In a sense, breathing is meditation by respiration without actually having to engage in meditation techniques. We'll examine the process of meditation, breath control, and the extreme benefits advocates purport to experience later in this chapter.

Fresh-Air Fiends

After all is said and done, simply getting a few deep breaths of fresh air can work wonders. Fresh air can help you to

- Achieve measurably lower levels of stress.
- Oxygenate your tissues.
- Improve circulation.
- Increase alertness.

- Diminish muscle tension.
- Reduce anxiety.

If you live in an area in which the air quality is poor, you are missing out. Your best strategy is to take frequent trips out of town, away from traffic and away from population centers. Get to the top of a small mountain where the air is clear and clean but not necessarily thin. Or take a walk in the woods, where trees and plants take in carbon dioxide and return oxygen to the atmosphere.

Normal room air is about 21 percent oxygen. Breathing air with a higher concentration of oxygen in and of itself does not make you feel any different. That 21 percent oxygen mix is more than enough for the hemoglobin in your blood to adequately distribute oxygen throughout your body. Likewise, the claims of oxygen-rich sports drinks and supplements don't hold water. Drinking oxygen is not any more effective than inhaling it.

Stress Alert

There's no physiological benefit to gain from ingesting "oxygen-rich" sports drinks prior to an athletic event, unless the consumer believes the beverages offer an advantage. In that case, they might afford a slight mental edge.

Effective Inhalations

You probably haven't thought much about innovative ways of breathing, yet there are some simple techniques you can practice anywhere to achieve surprising results. If you exhale two times as long as you inhale, for example, your heart rate begins to decrease as you exhale and slows down almost to a stop as you inhale. Hence, your arousal level (fight or flight) decreases, and you're able to more readily achieve a deep level of relaxation. You can use this technique, sometimes called two-for-one breathing, while exercising. People who practice this while walking or running notice an enhanced ability within minutes.

I Meditate, Therefore I'm Less Stressed

Driving back from a picnic, a friend once commented to me, "Why is it that those who seek some type of higher guidance or are on a spiritual quest generally are lightweights in business? Yet those who press along, unrelenting, with little time for reflection seem to own the large houses, drive the big cars, and basically control society."

Tranquillity Terminology

Meditation is a stress-reduction technique that has been around since words replaced grunts. It's a way of focusing on deeper thoughts and feelings by turning away from the distractions and tensions of everyday living.

Fortunately for those of us who seek a stress-free life, my friend's perception is, in a word, erroneous. It is becoming increasingly obvious that there's a way to fuse the quest for inner peace of mind and spiritual guidance with the quest for high achievement and social rewards. Today, even some of the high rollers can be found meditating.

How Does it Feel to Be One of the Beautiful People?

In 1959, Maharishi Mahesh Yogi first promoted transcendental meditation (TM) to Westerners. Meditation had been practiced in the Far East for thousands of years. It had even been practiced in the West in various forms and to a limited degree. However, TM (as it became known) popularized the ancient practice throughout a huge and influential generation of Americans—the baby boomers. Before TM, legions of Americans and Europeans had considered *meditation* to be something only practiced by strange holy men in India.

Calming Concept

Transcendental meditation is practiced by more than four million people worldwide, and is perhaps the best-known standardized method of meditation. It has been exhaustively studied and has been referred to by scientific literature more than 600 times since 1970. TM instruction is available in most large metropolitan areas.

In 1967, John, Paul, George, and Ringo, collectively known as the Beatles, became some of the Yogi's most devoted students. (Album covers and many of their songs thereafter reflected their newfound approach to life.) TM rose to the height of media attention and popularity in the U.S.

Early backlash media coverage about TM, however, suggested that its practitioners were part of a cult or, perhaps equally damaging, that TM was an excuse used by social outcasts (read "hippies") as a way of avoiding the rigors of real life.

Meditation Makes Its Mark

The scientific community began to take TM seriously enough to study the phenomenon. In the late 1970s, Dr. Herbert Benson of Harvard Medical School demonstrated that meditation could induce direct physical benefits such as reduced muscle tension, decreased heart rate, and lower blood pressure. In his best-selling book, *The Relaxation Response*, Dr. Benson identifies the "relaxation response" as the core of the meditation process. This relaxation response is your body's inbred physiological mechanism for diminishing or preventing the onset of your fight or flight process.

Today, more than two decades later, transcendental meditation and meditation of all types are regarded by scientists as effective methods for lowering blood pressure and relieving headaches, sleeplessness, and other chronic pain.

Meditational Magic

When highly motivated, go-getter types first begin meditating, they often find it disconcerting. Why? They are accustomed to "getting things done" and "seeing results." In meditation, they expect that something is going to *happen*. In meditation, however, nothing in particular is *supposed* to happen. There are no thoughts you are supposed to have or realizations that spring forth. You don't meditate to get from point A to point B. You meditate to meditate—the act of meditation itself is the reward.

Here and Now

Meditation facilitates your focus on the here and now—the present moment. This helps free you from outside distractions and enables your mind and body to "dialogue" with each other to a more harmonious degree. Experienced meditators achieve a state of relaxed awareness, sometimes referred to in New Age parlance as "the Zone."

Anxiety Antidote

Ah, the magic of meditation! By doing what appears to be nothing at all, you achieve a great amount of stress relief.

The Mechanics of Meditation

Meditation requires no special equipment or settings or any kind of physical prowess. All you need is a quiet place where you won't be disturbed. Many people begin meditating by devoting their complete attention to a word or a sound, called a *mantra*. One such sound is the syllable "Om." The sound is used to focus the meditator's concentration. A similar effect can be achieved by focusing on a candle flame, a mandala, or perhaps a simple image. Advanced practitioners need merely focus on the ebb and flow of their own breath.

Once focused, the meditator remains fully relaxed. The goal is to empty your mind, to free yourself from distractions, and to let the concerns of the world and your daily life drop away from you one by one.

Variation on the Meditational Theme

While transcendental meditation involves concentrating your mind and fixing your attention on a single word or image, other forms of meditation involve focusing your attention on where you are, what you're experiencing this moment, and the next, and the next. In either case, your goal is to step outside the day-to-day grind, moving beyond its ability to distract you. The fundamental difference of TM is that even your own body is considered part of that external world of distractions. You seek to transcend even your body's demands and sensations, however briefly.

Meditation's Myriad Gifts

Many people swear by meditation, citing it as the single best method for achieving an improved level of calmness and serenity. Others regard meditation as an important process for achieving the following goals.

- Better knowing one's self
- Viewing the world without judgment
- Being more accepting of others
- Getting closer to God

Calming Concept

Regardless of how you get started or the type of meditation you choose, your goal is to free your mind from accumulated tension and to reach a divine emptiness from which deep concentration and relaxation are possible.

The View from Inside

In a sense, meditation allows you to penetrate some of your own internal barriers and introduces you to what you're really feeling. It's as if the very same mind you've used every waking moment of your life steps to the side and becomes an independent entity, gently and easily observing the sensations the rest of you is experiencing.

The net result is an altered relationship with your inner being. Although in the past you might have shied away from distasteful or unpleasant thoughts, you now can develop a more nonjudgmental, almost dispassionate acceptance of whatever the world presents to you.

If you meditate often, you can learn over time to modulate your responses to potential external stressors. For example, if a project is dropped on your lap with short notice and you have only 45 minutes to get it completed, it's likely to be far less upsetting.

Meditation in Many Forms

The real beauty of meditation is that there's no fixed method or rigid procedure you have to follow to reap its benefits. You can enjoy the meditational experience even without engaging in its more traditional forms. For example, you can combine walking with meditation—what some call walking with spirit.

Hiking to Heaven

Have you ever gone on a strenuous daylong hike? By the end of the day, you're thoroughly exhausted but you feel great. Your muscles might be strained and your body aching, but your mind is at rest. What made this happen? Slow, purposeful walking affords many meditation opportunities. As you move along, you become aware of the swing of your arms and the movement of your legs. You feel your heels and your toes as they strike the ground. You become attentive to the way you're carrying your body and the rate of your breathing. In short, you've achieved a state of meditation.

Walking with Spirit

More than 140 years ago, Henry David Thoreau, noted author of *Walden*, contributed an article to *The Atlantic Monthly* in which he lamented to his readers, "I am alarmed when it happens that I've walked a mile into the woods bodily, without getting there in spirit." In other words, he was too preoccupied to appreciate his surroundings.

Preoccupation is the enemy of meditation. The secret to banishing preoccupation is to give your complete attention to where you are and what you're doing. Do you hear the crunch of the leaves beneath your boot? Do you smell the crispness of the autumn air? Do you hear the wind rustle through the branches overhead? Is the sun out? Does it filter through the foliage? Focusing on the details of your present surroundings forces you to engage in what you're doing *in the moment* and banishes the preoccupations and worries you've left behind in your workaday world.

Some "walking with spirit" advocates suggest focusing on a word or a phrase the way TM advocates do. This helps you stay centered and keeps your attention focused on the present.

While you're walking, try concentrating on one or more of the following phrases that spirit walkers frequently employ.

Stressbuster

By incorporating self-talk—positive affirmations that reinforce your personal growth and development—you can enhance the quality of your experience.

- Be calm.
- Be here now.
- Thank you.
- My heart is strong and healthy.
- I am at peace.
- Facing.
- Contentment.

Mind Yourself

Walking with spirit is a form of mindfulness, both of which are variations on meditation. Mindfulness, which Zen Buddhism calls mindful meditation, helps foster a state of relaxed awareness at almost any time and almost any place. You simply focus your attention on what you're experiencing at every moment.

To the degree you can, don't dwell on what you're going to do in the future or what you've done in the past. Rather, notice what's occurring right now in your mind, body, and surroundings. Slowly, you begin to experience a nonjudgmental and greater awareness of what you're doing or what you're experiencing. You don't forsake any responsibilities or cast your fate to the wind. Rather, you seize moments of your day to help you reawaken to the fullness of your life and your experience on earth.

Vivid and Accounted For

Mindful meditators report having a more vivid experience of what they are already doing. Hence, whether it's something as mundane as doing the laundry or as titillating as scaling Mount McKinley, the experience is heightened, enlarged, and made more enjoyable. One of the foremost proponents of mindfulness, Jon Kabat-Zinn, Ph.D., author of *Wherever You Go, There You Are,* suggests that you simply "tune in to the feeling ... the feeling of breath leaving your body. That's all—just feel the breath. Breathing and knowing that you are breathing."

If this sounds simple, it's because it is! How often, however, have you actually engaged in this? The answer is probably very little, if ever.

Meditation in the Mundane World

Meditation is something you can do even while engaged in the most mundane tasks. Take, for example, washing the dishes. Focus on the temperature of the water, how the sponge feels in your hand, the flow of water over your hand as you rinse a plate, the scent of the detergent. The key is to *mindfully* engage in something that you otherwise do *mindlessly* to help quiet the mind and to put your focus on the activity at hand.

Calming Concept

Zen Buddhist monk and philosopher Thick Nhat Hanh says, "If I am incapable of washing dishes joyfully, if I want to finish them quickly so I can go and have dessert, I will be equally incapable of enjoying my dessert. With the fork in my hand, I will be thinking about what to do next, and the texture and flavor of the dessert, together with the pleasure of eating it, will be lost. I will always be dragged into the future, never able to live in the present moment."

Writing as Meditation

"Shazam! Are you telling me I can sit at my computer, compose verse, and feel meditative effects?" Yes. At your PC, on fine writing paper, or on the back of a napkin, you can compose verse, lyrics to a song, an "Ode to Billy Joe," or whatever you choose. Such activity can yield the benefits of more traditional meditation.

Some people find comfort in writing to God. Others find it by writing to a loved one, even if that loved one is deceased. What you write never needs to be seen by anyone else. The benefits accrue from the simple act of having written it.

Stressbuster

Why not sit down and write yourself a letter—one that mentions how you're feeling, what you're experiencing, or particular obstacles you're up against. It will soothe you immensely!

If you're facing a tough time at work or in your domestic life and you feel stressed on a daily basis, writing about it can help in wondrous ways. While writing, you have to slow down and focus on the words, reading and absorbing what you've written. As your words appear on the page, you might find yourself thinking about their meanings in a new light. It can be an enlightening and cathartic experience.

The Three-Minute Meditation

In their book, *The Three-Minute Meditator*, authors David Harp and Nina Feldman explain that you can switch your stress "button" from overdrive to off in about 180 seconds. The authors explain that, whenever you keep your attention focused, you're actually engaging in a form of meditation. In that sense, we've all had lots of practice!

Hang gliding is a type of meditation for some people, according to Harp, while playing the piano or another musical instrument serves the same purpose for others. In each case, the practitioner is focusing his awareness on a single activity. The predictable outcome is less chatter of the mind, which usually is stress-producing chatter.

There are several methods for engaging in three-minute meditation. Here are a few to get you started.

1. **The heartbeat meditation**. Counting each of your heartbeats is a powerful way to focus your attention. Put your hand over your heart and, for at least a minute, count every time it beats. If you can hang on for three minutes, you'll be a different person than when you started. (Note: This exercise is not recommended for anyone with heart problems.)
2. **The flame meditation**. In a darkened room, focus intently for a couple minutes on a candle flame 10 to 15 inches away. If you find your attention wandering, call it back. No need to actively focus on what the fire looks like, the candle itself, what happened today, or anything else. Simply stare into the flame.

   When you've done this for three minutes (or as long as you can stand it), blow out the candle and close your eyes. You'll see images of the flame with your eyes closed, although it might change color or shape or move around. "Watch" the candle flame image for as long as you can. It might disappear and return. That's okay, keep concentrating. If you practice often, you'll be able to "view" the image for the same length of time that you actually watched the candle flame. When you're finished, you'll find you feel a bit more relaxed, more in control, and less stressed.
3. **The breath-counting meditation**. Sit comfortably in a quiet place. As you exhale each breath, mentally count to yourself, "Inhale, one. Inhale, two. Inhale, three," and so on. (This actually is harder than it sounds.)

   The moment you lose count, you have to go back to "Inhale, one…" That's okay; it happens to everyone. The nice thing about this meditation is that you can practice anywhere, anytime. The next time you're in a bank line or heading up to the top of the building in a slow elevator, mentally count your inhalations. By the time you're at the front of the line or at the top of the building, you'll feel better about the whole deal.

Anxiety Antidote

Even very brief meditational moments confer some benefit. They help you recharge your emotional batteries, slow your breathing rate, and clear your mind.

Musical Meditation

Music is well known for its ability to enhance meditation. Don your earplugs, put on a soothing CD, rest your head on a pillow, close your eyes to the world, and let the song take you where it will. You might doze off, you might daydream, or you might lie there like a limp fish. You'll be glad to be reclining, and you'll have far fewer cares in the world than when you started.

Some people add a few other elements to this easy routine such as engaging in deep breathing as a form of getting one's mind clear. Others visualize themselves performing well at work, in sports, with others, or someplace else in life. Some focus on a key word or phrase much like the TM advocates. Others simply lie there. It's up to you.

Centering: A Cousin to Meditation

To be centered is to be mentally, physically, and emotionally rested, relaxed, balanced, and comfortable where you are. Centering allows you to better direct your attention where you choose to direct it. Although centering is related to meditation, the goal is different—to enable you to be comfortably present prior to taking some specific action.

The rationale behind centering is that you'll be more effective at something if you are first effective at doing nothing. To achieve centering, find a comfortable place, close your eyes, and become aware of your surroundings. How do you feel? What do you hear? What are you thinking? In time, your body will relax, your mind will become more calm, and you will be better able to simply let things happen.

Calming Concept

The more centered you become, the deeper your understanding becomes of what is going on around you, and ultimately, the better your decisions become as to what to do next.

As you become more skilled in being centered, you can maintain the state while with other people, working, or participating in a sport. A good illustration of centering is that of health-care workers who, in the face of an obviously agitated patient, remain calm and understanding. You'll find that, when centered, you can remain calm and understanding even in distressing or difficult situations.

Feelings, Nothing More than Feelings...

You're probably decent at assessing your feelings, working to change them, or outright escaping them. What about simply learning to be with them? With meditation and most of the variations cited in this chapter, you forsake all efforts at analysis. Instead, you concentrate on the simple fact of your emotions.

If you're angry, simply notice that you're angry. Chances are, you can't stay that way for very long. On the other hand, if you try to determine why you're angry, if you analyze it, quantify it, look for cause and effect, or attempt the futile act of denying your anger or willing it away, you're bound to stay in that aroused state.

There's something about simply feeling what you feel that helps dissipate and dislodge unwanted feelings and helps heighten desirable ones. To regain control of your life, to reduce stress like a master, and to be more effective with others, it's vital that you regain your capacity to feel. Meditation and its various derivatives enable you to find a way to the depths of your emotional being and to yield to who you really are and how you really feel.

The Least You Need To Know

- Diaphragmatic breathing (from your stomach, not your upper torso) is the most effective method.
- The stronger and slower your inhalations, the better and calmer you feel.
- Meditation is a way of focusing on deeper thoughts and feelings by turning away from the distractions and tensions of everyday living. In its various forms, meditation can be a powerful stress-reduction technique.
- Meditation, in all its forms, can improve your resistance to stress while leading you to deeper personal awareness.
- Mindfulness fosters a state of relaxed awareness. You simply focus your attention on what you're experiencing every moment.

Chapter 20

Potions, Massage, Bubbles, and Beads

In This Chapter

- Stress-fighting supplements
- The gentle touch that means so much
- Get thee to a spa
- Bubbling your cares away

When it comes to reducing stress, don't forget to take stock of what goes in you and on you. It can make a world of difference in how you feel. There's a world of soothing, stress-relieving substances and therapies just waiting for you to try. So why wait? In this chapter, you'll learn about diet and dietary supplements, massage, aromatherapy and essential oils, and bath additives. Somewhere among all these alternatives, you're bound to find a few that work for you!

You Are What You Eat

Everything you need is at your local market. Fresh fruits, vegetables, and other foods supply all the nutrients you need to function properly and to keep stress at a low level. When it comes to eating healthy, however, most Americans, and increasingly people of other nations, fail miserably.

For too many people, fruits and vegetables are the fringe elements rather than the focus of their diet. Many people consume them in minute quantities or in so altered a form that they've been rendered virtually nutrition-less.

Stress Alert

Theoretically, you could eat your way to health, and you could eat your way to lower stress, higher energy, and greater productivity. The odds are good, however, that you don't.

Consider the Humble Potato

Think about this: By the time fast-food franchisers get their hands on a potato, process it, and serve it to you, it has been stripped of its food value. Instead, you get the high-fat, heavily salted atrocity known as the French fry. To top it all off, you get some highly sugared ketchup to dip it in!

Fast foods are convenient and cheap, but you're not getting much nutritional bang for your buck. When you consider what you eat combined with the *way* you probably eat it, you're looking at dietary disaster.

When you barely eat anything for breakfast, rush to work, eat your lunch at your desk, barely enjoy your dinner, snack on sweets all day long, and wolf down whatever looks good about an hour before going to bed, you're not doing your body any favors.

Maximizing Your Munchies

Ben Franklin knew what he was talking about when he advised his readers to make breakfast their biggest meal of the day. You need to fuel up to face the work ahead of you, but every meal is important. Here are a few meal-by-meal tips to keep in mind.

- Eat breakfast early and make it colorful—lots of fruits and vegetables. Avoid highly sugared cereals, Danishes, and other pastries.
- If you need a snack during the morning, make it something healthful. You've got lots of options: carrot or celery sticks, an apple, a banana, a granola bar, rice cakes, figs, or dates. Almonds, sunflower seeds, yogurt, tuna, soy nuts, dried fruits (apricots and prunes are good choices), and nuts also are nutritious and tasty.
- At lunch, strive to eat a variety of foods while keeping your meal light. Heavy carbohydrates will knock you out in the early afternoon. Proteins will give you energy, but if you're eating heavy meats, your body will have to divert energy to break them down.
- Our buddy, Ben Franklin, also had something to say about the last meal of the day: "Sup light." This runs contrary to standard practice in our society, but it is best. From a fitness, productivity, and stress-reduction standpoint, you're better off eating the majority of your calories at breakfast and the fewest at dinnertime.

Food Be No Refuge

If you can, avoid using food for comfort when you're facing a difficult home or work situation. Too many people confuse feelings of stress with feelings of hunger and, hence, eat more than they need to, more often than they need to, and more hurriedly than is good for them.

Eat in Leisure or Pay the Price

You're feeling stressed. You eat something healthy to alleviate the situation. If you eat poorly or too fast, however, you don't really get all you need from your food. So you stay stressed. That's a fact. A nutritionist once told me that, no matter how good the foods you eat might be from a nutritional standpoint, if you wolf them down, you'll barely gain any value. You see, when you're stressed, your body simply doesn't absorb as many vitamins from food as it would otherwise.

Stressbuster

Your Mom's advice is right on the money: Chew your food slowly! Even the healthiest plate loses much of its nutritional value when you eat too fast or you're too keyed-up before you eat. When it's rushed, your body can't absorb enough of the nutrients.

When you eat under duress, your body ends up excreting nutrients rather than using them to boost your immune system, to build up your bones, and to engage in other vital functions.

Getting More of the Good Stuff

You're probably wondering whether there's anything specific you could be eating to directly affect your stress levels. In fact, some foods do the trick better than others. Here are just a few.

- Turkey
- Chicken
- Seafood
- Nuts

All these foods help increase the production of the brain chemical serotonin. Low levels of serotonin have been linked to irritability and depression.

You also want to make sure you keep your magnesium level high throughout the day. Magnesium-rich foods include whole-wheat breads, raisins, and cooked spinach. (Popeye was right!)

Finally, drink a lot of water. Drink the proverbial eight glasses a day. When you're stressed, you perspire more than usual. This leads to dehydration, which leads to more stress.

Avoiding Those Pesky Free Radicals

As I've been stressing all along, *how* you eat makes as big a difference as *what* you eat—and not just because your body doesn't get a chance to extract all the vital nutrients in your food. Gulping down your meals also contributes to the production of *free radical cells*, which can compromise your health.

Free radicals contribute to the development of cancer, heart disease, and premature aging.

When you boil it all down, your mission is to begin taking vitamins and food supplements and to eat as healthily as possible. Make it a game if it helps. Although you might miss your sugared goop for a while, the payoff in vitality will be more than offsetting.

Tranquillity Terminology

Free radical cells are substances that latch onto normal healthy cells and corrupt them, mutating their DNA. Yuck! This sounds like cellular warfare.

Shall We Supplement?

Everyone's body chemistry is different, so there's no single "right" approach to taking vitamin or mineral supplements. Still, most of us can benefit from a good multivitamin supplement. Some nutrients are particularly useful aids in keeping stress in check. Vitamins B and C, for example, help nourish the adrenal glands, which release stress hormones as your body prepares for fight or flight or for the long-term but low-level insidious stress so prevalent today. Magnesium and calcium are two important minerals that help fortify your nervous system.

Have You Hugged Your Dietitian Today?

If you're concerned about your diet, one of the best things you can do for yourself is visit a good nutritionist or dietitian who will trace the following.

- Health history
- Current dietary habits
- Frequent illnesses and ailments
- Work situation
- Current stressors
- Typical eating patterns

After collecting this basic information, your nutritionist or dietitian can help you identify which vitamin supplements and dosages are right for you.

If you're the do-it-yourself type who likes to chart your own nutritional course, pick up a vitamin- and food-supplement chart at your local health-food store. Such charts identify the parts of the body each vitamin supports, the foods that contain those nutrients, and what happens if the body is deficient in each vitamin.

Consumer Expenditures on Health, 1997	
Alternative medicines and herbs	$27 billion
Unreimbursed physician services	$29 billion

Alternative Goes Mainstream

No longer considered quackery or "Grandma's remedies," alternative approaches to health and healing are gaining more respect from traditional practitioners—and even from insurance companies.

All of You ... Why Not Treat All of You?

Alternative therapies adopt a holistic approach to health and healing. In other words, they take into account nutrition, lifestyle, and mental and emotional well-being, not just medically recognized conditions and symptoms.

An Ounce of Prevention

The beauty of alternative health solutions is that they often are *preventative* as well as *curative*. Treatments frequently center around improving your way of life in addition to relieving the symptoms of whatever ails you. This is not to say, however, that non-traditional therapies are right for every medical condition, nor are the fields free from fraudulent advisors and practitioners.

If you decide to consult an alternative practitioner for vitamins, food supplements, or any type of health-related service, be sure to do the following.

- Do your homework. Research the field you are interested in and the reputation of the practitioners in your area.
- Search the Web. There are plenty of sites with helpful information such as the Office of Alternative Medicine (**altmed.od.nih.gov**) and the Rosenthal Center at Columbia University (**cpmcnet.columbia.edu/dept/rosenthal/**).
- Tell your physician about any alternative therapies you're trying, especially if you already are taking a prescribed medication. Certain herbs and homeopathic medicines might interfere with or react badly to traditional drugs.
- Ask for referrals and, if applicable, check credentials. Don't hesitate to question your practitioner about his or her training, experience, background, and so on.

Stroking Your Cares Away

When it comes to alleviating stress, not much can beat a good massage. Massage is a wonderful way to reduce stress and to promote greater alertness. It also will help you sleep better. From infancy to adulthood, massage is good medicine.

News from the Nursery

For much of the 20th century, it was commonly believed that pre-term babies should not be touched, since even the slightest shock might prove fatal, as reported in *Time* magazine. More recent research, however, has definitively shown that massage helps even the frailest of babies. In one study, pre-term babies who were massaged three times daily for at least five days were shown to gain weight faster, to sleep more soundly, and to exhibit greater alertness when awake.

Calming Concept

The simple act of touching is good for alleviating pain and accelerating healing. Practitioners of therapeutic touch say it works because they transfer some of their universal life energy to others who are sick or in need of healing. In some hospitals, nurses routinely use therapeutic touch to help patients relieve pain and achieve more rapid recovery.

Massage Goes Mainstream

For adults, the effects of massage are no less miraculous. Scientists have confirmed that massage can boost your immune system and can dampen the effects of harmful stress hormones while increasing the levels of serotonin in the brain—and you know what that's good for. Massage also can reduce blood pressure and can promote sounder sleep among adults.

On the strength of such studies, many Fortune 500 companies that once would have scoffed at the idea of bringing massage therapists into their hallowed halls are now including massage therapy as part of their benefits programs. At Boeing, for example, the massage-therapy program has reduced the number of reported headaches, back strains, and feelings of general fatigue among employees.

The Mechanics of Massage

How does massage work? Sandra Blakesee, writing in the *New York Times* (11/24/94), reported that people have a special pathway of nerves that send pleasure signals to the brain when the skin is gently stroked. The pathway is present at birth and might help infants distinguish comfort from discomfort.

Some researchers now consider massage to be a key component in maintaining overall health—as important as maintaining a proper diet and exercising regularly.

If you feel totally stressed out at the end of the workday, head off to a certified massage therapist for some quick relief. You can achieve dramatic results in just a one-hour session.

It makes sense. After all, every nerve cell in your body is connected in some way to every other nerve cell. It stands to reason that the direct stimulation you receive from massage will impact your total being.

Anxiety Antidote

Humans have separate nerve networks for detecting pain, temperature, and touch. Each nerve has more than 1,000 fibers that help pick up signals from receptors in the skin and the muscles.

Research bears that claim out. Tiffany Field, Ph.D., who works at the Touch Research Institute of the University of Miami School of Medicine, has shown that even your brain waves are altered by massage. In an experiment she conducted, workers who were massaged for 15 minutes twice a week had greater levels of alertness than a second group who merely did relaxation exercises for the same amount of time.

A Family of Disciplines

If you're ready to take the plunge into massage therapy, you've got a lot of options from which to choose. Here's a list of some of the massage-based therapies you might consider.

- *Deep-tissue massage* helps alleviate painful muscle aches and spasms or trauma around joints. A skilled masseuse can ease inflammation by pressing excess lactic acid and fluids from the muscles. It's particularly useful when it's done within a day or two after injuries and sprains.
- *Swedish massage* offers long, slow, soothing strokes. If you've had a tough day at the office but aren't otherwise feeling chronic pain, Swedish massage might be your cup of tea.
- *Trigger-point massage* involves stretching out and prodding along sensitive spots in one part of your body that might cause aches and pains in another part of your body. You've actually done this for yourself on occasion when you rub the back of your neck to alleviate a headache.
- *Sports massage* combines a variety of massage techniques to reduce fatigue and soreness and to prevent injuries, strains, and sprains.

Finding Your Dream Masseuse

Forget the old days when the word "massage" conjured up images of a seedy parlor in the bad part of town. Massage therapy is now so mainstream that even the smallest communities are likely to have at least one or two locations. Open the Yellow Pages to

Stressbuster

To make sure you're working with a professional masseuse, visit **www.amtamassage.org**, the Web site of the American Massage Therapy Association in Illinois. The AMTA (847-864-0123) provides a list of qualified therapists throughout the United States.

Massage. You're looking for a certified massage therapist (CMT)—someone who's had the necessary training to guarantee good results.

CMT's Do It with Soothing Strokes

In addition to professional certification, half of the 50 states require masseuses to be licensed. Even if you live in one of the nonlicensing states, certification means your masseuse has had some pretty impressive preparation. Candidates for certification must have completed 500 hours of formal training including course work in physiology, anatomy, and ethics. The test for certification is administered by the National Certification Board for Therapeutic Massage and Body Work.

The cost for an hour with a CMT ranges from $40 to $90 (possibly more in major metropolitan areas), and it can run much higher for same-day scheduling. Many people swear by their masseuses and keep regular appointments on a weekly or biweekly basis. Even if you only schedule yourself once every couple months, the benefits will be impressive.

Anxiety Antidote

Nowadays, it's easy to find a chiropractor. They operate in virtually every community in the United States. Some practices are so popular that the waiting time is weeks, if not months, to get an appointment.

Push Me, Pull Me: A Visit to the Chiropractor

Now an established therapeutic option, chiropractics has had a long and stormy history in America. Its original advocate, D.J. Palmer, might have gotten his original inspiration from his father, who alleviated another man's deafness with a measured blow to the back.

Palmer spent decades promoting his new therapy, but it wasn't until 1963 that New York issued the first chiropractic license. That same year, however, the American Medical Association's Committee on Quackery launched an all-out attack on chiropractics. The committee publicly branded it as an "unscientific cult."

Texts, Lies, and Videotape

Over the next 25 years, the AMA went so far as to falsify data in studies of the results of chiropractics. It also sought to keep books, articles, and literature out of texts and traditional literature about medical careers. Nevertheless, by 1973, visits to chiropractors nationwide had doubled. Today, there's clinical proof that chiropractors are more effec-tive at easing back pain, especially in the first month of treatment, than traditional medical doctors.

Check Around

When seeking a good chiropractor, your best bet is to check with the certifying and licensing agencies in your area. Also, ask around. It's quite likely that one of your friends can give you a referral. When you call a chiropractor for an appointment, ask for the names of some of his or her patients who might provide references.

Easing Your Aches with Acupuncture: Stick It to Me

Acupuncture has been practiced in Asia for more than 5,000 years. The West, however, only recently has taken it seriously. Current popularity stems from Secretary of State Henry Kissinger's visit to China in 1971. From there, the procedure gained a measure of recognition in the U.S.

Traveling with Kissinger's delegation to China was *New York Times* reporter and popular columnist James Reston. While in China, Reston required an emergency appendectomy after which he was treated with acupuncture. On his return to the U.S., Reston wrote an article singing the praises of this procedure.

Clearing Out the Half-Truths

The National Council Against Health Fraud disputed the claims Reston made in his article. It revealed that Reston was conventionally anesthetized during and after his appendectomy and that acupuncture was used only to treat postoperative cramps. The American public, however, began to embrace acupuncture, believing it's restorative powers were nearly miraculous.

For a time, rumors and half-truths about the effectiveness of acupuncture spread like wildfire. Victims of cancer, heart disease, and other crippling ailments suddenly believed their salvation had come.

Calming Concept

The thin, sharpened needles used in needle acupuncture can be inserted into specific nerve junction points on the body to help relieve pain after major surgery or dental procedures or to control vomiting and nausea caused by cancer chemotherapy or pregnancy. A panel of experts at the National Institute of Health has concluded that there's "clear evidence" that acupuncture is effective in all these treatments.

West Finally Accepts East

Eventually, time and testing cleared the air. It is now known that acupuncture can indeed help relieve a variety of medical infirmities. Scientists believe that knowledgeable and precise placement of acupuncture needles helps engage pain-blocking endorphins.

In 1997, the U.S. Food and Drug Administration ruled that acupuncture needles are safe and effective for medical use in the hands of a qualified practitioner. Today, more than 3,000 physicians practice acupuncture across the U.S.

Spas and Such

On every other scenic highway in America, you'll find a vacation spa. Depending on where you go and what you want to pay, your experience can be anything from stress reducing to sublime beyond words. The programs you encounter might last a single hour or days on end. Although every spa has it's own distinct program, here's what you might expect to experience.

Welcome to Nirvana

At a certain spa in Virginia, you're led to a private room where the sounds of the outside world are completely muted. A spa professional asks you to take a whiff of different scents to determine which one is most pleasing to you. It'll be used during your massage, the first of many therapeutic treatments you'll receive during your visit.

Relaxing Measures

Your massage is a total-sensory experience. You lie in a candlelit room on an ergonomically designed cot, listening to soothing New Age music and relaxing under the deft touch or your professional masseuse. Many therapists start at the top of your head and work their way down to your feet. Once this is done, you might be placed in a chair where your spa professional now continues with a frontal massage including your legs, arms, and face. Following the massage, you then might be led to a whirlpool bath or shower to relax a while under the gentle waters.

Working on the Surreal You

Spa programs offer much more than massages. Other popular therapies include facials and hot-oil hair treatments. Most likely, you'll be offered a refreshing drink of yummy carrot juice, papaya, or some other concoction designed to replenish the fluids you might have lost during your spa experience. Depending on the program you've chosen, other available treatments might include

- Aromatherapy.
- Manicures and pedicures.
- A hydromassage bath.
- A Swedish shower.
- Mineral baths.
- An herbal wrap.
- An herbal steam shower.
- Shampoos.
- A hair cut, coloring, or styling.
- Body waxing or body polishing.
- A body masque or scrub.
- Reflexology.
- Polarity therapy.

Tough Guys Don't Spa

Until lately, men have been far more reluctant than women to try the spa experience. The men who give it a try, however, generally become advocates. They discover that their perpetually stiff necks don't need to stay that way. That aching back, that shoulder tension, and that nagging feeling in the back of the thigh just melt away.

Stressbuster

Once a man gets into a spa (usually for a massage), he's far more likely to give the other services a try. Even the toughest men have been known to submit to skin cleansing, moisturizing masques, and facial scrubs. Some brave souls even try body waxing.

Feet First

Reflexologists have long advocated that your foot, particularly the bottom of your foot, represents your whole body in miniature. Manipulating your big toe, for example, can help relieve headaches. Kneading your left arch allegedly alleviates stomach aches. It might come as a surprise to learn that scientific research backs up these claims.

Reflexologists use a detailed diagram that shows how the areas of the foot correspond to the different areas of the body. They work to both soothe and relieve, and you'll be amazed at what they can do for your total body just by working with your foot.

Anxiety Antidote

If you've never been to a reflexologist, you're in for a totally renewing experience. He or she will awaken in you feelings and sensations you didn't even know you had.

Don't worry if you're ticklish on the bottom of your feet; that concern soon passes. You'll begin to experience a connection with other parts of your body as your reflexologist manipulates your feet to successfully relieve strains and pains you've been living with for years.

Manipulation Galore

Beyond reflexology, a host of other disciplines await. One or more of these might be exactly what you're looking for.

- **Shiatsu.** A Japanese form of massage in which the therapist uses his elbows, thumbs, knuckles, and anything else to manipulate certain energy points in your body and get them moving again.
- **Rolfing.** People who knead people, rolfers work on your fascia—the pliable web of connective tissue encasing your body—to realign your body and to give it better balance. After several sessions, you'll feel lighter, more aligned, and able to breathe easier, among other outcomes.
- **Alexander technique.** While you stand up, a specialist strategically touches your back, neck, and shoulders to gently correct your posture. Then, through simple exercises you do on your own, you reinforce and retain the posture that gives you the best alignment and the most energy.
- **Feldenkrais technique.** Using pushing and pulling techniques, the practitioner rhythmically and symmetrically manipulates your torso and limbs to reeducate your body so it moves more efficiently.
- **Traeger technique.** The practitioner uses light massage and physical manipulation to transfer energy from himself (or herself) to you. The physical touch is designed to release blocked energy, ideally leading to physical and mental relief.

Stressbuster

You can combine the effects of aromatherapy with massage by using scented oils. You also can add a few drops to your bath and settle in for a soothing soak.

For oodles of information about these and other disciplines, visit the book section of any health-food store or look in your local Yellow Pages under Massage Therapy and Holistic Healing.

The Nose Knows

Ahhh, the smell of pine (or lemon or lavender)! Many natural substances can help you feel calm and serene. And it's no wonder. Smells stimulate your olfactory sensors and are powerful triggers for memory and moods. This fact is the basis for aromatherapy—a technique quickly gaining popularity across the U.S.

Stress Relief Through Your Sense of Smell

Scents *do* make a difference. Dentists, of all people, have found that, when they scent their offices, patient resistance and fear seems to diminish. Even patients having root canals exhibited less anxiety and higher levels of relaxation when they were treated in rooms primed with soothing scents. They even reported feeling less pain! If it can work for root canal patients, it surely can work for you.

Back to the Brain

Aromatherapy works because your olfactory nervous system is directly connected to the brain. Unlike your other senses, which have to be translated before your brain can recognize their signals, aromas are immediately and directly processed by the brain.

How powerful is your sense of smell? Real estate agents have long advised their home-selling clients to bake bread or cookies just before potential buyers are due to drop in. They know that homes with the subtle scent of baking sell more readily than they would otherwise. Dr. Alan Hirsch, Director of the Smell and Taste Treatment and Research Foundation in Chicago, says that "You do not have to be consciously aware of an aroma for it to have an effect."

Anxiety Antidote

Aromas trigger the brain to dispatch chemical messengers called neurotransmitters, which control brainwave activity and patterns, blood pressure, breathing, heart rate, glandular activity, hormonal production, and you guessed it ... stress levels.

The Power of Pungency

Aromatherapy has been used medicinally and therapeutically for thousands of years in Asia and the Middle East, but it is a relatively new phenomenon in the West. In the late 1930s, a French perfume chemist named Rene-Maurice Gattefosse experimented with many aromas in search of their medicinal and psychological effects. Since then, the aromatherapy movement has picked up steam. In present-day Europe, many countries have incorporated licensed aromatherapists into the medical mainstream. These professionals prescribe the use of essential oils in place of or in support of traditional medicines.

There are no licensed aromatherapists in the United States, nor is there a professional certifying body. Nonetheless, hospitals use aromatherapy to help calm expectant mothers and to soothe them after they have given birth. You can walk into virtually any health-food store and be treated to a variety of oils and essences, each purported to have its own special effects. Wall charts and scent guides abound.

Flower Power

Aromatherapist Penny Rich, author of *Practical Aroma Therapy*, observes that, when you bring flowers to a friend or a loved one who is bedridden, you're actually engaging in aromatherapy and helping them feel better:

> The essential oils that give the smell to a bouquet of jasmine, roses, geranium, and lavender ... all contain chemicals that relax the nervous system and instantly improve spirits.

Rich says that using pure essentials, however, is more effective because their high concentration of scent has a more pronounced effect on both the mind and body than can be achieved by simply sniffing a bunch of flowers.

Support from the Scientific Community

So-called folk remedies, including aromatherapy, have been increasingly substantiated through research and development. Starting in the 1980s, biochemists began isolating scores of ingredients in the essential oils and cataloging what specific properties each has.

Delivery Mechanisms

How do you get the most out of essential oils? First, refer to an aromatherapy chart to determine which essential oil is right for you based on

- Your body chemistry.
- What you're experiencing.
- What you want to achieve.

Next you need to decide on the form of aromatherapy in which you want to engage. You can buy beauty treatments that include essential oils, you can include a drop or two in your bath, or you can permeate a room with a scent using your room vaporizer. One simple technique is to put a drop of an aromatic oil on the light bulbs in your room. The heat from the bulb will release the scent. Other methods include

- **Room sprays.** Simply mix a few drops of an essential oil in an effective pump-action spray bottle, shake before using, and then spray lightly into the air.
- **Wood fire.** Aromatherapy advocates suggest heating a scent to get a fuller effect. Pour a few drops of an essential oil onto wood 15 minutes before lighting a fire. The heat will release the fragrances throughout the room.
- **Inhalation.** Add a few drops to a bowl of boiling water, cover your head with a towel, bend over the bowl and inhale deeply for five minutes. "The steam helps open up pores and lets oil enter the skin so it's a good way to enjoy a facial," says Penny Rich.

Bathe Your Cares Away

Here's an old favorite for your stress-relief strategy: a long, hot bath. By all means, include bath beads, essential oils, bubble baths, or what have you and then simply sit and soak. Some particularly effective bath oil additives include oil of malacia and lavender.

Dr. Avery Gilbert, who is based in Sacramento, says, "Because the bath engages almost all the senses, it is a powerful way to influence our moods." The key to getting the most from your bath, according to Gilbert, is to tune "into your desired emotional state or mood. Once the desired bathing mood has been identified it can be enhanced through sensory inputs."

He suggests adding the glow of a flickering candle or the relaxing sound of soft music. If you elect to put a few drops of essential oil into your bath, you need only to lie back and soak for about 15 minutes. The steam and warmth of the bath helps evaporate the oils and intensifies the aroma. It also speeds up oil absorption. You come out of the bath with softer skin and a calmer mind.

Calming Concept

Cleopatra bathed in all kinds of oils. The Romans built lavish public baths throughout their wide empire. Mary Queen of Scots filled her tub with hot wine. The French soothed their weary bones in the natural springs that dot their countryside. The Japanese still maintain ancient, intricate bath rituals.

Rubber Ducky, You're the One

Lest you think that using your bathtub for stress reduction is undertaken by one gender only, or by the kinky few, consider the following. *Drug Store News* reported in mid-1997 that one out of six households in America regularly turned to bath beads, bubble bath, or liquid bath additives to remedy stress.

Bath beads and bath additives generally come in a wide variety of options. Walk into stores such as Bed, Bath, and Beyond, The Body Shop, or the bath section of any full-line department store—you'll have more than enough options. Fruit scents are widely regarded as calming. Jasmine, citrus, and lavender are considered to be energy boosters.

The Least You Need To Know

- Most of the vitamins you need can be found in the fruits and vegetables section of your supermarket. Add a multivitamin for insurance.
- Several times a year, if you can stand it, treat yourself to a spa weekend.
- When it comes to massage, a willing and able significant other can do wonders for you.
- Chiropractics and acupuncture, once considered to be on the fringe of respectable medicine, now are considered to be mainstream pain- and stress-reducing therapies.
- Aromas have a powerful impact on how you feel. When you find one that works for you, use it!
- A relaxing bath works as well as anything to reduce stress.

Chapter 21

Can We Talk?

In This Chapter

- Just talkin' to yourself
- Turning to heaven for help
- Spiritually speaking
- You gotta have friends

Speech is such a powerful tool. It can be destructive, or it can be an important means for combating stress.

Speech can be used in many different ways to alleviate stress—from self-encouragement to confiding in a friend, from general spirituality to formal prayer. This chapter discusses how your capacity for language opens you up to some of the most immensely powerful stress-reduction measures available on earth—if you'll only open yourself up to use them.

Be Kind When You Talk to Yourself

Did you know that 80 percent or more of your internal dialogue focuses on your shortcomings? Most of what people say to themselves is negative.

- "What a dummy I am! I can't believe I just said that!"
- "I know I could have done better. I'm always messing up!"
- "I'd like to talk to that person over there, but I'd probably mess up."

Tranquillity Terminology

Self-talk is a way to use internal dialogue to empower yourself, to reinforce positive goal qualities, and to tighten your focus on your goals.

Don't beat yourself up if you've ever said anything like this to yourself. *Do* try to change it. The technique of *self-talk* is a great way to make that change. The key to making self-talk work for you, particularly with regard to reducing stress, is to be more conscious of what you say to yourself.

Say Something Nice

Shad Helmstadder, Ph.D., in his ground-breaking book *What to Say When You Talk to Yourself,* says that the quality of our lives—let alone the amount of stress we experience—is dependent on self-talk. All day long, the little voice within us is saying things like "I shouldn't have done that" or "I'm not good at this." This kind of talk is like a self-fulfilling prophecy. What we believe of ourselves often is what we end up doing.

Shaping Your Own Destiny

Dr. Helmstadder says that, if you were told at an early age that you're no good at a particular skill, chances are you might have convinced yourself it's true. Hence, you go about your life collecting evidence to confirm this erroneous notion that was planted by another person, finally making it your own. "Well, of course I'm no good at XYZ. I've never been good at it." Such self-limiting pronouncements need not be your destiny.

The woods are full of people who've had negative feedback from their parents, teachers, or friends but who nonetheless went on to achieve spectacular success in that very discipline. How did they overcome their negative programming? They engaged in positive self-talk. They continually gave themselves messages like these.

Stress Alert

Be careful what you say to yourself. Negative self-talk directs our lives in ways we would not allow if we were conscious of what was going on. Each negative statement limits what we can accomplish.

- "Sure, I can do it."
- "It's not that hard."
- "This is something I want to achieve."
- "If I put my mind to it, I can do anything."
- "I choose to be good at this."
- "This is fun."
- "The more I practice this; the better I get."
- "I've succeeded elsewhere, I'll succeed here."
- "With a little help, I can make this work."

Sounds easy, doesn't it? Don't get too cocky! Although your intentions might be good, the common human experience is to fall back on old habits at the first sign of trouble. If something goes wrong, your little voice goes back to saying "I knew it ... It was only a matter of time until I failed."

See the Whole Picture

The problem with merely reflexive self-talk is that it fails to take the bigger picture of your life into account. Let's take a look at how this works.

Let's say you've got a big, 25-step project ahead of you. You start out saying "I can do this!" and get to work. After you've completed the first 10 steps, you have a setback. How does the initial self-talk stand up? Not well.

Stressbuster

Practice your self-talk whenever you can. It's most effective when it becomes automatic.

Wait a minute. You've successfully completed 10 steps, right? A more productive self-talk strategy would be to acknowledge each and every step along the way to the project's final completion. That way, you've got 10 positive statements under your belt, and your one slipup is far less devastating. You can easily recover from the setback and get back on track.

Catch Yourself on the Fly

Helmstadder advises catching yourself in the moment and offering positive self-talk as often as you can. Pretend you have to learn to operate some new equipment at work. You're finding it slow going, and you're getting totally stressed out. What message are you probably giving to yourself internally?

- "I can't stand this."
- "I'd rather be someplace else."
- "I don't think I'm going to do well at this."

What could you be saying to yourself?

- "I easily accept this challenge."
- "I've mastered harder things than this."
- "I am going to be more productive because I know how to use this to the best advantage."

By letting positive, self-boosting statements into your internal dialogue, you enhance the learning process, experience less stress, and feel far better about yourself.

Putting Your Self-Talk on the Record

You need considerable support to overcome years of negative self-talk programming. One way to facilitate your self-talk is to make a list of positive supportive statements to use when you need them. Write them down or even make a cassette tape of them.

It makes sense to play such a cassette every morning so you start the day with positive programming. You can reinforce the message by playing the tape periodically throughout the day. You might even find it helpful to make several tapes, each with a different positive self-talk, to bolster your efforts.

Supporting Yourself Every Step of the Way

The most effective way to reprogram yourself positively is to make a point of noticing the small victories you achieve. As you increase in confidence, you're more prepared to tackle higher-order stressors. You also can combine self-talk with other techniques such as visualization to enhance your experience. Perhaps one day you'll be able to simply sail through most of what used to rattle you to the core.

Let Us Bow Our Heads

If you've used prayer throughout your life to feel closer to God, you might have experienced corollary benefits such as a calmer mind, reduced stress, and even a greater tolerance for pain. For many people, prayer is one of the most powerful stress-reduction measures available. What can prayer do for you in terms of managing stress?

- Prayer can lower your blood pressure.
- Prayer can help you live longer.
- Prayer can help you heal faster.
- Prayer can help you have greater peace of mind, both daily and in the long term.

Researchers are only beginning to understand the power of prayer. Incredibly, several studies indicate that distant prayer—praying for another—actually can be effective.

Calming Concept

Time magazine cited a study that found that heart patients were less likely to succumb to their illness when "designated well-wishers prayed for them—though the *patients didn't know* the experiment was going on."

Prayer-Based Healing

Psychic healing, mental praying, nonlocal praying, and prayer-based healing—they all involve one person praying on behalf of another. Lest you dismiss this as superstition, keep in mind that startling evidence supports some psychic-healing claims. Nonetheless, even scientists who have viewed experiments at close range have trouble intellectually accepting what has happened.

Larry Dossey, M.D., has witnessed firsthand the miraculous effect of prayer-based healing. One of his patients had metastatic lung cancer. The situation looked hopeless. The patient chose not to have any surgical or medical procedures. Rather, his chosen therapy was prayer, offered around the clock by members of his congregation at church. Throughout all the visiting hours, members of his church were at his side, praying for him. After a few weeks, Dossey sent him home for what the doctor felt were his final few days.

I'm Baaaack

A year later, Dr. Dossey reencountered the patient, who was back in the hospital with a bad case of the flu. Amazingly, the patient's chest x-rays showed no sign of his old cancer. Dr. Dossey knew that the only therapy this patient had accepted was prayer. When he sought other medical opinions, he was simply told that these things sometimes happen.

Dossey wasn't satisfied by the explanation. He says it took him many more years to accept the reality that prayer-based healing could have powerful, miraculous effects. Over time, he came to recognize that this might be a case in which scientific knowledge is inadequate for explaining this or similar cures. After all, at one time the finest scientific minds in the world refused to believe that the moon influenced ocean tides, that the sun revolved around the earth and not vice versa, and that the earth was round and not flat.

Anxiety Antidote

Since the late 1980s, medical researchers have undertaken experimental research on the effectiveness of prayer in healing. So far, the evidence tends to confirm that prayer-based healing has dramatic effects on the patients for whom the prayers are offered.

Confounding the Scientists

For more than 100 years now, scientists have been confronting incidences of prayer-based healing. One of the first fully documented studies was published in 1988 by Randolf Byrd, Ph.D., of the University of California at San Francisco. In Byrd's study, 393 heart attack patients were divided into two groups at random.

Both patient groups received standard medical care, but the members of one group also received the benefit of daily prayers from born-again Christians who volunteered to participate. Neither Byrd nor any of his staff knew which individual patients were assigned to which group.

It was only after the clinical study ended that Byrd reviewed patient records. At that time, he found that patients in the prayed-for group required fewer antibiotics, were less likely to experience congestive heart failure, and developed fewer incidences of pneumonia than patients who only received standard medical care.

Do You Believe in Miracles?

Is the success of prayer-based healing evidence of miracles? Or can it be explained in other ways? Some skeptics point to nonreligious factors that might explain prayer's success. For one, a religious community provides strong social support to its members. A patient who knows others care about him has a distinct advantage over someone lying in a hospital bed with no one around. Other skeptics point to the fact that people who are devoutly religious are less likely to smoke, drink, stay up late, and so forth.

Stress Alert

Healthcare workers need to know more about prayer-based healing. They should be receptive to the idea that religion can help improve a patient's general health.

Nevertheless, researchers are finding that, even when obvious lifestyle differences are taken into consideration, people who pray have a distinct advantage over people who don't in terms of longevity and overall health. For people who engage in prayer-based healing for others, the benefits are no less palpable.

Praying Your Way to Mental Health

Psychiatrists also have started to acknowledge the link between prayer and healing. Many feel religious faith can be an important factor in recovering from emotional illness. They recognize that having a strong religious faith can have a dramatic impact on a person's lifestyle and long-term mental-health prospects.

Bless This Stress

Dr. Herbert Benson, author of *The Relaxation Response*, is studying the relationship between prayer and relaxation. His premise is that prayer can reduce stress in much the same way that meditation does—by slowing the heart rate, lowering blood pressure, and decreasing levels of stress hormones such as cortisol (which has been shown to play a part in robbing immune cells of their disease-fighting abilities).

Benson has found that repetitive prayer combined with the expulsion of intrusive thoughts can lead to distinct physiological changes akin to relaxation. He has published his findings in a book titled *Timeless Healing*. He says, "The influence individuals and their minds, emotions, and beliefs can have over their healing is being neglected."

Calming Concept

With a reduced respiration rate and a calming of the mind, prayer-induced relaxation is beneficial in treating chronic pain, insomnia, anxiety, some forms of depression, hypertension, and even cardiac rhythmic irregularities.

Dr. Benson also observes that all forms of prayer can be equally effective. You don't have to direct your thoughts in a certain way, practice a certain religion, or adhere to a particular belief system. In short, all you have to do is pray.

Don't Knock It if It Works

Prayer and prayer-based healing are not without their critics, but even skeptics tend to concede that faith can have an impact on your health. One of the most prominent critics of prayer-based healing is Dr. Albert Ellis, president of the Institute for Rational Emotive Therapy. Ellis maintains that patients who benefit from prayer do so because "faith bolsters their immune system" and not because there's any type of divine, paranormal, or direct physiological intervention.

Perhaps he's right—but what does it matter? If prayer is effective in reducing stress and alleviating other ailments from depression to heart disease, is it so important to understand the mechanism behind it? It costs nothing, it requires no special skills, and it works. How often in life do you encounter such a bargain?

Get Me to the Church on Time

It's not just prayer that can help in stress reduction. Going to church helps in other ways as well. An article in the *International Journal of Psychiatry in Medicine* reports that attending religious services can help lower blood pressure and that monthly church visits improve the mental health of the elderly. Although more research is needed to understand the links between attending church services and improving your health, it appears that the social part of attending services with others is highly important.

Praying for Peace of Mind

Whether or not you buy into the healing power of prayer, it's hard to deny that it can help lift your spirits, renew your vision, and replenish your soul. Prayer can help you focus your thoughts and reinforce and strengthen some of your deeply cherished values. It can serve as an inner source of strength and can help illuminate long-held dreams. Even people who irregularly attend church services report the feeling of being renewed and transformed.

People report that they're better able to forgive others following prayer. Some even report that they are less inclined to surround themselves with material benefits. Many feel more charitable after praying.

Anxiety Antidote

Some people report that prayer helps them be a better spouse, parent, son, or daughter. From the standpoint of reducing stress, if *any* of this is true, perhaps it's time to discover—or perhaps rediscover—the power of prayer in your life.

The Spirit Within You

Formal prayer is only one spiritual route to healing. Up to one-third of all Americans and increasing numbers of people around the globe are now taking a spiritual—but not necessarily religious—view of life. Spirituality has, in many respects, become a mass movement. More and more people are recognizing that their life is connected to the lives of other people and to all other living things in the universe.

Dr. Wayne Dyer suggests that, rather than viewing yourself as a physical entity having a spiritual experience, you should consider viewing yourself as a spiritual being having a physical experience through your body and life here on earth—a captivating thought, no matter what your predisposition.

The Spirit Is Always Free

First-person testimony from people who were incarcerated under grueling conditions, such as Admiral James Bond Stockdale and Captain Jerry Coffee during the Vietnam War, confirms that, under the most gut-wrenching, stress-inducing physical ordeals, your spiritual self can remain free and unshackled.

You're in Charge the Moment You Choose to Be

Stockdale, who endured seven years in Hanoi under the most barbaric conditions, drew upon his study of philosophy, in particular the ancient Greek Stoics, to survive. He took heart from the Stoic belief that no one can control the inner you without your permission. Captain Jerry Coffee, similarly incarcerated for seven years in Hanoi, drew upon his faith in God, country, and family to endure a hellish existence earmarked by confinement, brutality, and deprivation.

Spirit and Healing

The results of such aforementioned experiences, succinctly documented in best-selling books, essays, and keynote speeches, have helped marshal a wave of disciplines that draw upon one's inner spirit in the face of highly challenging situations.

Calming Concept

The gurus of nonsecular spirituality—such as Dr. Deepak Chopra, Dr. Wayne Dyer, Marianne Williamson, and a host of others—preach the gospel of recognizing that there's more to your existence than your physical shell. They claim you are not your body; you are simply inhabiting a body during your time on earth.

At Houston's Mind/Body Medical Institute, a part of Memorial Hospital, Mary Jane White, a psychotherapist and wellness facilitator, says that they focus on healing the whole person, "the physical, the psychological, the social, and the spiritual," although nothing they do is directly religious.

There's also a growing awareness among Western doctors and their patients that spirituality, including attitude and outlook, plays a vital role in a person's physical health. Dr. Herbert Benson has said that he's seen people overcome lifetime habits, albeit with the assistance of trained professionals, that dramatically and irrevocably "change one's outlook and improve one's health."

The Whole Is Greater than the Sum of Its Parts

The traditional Western philosophical and scientific view that divides the mind from the body is continually being challenged these days. Less stress, the absence of disease, and optimum health are now seen as stemming from a *balance* of the mind and body, of thoughts and feelings.

As science recognizes more and more links between stress and disease, there's a growing appreciation for the healing power of the human spirit. What constitutes the human spirit? Ask people who have come through horrendous illnesses or bone-shaking, catastrophic experiences. They will tell you that they were able to draw upon inner resources to help them unblock their path and make their way back to health. These resources include such everyday traits as optimism, imagination, patience, tolerance and compassion, creativity, faith, and courage.

Reaching Within Yourself for Strength

As the world around you gets more hectic, your ability to draw upon inner strength to achieve calmness and serenity will take on an added element of importance. Beyond helping you become more calm, focused, and directed, your spiritual self actually can provide you with greater energy and stamina. You see this every day. A long-distance runner who doesn't seem as if he's going to make it suddenly draws upon some inner reserve that enables him to finish with a flourish.

Drawing upon the Spirit

Suppose you want to draw upon the spirit within you, to not only sail past stressful situations but to attain a higher quality of life. Here are some ideas to get you started on that noble pursuit.

1. **Be honest with yourself.** On occasion, everyone displays intolerance, envy, impatience, and a host of other negative traits. To be more fully at peace with your inner spirit, acknowledge that there's a side of you that certainly could stand some improvement. This aspect of your life does not mean that you're a bad person or that you're somehow less than worthy.

   The more you're able to acknowledge this part of yourself and bestow upon yourself the compassion and tolerance that you strive to offer others, the less often these aspects of yourself will actually emerge. Your greater comfort with your overall being renders them less effective.
2. **Renew thyself.** Renewing yourself spiritually is vital. Everyone on occasion needs a sense of stillness, a place of quiet, and a time for reflection and renewal. Some people find that a drive out to the mountains works wonders. For others, visualization (see Chapter 18), meditation (see Chapter 19), and many other alternative activities (see Chapter 20) work as well.

   For you, renewal of the spirit might come through activities as simple as a walk in the woods, a long steam bath, or even reading poetry. It's different for everyone.
3. **Find your bliss.** What makes you happy? What do you feel is beautiful? Each day, you have the opportunity to find and dwell upon the beautiful aspects of the world and your life.

Learning to Live in the Moment

Unquestionably, all is not right with the world, and you could spend an entire lifetime focusing on everything that could stand to be corrected. Renewing your spirit, however, means allowing yourself to enjoy some of the pleasures in life. Get curious; let your imagination run wild. Perhaps it's time to visit a museum or, better yet, a children's museum. Jump into a pile of leaves, pour bubble bath into your bath water (see Chapter 20), pet a kitten, or feed the ducks in the park.

Stressbuster

In the workplace, people who are able to draw upon their inner strength might go unnoticed until a crisis arises. Then they display their remarkable ability to stay relatively calm, to keep a clear focus on the task at hand, and to provide guidance to others.

Getting a Little Zen

Living in the present can be an intensely spiritual experience, but it's an unfamiliar concept in Western society. Thich Nhat Hanh, a Zen Buddhist monk from Vietnam, has helped people all over the world achieve this state. At his retreats in Asia, Europe, and North America, he teaches people to achieve a greater sense of spirituality through the use of the body and the mind.

Stress Alert

Whether you like it or not, the effects of negative emotions are manifested physically. As you learn to recognize your physical state, however, you can help yourself get clear of past emotions and more fully experience what's before you now.

The pace of life around Hanh is slow and deliberate. Students practice walking mindfully, gently breathing, even feeling the wind against their faces. By focusing on the pure sensation of the moment and not being caught up in the past or future, a present reality begins to emerge.

After several days of focusing exclusively on what is present, you find yourself less immersed in thought and less preoccupied.

- You become more conscious of your breathing.
- If there's a smell in the air, you're aware of it.
- Food takes on fuller, richer taste.
- Each moment becomes precious.
- Silence is a gift.

If you choose to experience awareness of God, it comes readily. Wherever you are, the world around you takes on a vibrancy. Colors deepen, and you experience sensations that you missed before.

Your Body Plays a Part

Hanh, like many other spiritual leaders, teaches you that your physical self (your body) plays an important part on your path toward greater spirituality. You are, after all, here on earth at this time in the physical shell called your body. You cannot deny its existence any more than you can deny that the sun warms the earth through its radiance. So use all your senses, all your faculties, all your experience, and all your physical sensations.

As you get more fully into the present moment, you begin to let go of your judgment. You come to realize that, when you judge another person, you experience less energy and expose yourself to the potential for physical ailments. Hanh teaches breathing techniques that you can use to reduce the physical tension that accompanies anger and judgmental attitudes. As the tension dissipates so do the negative emotions. Eventually, you can feel at ease, content, and even tolerant.

Getting There for Yourself

If you encounter someone who is skilled at living in the moment, they have an immediate impact on you. This person is more spontaneous, more fluid, more alive. He or she looks you in the eye, is with you, hears you, experiences you. Such people can seem almost magical.

What is their secret? They're carrying less stress, less hurt, fewer emotional scars. To achieve this state, you need to learn what they know—how to attend to the present moment.

Stressbuster

If you have a huge project at work and it's stressing you out, listen to a "present moment" tape. You'll find it's far easier to accept where you are in the project, how much time you have left, and what it will take to complete it.

Once again, cassette tapes can be enormously helpful in achieving the experience of the present moment. Such tapes, which might range anywhere from 15 to 45 minutes per side, require only that you sit in a chair in a quiet, undisturbed place, focus on the message you hear, and do what is asked of you.

Sometimes you will repeat verbally or mentally a particular statement or focus on a particular image. In this respect, the process is much like visualization. However, the script on the tape dictates what experience you're likely to encounter. You can find useful tapes in health-food stores and bookstores.

Present-moment tapes remind you of the overriding reality that today is just *this* day, *one* day. You can only do so much, and there likely will be other days.

People Are Talking

Thus far, we've covered various forms of dialogue including prayer to God, communicating with spirit and nature, and positive self-talk to your subconscious. To close this chapter, let's briefly examine the stress-reducing potential of talking to others.

A Friend Every Day Keeps the Doctor Away

You and your friends laugh together, cry together, watch TV together, gossip together—and keep each other healthy, too! It does make sense. After all, your friends are your support system. They are there for you when you need them, and that's a great stress reliever.

Studies show that having a wide social and personal network of relationships does indeed reduce your chance of getting sick. When you do fall ill, it improves your chances for a full and speedy recovery. The next time you're feeling a little under the weather, have a bunch of your friends over for a little repartee.

As Good as a Witch Doctor

In *The Psychological Society*, author Martin L. Gross concludes that "the modern industry of psychology in America was no more effective in treating patients than witch doctors in Africa were in treating people who came to them." The key to success appears to be that the patient believes in the doctor's healing powers—be it a psychiatrist or a witch doctor. By the same token, a trusted friend or a relative with whom you can discuss your problems can be equally effective.

Calming Concept

When you talk to someone else about what's stressing you—whether it's a counselor, a spouse, or a friend—you begin the process of alleviating your feelings of stress and anxiety. Since language first developed, talking to another person about your woes often has proven to be therapeutic, even if the listener didn't offer any significant verbal response.

If You Were Here, I'd Say...

You don't talk to someone about what's stressing you because you hope to find a solution then and there. You do it because discussing the stressor moves you closer to its resolution. The mere act of talking out your problems and knowing another person is on the receiving end is comforting. Amazingly, that other person need not even be present! As you learned in Chapter 19, composing a message to someone, either verbally or written, can offer the same benefits.

And Another Thing I Want Me to Hear

Even talking to yourself (by conscious choice, not because you've gone daffy) using focused, direct dialogue can be of great value. When you do this, you get a chance to explore the issue from new angles.

I'm not referring to self-talk here. I'm talking about simply vocalizing a problem—talking it out, out loud. Sometimes just hearing it spoken aloud can help you identify something you had overlooked or had not considered. Things become clear, and your stress related to the issue often subsides. It doesn't seem so insurmountable.

The Least You Need to Know

- Catch negative self-talk and replace it with something positive.
- The phenomenal effects of prayer on healing are a scientific reality. Prayer can help you alleviate stress.
- Rather than viewing yourself as a physical entity having a spiritual experience, consider viewing yourself as a spiritual being having a human experience.
- If you feel stressed, talk to someone who is good at listening.

Chapter 22

Let's Get Physical: Yoga and Exercise

In This Chapter

- Contorting toward calmness
- Get thee to a fitness club
- Stretching your way to health
- Move it or lose it

The role of exercise, any kind of exercise, in improving your fitness is well known, but it's equally important for reducing your stress. It stands to reason that a healthy, well-functioning body is less prone to aches, pains, and discomforts—all stressors. And as you now know, the rush of endorphins set off by exercise is a great mood elevator. This, again, means stress relief for you.

In this chapter, you'll learn all about some great exercise-based approaches to stress relief. In particular, you'll learn about the therapeutic value of *yoga* in promoting your physical, mental, and spiritual well-being.

The Yoga Boom

The practice of yoga goes back five to seven thousand years, when it was developed as a part of the Hindu religion. It has long had advocates in the West, but it truly went mainstream when Jane Fonda's *Yoga Exercise Workout* hit the top of Billboard's health and exercise video chart. By some estimates, today more than four million people practice yoga in the United States alone.

Much of the Western practice of yoga can be traced back to the Indian Swami Sivananda, who was educated in the West and practiced medicine in England. Sivananda studied the traditional form of yoga back in India, detailing every movement and posture so he could teach it to Westerners.

Tranquillity Terminology

Yoga is a Sanskrit word meaning "union." It signifies the fundamental link between mind and body.

Later, he founded a center in India dedicated to the study of yoga and its philosophy and practices. The Beatles visited there nearly a half a century later when they went to study meditation with the Maharishi. Sivananda is credited with training several yoga teachers who were highly influential in attracting advocates throughout Europe and America.

Something for Everyone

The idea of yoga is to awaken the mind, to feed the body, and to rekindle the spirit—to create a union between mind and body. The masters tell us that 10 to 15 minutes of basic yoga exercises a day can enable you to feel more relaxed at work, to concentrate better, to have a healthy appetite, to have better sex, and to sleep more soundly.

Although some yoga exercises can be difficult to master, there is something for everyone among the more than 1,000 different postures.

- Dancers can practice yoga to increase their energy and to improve their stamina.
- Business executives can use it to stay calm and balanced in a hectic environment.
- Athletes can use it to improve performance or to recover more quickly from an injury.

Ready for Prime Time

As holistic approaches to wellness grow in popularity throughout the West, and as scientific studies further corroborate and enhance the medical community's understanding of the benefits of yoga, more programs and more yoga therapies are likely to be embraced by institutions in every community.

Integrative yoga therapies, which combine the wisdom of the masters with recent advances in mind-body medicine, are already popular within wellness programs at progressive health, corporate, government, and educational institutions. They are used for treating everything from high blood pressure, eating disorders, heart ailments, anxiety, and depression to simply and effectively enabling everyday career professionals to feel more calm and at ease.

Here are some of the immediate benefits of yoga.

1. Dynamic stretching helps alleviate tension throughout the body. Even first-timers report that they feel lighter and freer after a workout and that they are more easily able to sit, bend, stand, walk, and move.
2. The focus on breathing during yoga helps participants have a greater awareness of their body on many levels.
3. Improved posture is achieved through movements, twists, and contortions that help lengthen and strengthen as well as tone muscles in the body. Participants report feeling stronger, more graceful, and invigorated.
4. The meditation component of yoga helps participants calm the mind and enliven the brain. Yoga masters are able to achieve considerable inner peace. Even first-time participants report feeling a level of inner contentment that they had not anticipated.

Anxiety Antidote

A yoga master will not do anything harmful to his body or to his mind, nor will he do anything unnatural.

Work In, Not Out

If you're only accustomed to Western approaches to exercise, yoga can seem strange at first. There's no emphasis on working up a sweat or straining to the limit of your endurance. Whereas Western exercise often is characterized by exertion, yoga is characterized by *control*—the ability to perform and maintain a posture for an extended period of time. That's why it can look deceptively easy to first-time students.

If you are reasonably fit and dexterous, most of the basic yoga postures are well within your capability, certainly after a few weeks of practice. Some, however, require an extraordinary degree of flexibility, and it might take some time before you achieve the physical mastery required to perform them.

Dexterous Me

As you take one class after another, you begin to get more limber and more dexterous. The effect of the performance of each posture is cumulative. With each successfully mastered pose, you become more able to execute truly challenging postures.

As you become more adept at various postures, you develop greater conscious control of your breathing, and you benefit from a physiological cleansing as well as a mental cleansing of sorts. You also feel more encouraged to try the more difficult postures, some of which might have looked outright weird, and all but impossible to you when you first became exposed to yoga.

Yoga Basics

The *Yoga Journal* estimates that more than six million people in the United States have tried yoga in one form or another. The following are among the more popular forms of yoga practiced here.

1. Raja yoga is the purely meditational aspect of yoga—disciplines of breathing and contemplation designed to enhance your spiritual growth.
2. Hatha yoga is designed to strengthen and relax the body. Hatha yoga involves a variety of elaborate exercises—contortions—such as back bends, spinal twists, and head stands. All of these help improve posture, promote calmness and relaxation, and help a person feel "lighter." Some Hatha yoga instructors integrate meditation and breathing exercises into the practice. Below are a few styles of Hatha yoga.

   - Kundalini yoga involves combining various posture techniques with meditation, chanting, and considerable breathing exercises. There's a strong devotional aspect to Kundalini yoga.
   - Ashtanga yoga is for the athletic. Here, through a series of postural exercises, a person seeks to purify, strengthen, and stretch the body. A typical session might begin with a brief chant followed by a long series of exercises executed in rapid fashion with little time in between. Ashtanga can be intensive and, hence, is not for the meek.
   - Iyengar yoga draws upon postures and contortions practiced in Hatha yoga. The goal is to improve upon bodily alignment in order to isolate and refine muscle movements and to achieve greater muscular precision. There might be little or no chanting or meditation. Students focus on practicing the various poses repeatedly to achieve higher and higher levels of precision.

Regardless of the type of yoga you practice, the variety of poses, postures, and stresses helps keep your body limber. The slowly controlled moves in combination with breathing help keep the mind calm.

The Teacher/Student Relationship

The teacher-student relationship in yoga is paramount. The pupil or student must observe the teacher intently because the teacher is the complete and only model for the correct poses.

Calming Concept

In the United States, there are many certification programs, but there are no licensing requirements by law needed to teach Yoga. You should employ the same principles in finding a good yoga teacher as you would in finding a good practitioner of any art or science. First, ask around. What are the most popular classes? Chances are the instructor is good, and that's why so many students sign up and attend.

Continuing Ed

Thanks to yoga's broad popularity, classes are easy to find no matter where you live. Check with your local Y, community center, or gym. The American Yoga Association, on the Web at **users.aol.com/anyogaassn/aya**, provides free guidelines for how to find a yoga teacher. They also can be reached at 941-953-5859.

Before signing up, ask the teacher whether he or she studies regularly with a master instructor. Yoga is an involving art; no one, even at the top, ever stops learning. Be skeptical if you've encountered a teacher who feels he or she has "completed" their course of study.

It's also essential that your instructor have fundamental knowledge of the major muscle groups and body systems. This is because it's easy to rip, tear, rupture, or strain something in your body if you attempt a posture beyond your current level of ability. Observe how the instructor approaches safety issues before each posture or exercise. If you feel pain in a joint area, don't hold a stretch—no matter what the rest of the class is doing.

Principles of Yogic Practice

Each posture (*asanas*) you undertake during your class is designed to stretch or flex one or more muscle groups. It then is followed by a counter-posture, which is chosen because it works an opposing muscle group. In other words, if your first posture stretches and extends the muscles of your back and shoulders, the second will contract that same set of muscles. This alternation between the flexing and extending of your muscles is consistent with the philosophy of duality that underlies all yogic practice.

Tranquillity Terminology

In yoga, all the positions—from the famous "lotus position" to simple facial grimaces—are known by the Sanskrit word for posture: **asanas**.

Similarly, yoga classes are never competitive. There's no room in yoga philosophy for the idea of pushing yourself to your limits. Rather, growth in the discipline is expected to be gradual. It is not unusual for a student to take several weeks developing the flexibility he or she needs to execute a particular posture. Yoga practitioners recognize that trying to push themselves too far, too fast is a violation of yoga's essential precepts.

Men and Yoga

At first blush, many men are unwilling to consider the idea of yoga let alone attend a session. For them, the term might conjure up visions of swamis tossing flowers in the air as mindless, chanting followers dance in a procession behind them. Then, too, they might be reluctant to try a discipline that requires a degree of flexibility and dexterity that they don't possess as a result of their previous sports and exercise experiences.

If you are a weekend warrior, for example, whooping it up on Saturdays and Sundays without doing extensive stretching, you might have pulled your spine out of alignment, shortened tendons, and experienced back pain. The same goes if you've been weight lifting for years. During initial yoga sessions, you might feel inflexible or downright weak—and therefore reluctant to continue. Such feelings, however, are solid reasons for continuing with yoga, so your body is strengthened in the areas where it most needs it.

Get Aligned, Brother

Researchers have found that yoga helps draw fluids into stiffened joints while loosening up the spine and various ligaments throughout the body. Repeated practice actually can help to realign your spinal column, improve your overall posture, enable you to stand more erect with ease, help you appear taller, enhance your endurance, and encourage deeper and more satisfying breathing.

Men who have long engaged in vigorous workouts at the gym or in team sports often experience muscle soreness following such activities. This is due to a buildup of lactic acid in their muscles caused by the kind of exertion required by the exercise. The various yogic stretches, on the other hand, require your body to respond with oxygenated blood. This helps your muscles stay active longer while flushing out excess lactic acid and heading off the otherwise predictable next-day soreness.

Calming Concept

One of the great paradoxes experienced by gung-ho career achievers who engage in yoga is that, by learning to quiet the mind, they gain ample opportunities for expanding it.

A long-time jogger confessed that, once you get into it, yoga can be a more well-rounded and satisfying form of exercise than you might imagine. It reaches parts of your physical and mental being that other forms of exercise sometimes don't reach, leaving you recharged, refreshed, and noticeably calmer to others.

Stressbuster

If you tried yoga on several occasions and, for whatever reason, found it's not your cup of tea, engage in something else that helps limber you up, stretch you out, and relax your mind and body.

Stretch and Be Saved

Yoga is not the only exercise regimen that foregoes the exertion of intense workouts. Simple stretching seems to be a vital component of health and fitness, and it's certainly a great stress reducer. Yet studies conducted thus far on the subject have failed to identify the precise benefits of stretching. People who engage in stretching, however, do so because it feels good. You get instant results, and it prepares you for other, more strenuous activities.

Even if your primary form of exercise is of the strenuous type, stretching is important. Muscles can become too tight from working out too hard—you've probably experienced this before. Any time you engage in activities that require prolonged muscle contraction, your muscles become increasingly tight. Once you stop, your muscles still remain somewhat contracted. If you leave them in that state for too long, they'll get sore and fatigued because this is an unnatural position. For this reason, stretching exercises done before and after a workout yield benefits.

- Stretches before a workout help warm up and loosen up the body and prepare it for more vigorous physical activity.
- Stretching afterwards enables tightened, constricted muscles to revert back to their resting length.

Use Me

The funny thing about muscle groups is that they also get tight from *lack* of use. If you've ever sat in front of a computer screen for hours on end, you know that the back of your neck and your shoulders can become taut. If you hunch over or slouch at your chair, you might be rounding your shoulders. This results in the contraction of your pectoral muscles.

If you don't stretch your pectoral muscles back to their original resting length, they get even tighter. Then, in an attempt to compensate for this constriction, your opposing muscles in your upper back become overstretched and overstressed. If this situation goes on for years, these muscle changes become permanent. This leads to round shoulders, frequent soreness, and strain.

That in itself wouldn't be so bad, but muscle tension also triggers the body's fight or flight mechanism. Think of it this way: If a muscle is tight, it signals the brain to prepare the body for stress. The brain returns the signal to the muscles, telling them it's time to tense up to an even greater degree.

The net result is that you feel stressed and sore. Simple stretches can ease the tightness and soreness that confine your body to rigid, unrewarding postures.

Loosen Up and Win

Loose muscles are more active muscles. They are more able to engage in the full range of motion of which they are capable.

Calming Concept

When you see someone graceful enter the room, what you're really seeing is someone who has a full range of muscular motion. This enables the body to move with less resistance and, hence, greater ease. You might encounter a dance instructor, a yoga teacher, or simply a jogger on the side of the road who seems to be in perfect harmony in his or her movements. If you try to guess the age of these people, you might be off by as much as 10 to 20 years.

Flex with Me

Regular stretching leads to flexibility. Being flexible makes a dramatic difference in how you feel on a daily basis and in how much energy you have at the end of the day.

That's why, if you're stuck at a desk for eight hours a day, it's a good to get up and take a walk at least every 20 minutes or so or whenever you get any internal cue to do so. People who ignore such cues and keep sitting—even though a part of them knows they need to get up—end up paying a hefty price: an aching back, reduced flexibility, and all-round discomfort.

Stressbuster

Although new methods of stretching with highfalutin' names such as proprioceptive neuromuscular facilitation or active isolated facilitation are starting to show up, most of them rely on the good ol' principles of stretching.

Your flexor muscles at the top of your legs enable you to make a lap when you sit down. If they are contracted or stiff, they prompt your pelvis to tilt forward. This pulls your spine out of alignment and leads to lower-back pain. This is why, when you sit in a chair too long without moving and then get up quickly, your back sometimes feels weak.

Yoga, stretching, and other exercises that promote flexibility enable you to sit more comfortably for longer periods of time and then get up ready for activity.

Going for the Gym Toys

There's lots of exercise equipment on the market these days, from Suzanne Somers' infamous Thigh Master to rowing machines, stair-climbing machines, and who knows what else. It's true that you can enhance the productivity of your work out with some of the devices you see advertised on television. The problem with them, however, is twofold. First, for every worthwhile machine or appliance that might be of benefit in keeping you limber and loose, building muscle, reducing fat, and so on, there are many that won't be. Second, it's easy to get caught up in the advertising moment, so to speak, and commit yourself to purchasing expensive equipment that you'll use once or twice before abandoning it to gather dust.

If It's in the Gym, You Win

You're better off using the equipment in your health club. These places are in the fitness business, so they're going to have the equipment most likely to afford you the benefits you seek. In addition, instructors are available to show you how to use the available equipment. They can even help you put together a routine that cycles through several different pieces of equipment to give you the best possible workout.

I've worked on weight machines at health clubs for more than 15 years, and I can tell you that each device designed to strengthen specific muscle groups or to limber and loosen up specific parts of your body yields it's own mini-benefits. I feel a sense of accomplishment and relaxation following my visit to each piece of equipment. There's even a heightening of relaxation between working out with one piece of equipment and the next.

In the Bounds

Most health clubs arrange their equipment in rounds. This means you start on one piece and move successively around to each of the other pieces during the course of your workout. By the time you're done, if you've pushed yourself, you feel a little spent but definitely calmer and glad you did it. Whatever stresses you experience before starting invariably seem less so by the time you're done.

Get Up and Get Moving!

In exercise, as in everything else in life, it's a case of different strokes for different folks. Only you can decide what type of exercise is right for you, but there's no denying that a regular exercise plan will do wonders for your health during stressful times. Unfortunately, exercise usually is the last thing most of us want to do when we're overwhelmed with too much work—even though it's one of the best techniques available for reducing stress.

Change Your Perceptions

During high-pressure episodes, you're likely to think of going to the gym (or yoga class or aerobics class) as just one more chore in an already overloaded day. That's self-defeating. Mary Marcdante, based in Del Mar, California, is the author of *Mother, Tell Me True: Conversations to Strengthen, Heal, and Celebrate Your Relationship with Your Mother*. She says, "to change your attitude about exercise, think of it as movement, and just move your body a little bit more every day." Marcdante poses this question: Why do you think music conductors live longer than other professionals? She suggests it's because they're constantly moving their arms to music. This creates aerobic energy and keeps their hearts healthy.

A Little Is Lots Better than None

"Movement keeps your heart and lungs strong and circulates more oxygen through your body," says Marcdante. She cites an independent study done at Harvard University. The study indicated that even mild exercise can have dramatic effects. Another study followed 84,000 nurses over a 20-year period. The findings stated that 30 minutes of exercise done five to six times a week reduces your chances of heart disease by 40 percent compared to those who don't exercise.

"But I'm so busy! I don't have 30 minutes to exercise," you might say. Sure you do. Just divide your exercise into smaller units. The Cooper Institute for Aerobic Research found that short bursts of exercise are just as beneficial as long sessions, as long as the total amount of "elevated heart-rate" exercise during the day adds up to at least 30 minutes. The great news is that chasing after children, gardening, mowing the lawn, and cleaning closets all count as time spent exercising.

Leave That Chair

What about at work when you're sitting at a desk job? Marcdante says you can still find time to move. Most people have two formally scheduled breaks of 15 minutes during the day, a half hour to an hour for lunch, and a few minutes to use the rest room. Just as some people don't take their annual vacations, however, some people don't take their work breaks. Don't be one of them. Breaks are fundamental tools in managing stress.

If you work right through your breaks and your lunch, you can end up creating more stress for yourself. The following are four routines Marcdante suggests using during your work week to manage your stress more effectively.

1. Use one of your breaks for a 15-minute brisk walk outdoors. Take 15 minutes of your lunch for another brisk walk after you finish eating. Total time: 30 minutes! Then, when you bend over to get a drink at the water fountain, just before you take a drink of water, tighten your abdomen and your buttocks and hold it while you're drinking.
2. Keep 5- or 10-pound barbells underneath your desk. Every hour, take a 3-minute break to do arm curls and leg lifts with the barbells. Total time: 30 minutes! Also make it a habit to stretch every time you get up from your desk. Stretch your arms up in the air until you feel your ribs move.
3. If you work in a high-rise, take a break once every hour during your 8-hour workday and walk up the stairs for 3-minutes and 40 seconds. Total time: 30 minutes!
4. Set your radio or CD player to wake you up in the morning. When you get out of bed, slowly stretch to the first song. Then pick up the pace and dance for one song (about 3 minutes for each, 6 minutes total).

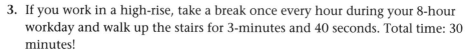

Stressbuster

While you're on hold on the phone, do 10 standing leg lifts or sitting leg-extenders at your desk.

A Little Exercise Exotica

Now, if you're really feeling bold at work in the morning, once every hour for 1 minute do what Marcdante calls the "snorting rhino belly breath." Then, in the afternoon, do the "mountain pose" for 1 minute once an hour.

- **Snorting rhino belly breath:** Keeping your mouth closed, blow short bursts of air out through your nose and pull in your stomach muscles at the same time. All the while, focus your awareness on exhaling. Your lungs will naturally draw the air back in.
- **Mountain pose:** Either standing or sitting, raise your arms up over your head. Clasp them together just above your head with your wrists resting on your head. Reach as high as you can and, as you straighten your elbows, take a slow, deep breath through your nose (on a count of eight). Raise your heels off the ground as you exhale through your nose,

Stress Alert

Sitting motionless at your desk is a surefire recipe for a stiff neck and back pain. Rearrange yourself in your chair every 15 minutes, even if it's just to uncross and recross your legs.

keeping your hands clasped. Bring your wrists back down to the crown of your head and lower your heels to the floor.

When you get home, turn on the radio or your CD player again and dance to two songs (about 6 minutes total). Take a 10-minute brisk walk outside after dinner. Total time: 30 minutes!

The Fail-Safe

If you find yourself unwilling or unable to sign up for classes—whether yoga, stretching, or anything of that nature—and you don't want to go to a health club or lift weights, at least get yourself in motion.

A light jog at 12 to 14 minutes per mile (no faster than a brisk walk) can do wonders for you. Research has shown that, if you exercise as little as 30 minutes every other day, you aid your cardiovascular system, boost your immune system, and help diminish stress.

If jogging isn't for you, how about a brisk walk? Walk at a pace that's comfortable for you but that's not so easy as to be considered a stroll. A useful and reliable indicator of whether you're working out too hard is your ability to converse. You should be able to walk with a buddy at a brisk pace but still be able to maintain a conversation.

Walking for 30 minutes a day is the perfect exercise if you have no other opportunity to exercise that day or if you don't normally engage in exercise. If you can swing your arms to and fro, all the better.

Calming Concept

It pays to take off your thinking cap when you're running. Researchers from the University of Alabama at Birmingham found that runners who simply took in the scenery and avoided thoughts about work were more energized and less tense after their workouts. The same study found that runners who concentrated on how they were feeling as they ran were less invigorated and more fatigued during their workout.

Although repetitive motions, such as typing at a keyboard, lead to problems such as carpal tunnel syndrome, walking is one of the few things that *Homo erectus* has been designed to do endlessly. Wherever you are and however stressed you feel, walking for a while will bring relief.

The Least You Need to Know

- Yoga confers a vast array of physical and mental benefits to those who engage in it regularly.
- If you only have five minutes to engage in a simple yoga position, the benefits will still accumulate.
- Stretching before and after a workout, either in a class or by yourself, helps keep muscles in their natural, relaxed position.
- Even mild forms of exercise, if engaged in for 30 minutes daily at least three to four times a week, offer distinct physical and mental benefits.
- Walking is one of the few activities human beings can engage in endlessly without undue risk of injury.

Chapter 23

Peace of Mind Through T'ai Chi

In This Chapter

- The slow-motion way to less stress
- The yin and the yang of it
- Short and long programs
- Do what you enjoy

Suppose there were a slow-motion form of stretching combined with some boxing maneuvers that you could easily practice everyday, even if just for five minutes. Suppose it yielded a variety of health and fitness benefits. Suppose, after the first few times you tried it, you felt a marked reduction in stress. Would you be willing to give it a try?

Today that very discipline is enjoying a great boom in popularity across the country—it's known as T'ai Chi. In this chapter, you'll learn about this stress-busting, calm-inducing martial art and philosophy.

A Martial Art and a Philosophy

T'ai Chi Ch'uan, or T'ai Chi as it's more popularly called, is not just a martial art. It's also a philosophy that, in one way or another, attempts to explain just about everything in the universe. It's designed to help people achieve a more even temperament and a more tranquil mind.

The best Chinese sources indicate T'ai Chi originated in the Chen family of Chenjiagou, China in the seventeenth century. The patriarch of the family was Chen Wang-Ting, a general who devised martial arts routines in his spare time. Anecdotally, it was devised by Zhang San-Feng, a Taoist monk of the thirteenth century. T'ai Chi proponents swear it's the best physical and spiritual workout available. In its purest form, T'ai Chi training mandates that practitioners devote themselves to the service of others.

Opposites Attract

As is true of many Eastern disciplines, the philosophy that underlies T'ai Chi is based on the opposing but complementary concepts of *yin* and *yang*. Basically, yin is understood as the receptive principle and is associated with Earth, while yang is the creative principle. Everything on earth, including you, possesses yin and yang. Although they embody opposite forces, they work in harmony throughout the universe. Your spiritual and physical well-being is dependent on bringing these two forces into balance.

> DEFINITIONS
>
> **Tranquillity Terminology**
>
> The dual Eastern concepts of **yin** and **yang** refer to the opposite but complementary principles that underlie all of life.

A Dance and a Drill

The quest for this balance is reflected in the physical discipline of T'ai Chi. Proper execution of the T'ai Chi program enhances your powers of concentration, improves your effectiveness in decision making, and increases your level of alertness. Some of the popular and classic books on the topic include:

- *Embrace Tiger Return to Mountain: The essence of T'ai Chi* by Chung-liang Al Huang
- *T'ai Chi Ch'uan for Health and Self defense* by T. T. Liang
- *The Dao of Taijiquan: Way to Rejuvenation* by Jou, Tsung Hwa

As an exercise, T'ai Chi bears some resemblance to classical dance, although it is actually more like a drill. It is designed to balance the muscles and joints through movement, deep breathing, and manipulation of the diaphragm. These movements have an impact on the central nervous system, which presides over the efficiency of operations of the organs within your body.

You begin to receive the benefits of T'ai Chi by practicing its slow, careful, graceful movements that help foster a sense of internal peacefulness. Because students have to concentrate intently on correctly performing the various movements, their external distractions tend to fall by the wayside. That alone is a stress-relieving boon to us all.

Proven to Be Safe and Effective

Over the years, studies have shown that regular T'ai Chi practice helps reduce anger and frustration, depression, confusion, and anxiety. A 1991 study indicated that there might be a correlation between the principles of T'ai Chi and widely accepted components of modern psychotherapy, particularly in the way they envision the importance of harmony, balance, simplicity, and the ongoing interactions between the human body and its environment.

Schools Days, School Days

Many martial arts enthusiasts believe that karate, tae kwon do, and other martial arts are actually easier to learn than T'ai Chi. The primary goal of mastering these disciplines, however, is self-defense. T'ai Chi, on the other hand, has as it's focus the attainment of a state of harmony between the body and mind, heart and spirit.

Calming Concept

It is said that T'ai Chi can improve your health as well as your disposition. In addition, its philosophical components can enhance your sense of well-being by helping you achieve a state of spiritual clarity.

A Hit with All Ages

T'ai Chi is popular with men and women and both young and old because there are few strength, speed, or endurance impediments to a person's enjoyment and mastery of the discipline. T'ai Chi can be enjoyed by nearly all participants. Everyone has the opportunity to experience a sense of mastery.

T'ai Chi improves balance and strength—a real boon for older adults. Keep in mind that bone-density loss, a natural consequence of aging, leads to brittle, fragile bones. Falls, therefore, can be extremely dangerous. A fall might mean broken bones that heal very slowly. A study reported in the May 1996 *Journal of the American Geriatric Society* indicated that the improved balance that can be achieved through T'ai Chi can decrease an older person's risk of falling by 40 percent! No wonder so many senior centers make instruction in T'ai Chi available to their clients!

Other benefits of T'ai Chi include improved flexibility, relief of the joint pain that accompanies arthritis, and a reduction in the severity and incidence of migraines and stomach disorders. All this and stress relief, too!

Calming Concept

No expensive or special apparatus or equipment is necessary to practice T'ai Chi. You just bring yourself and that's plenty. People of all mental and physical capacities can benefit from the repetitive and rhythmic movements.

It's All in the Movement

As previously mentioned, T'ai Chi movements are slow and deliberate. Like the symbol that has come to represent T'ai Chi, the movements flow from one to the next in uninterrupted fashion.

Now, Class!

A typical T'ai Chi class, containing anywhere from 15 to 30 students, is held in a large, open space. Lots of room is necessary because some of the movements involve sweeping gestures. The instructor begins by demonstrating the initial stance. In this position, you go through a series of warm-up movements to loosen your muscles and joints in preparation for the start of the program.

Stressbuster

As a student engages in the discipline of T'ai Chi, he or she is encouraged to exhibit joy whenever he feels it. A grin, a chuckle—any such expression is encouraged.

Proper breathing is another preliminary to a T'ai Chi workout. Inhale deeply through your nose, filling your lungs completely before releasing the breath in a long exhale. The goal is to establish a natural, easy breathing rhythm that will be sustained throughout the exercise to come.

Mastering Your Breathing

Proper breathing is important for many reasons, not the least of which is that, by focusing on your breathing, you are better able to establish an awareness of what's going on throughout your body during the course of the exercise.

Going with the Flow

Properly speaking, T'ai Chi consists of a series of 128 individual movements performed in a seamlessly executed sequence that is broken down into separate sets. A typical performance of the sequence takes from 40 to 50 minutes, in which time all movements are executed.

The T'ai Chi instructor models each of the movements for the class, demonstrating the proper execution. All movements in T'ai Chi must be circular, gentle, and smoothly carried out.

Quantity over Quality Only at First

Novices are initially taught the entire routine so they gain a sense of the way the movements fit into one another. At this level of instruction, the primary goal is for the student to learn the sequence itself. Don't stress yourself out if you can't quite manage each movement perfectly.

Later, the quality of your performance becomes your primary focus. Each movement has its own specific details. The exact specifications for posture, how shoulders are balanced, the positions of the feet and hands, and so on are all important. All this would confound a beginner. The emphasis is placed on the fine points only after you've gotten comfortable with the sequence itself.

Eventually, however, you will begin to spend time perfecting your technique—practicing a single movement or set of movements over and over until execution comes smoothly.

When the session is over, the lingering notion of relaxation and contentment will accompany and benefit everyone who participated.

Recommended Daily Requirement

You should perform a complete T'ai Chi routine twice a day, once in the morning and once in the evening. There are no hard and fast rules, however, unless you seek to become a master at the discipline. You still can achieve many of T'ai Chi's benefits even if your schedule permits only one performance a day.

If time is limited, rather than running through the whole routine, practitioners will focus on basic components such as proper breathing, hand techniques, foot movement, and so on.

When Time Is at a Premium

In 1956, T'ai Chi masters in China introduced a simplified version of the traditional 128-step routine. This new and simplified version of T'ai Chi was not merely some latter-day, stripped-down version of the original. Instead, it was based on a well-thought-out system of integrated movements.

Calming Concept

As with many centuries-old disciplines, it's hard to know exactly when T'ai Chi started. Its rudimentary origins are from about one thousand years ago. The more formal structure, the movements of which are still evident today, originated in the Hunan Province of China around the year 1650. (For you Eastern civilization buffs, during the late Ming and early Qing dynasties.)

24 Steps to Nirvana

This simplified version has 24 separate movements. Like the longer, traditional form, it begins with relatively simple motions and progresses to the more complex. Simplified T'ai Chi requires only five minutes to complete. As participants become masters of the simplified form, they are better able to learn the long form.

You've probably seen people practicing simplified T'ai Chi. That woman in the corner of the health club or that man at the back of the exercise field might be going through the motions. They might look as if they're engaging in some form of graceful pantomime, occasionally with one foot off the ground or extended, arms moving in methodical, circular motions, oblivious to their surroundings.

Keys to Its Popularity

The burgeoning popularity of T'ai Chi is easy to understand. Because it is a self-paced, noncompetitive activity, newcomers to the discipline are less likely to feel intimidated at first. The set routine of integrated movements, once learned, frees you from the self-consciousness of trying to anticipate what you're supposed to be doing next.

Stressbuster

The movements as performed by a T'ai Chi master can seem like poetry in motion. One instructor likens traditional T'ai Chi to "swimming on dry land." Another regards it as martial arts movements combined with a form of standing meditation.

Your Own Pace

There is no competition among participants. Ego has no place here. You do what you can and what's right for you—do not strain yourself. New students are encouraged to take it easy at first. Form and focus are more important than exertion and strain.

On Your Own

When you're familiar with the program (long or short), T'ai Chi is a convenient discipline to practice on your own. Practicing on your own offers a degree of flexibility—you can focus on perfecting one or more movements, or you can run through the entire series. The objective in all instances is to develop consistent patterns of movement, to follow the routine, and to engage in the movements automatically and effortlessly.

Calming Concept

The predictability and the sameness of T'ai Chi is enjoyable and rewarding for many students.

Not Just for Feeling Good

Mastering and refining each individual movement and remembering the entire sequence comes only after considerable practice. Students are taught early on about the importance of understanding the underlying T'ai Chi principles. These principles aren't simply a series of feel-good exercises. Rather, T'ai Chi is movement intertwined with philosophy, rooted in humankind's fundamental understanding of the universe and embodied by the single practitioner. T'ai Chi, in other words, is ultimately a way of life.

2-4-6-8, We Know How to Concentrate

Concentration is the key to effectively performing T'ai Chi. Improved concentration often leads to enhanced performance in other sports and activities, even in academic studies.

The Health Benefits of T'ai Chi

Can T'ai Chi improve your health? You bet it can. A study published in the *Post-Graduate Medical Journal* indicates that T'ai Chi can hasten the recovery of heart attack victims.

In the study, 126 cardiac patients with an average age of 56 were divided into two groups. One group attended aerobics classes; the other attended T'ai Chi classes. After five weeks, both groups showed reduced blood pressure. The T'ai Chi group, however, also showed reduced systolic and diastolic pressure. Because the time period directly following a heart attack is critical for the survival and long-term health of the patient—and because many such patients are too elderly or frail to participate in higher-impact exercise programs—T'ai Chi was judged to be a more suitable course of exercise.

Calming Concept

Through T'ai Chi, a person is able to achieve a lower heart rate and decreased blood pressure. These come about as a result of improved coordination of the body, the nervous system, and the circulatory system. This helps promote a sense of calmness and the ability to withstand stress.

The Antidote to Injury

Stressbuster

A full T'ai Chi session roughly equates to walking at four miles per hour for one hour or engaging in ballet for the same time period.

Every time you injure yourself, whether you regain complete health or not, your body stores a memory of the trauma. As the theory goes, your subconscious creates its own form of protection around the formerly injured area by deflecting stress to stronger areas. This creates an imbalance. Pent up areas of stress can lead to inflammation.

Slow, measured steps such as those fundamental to T'ai Chi can help restore balance while concurrently stimulating your circulatory, respiratory, nervous, lymphatic, muscular, and skeletal systems. Because effective breathing is emphasized, students learn to open their chest areas; to engage in deep, lung-expanding, diaphragmatic breathing; and thereby, to facilitate oxygenation of their body's cells.

A Great Gait

Regular practice of T'ai Chi helps you lengthen the spine, which has a variety of beneficial effects. Your natural walk becomes more relaxed and more efficient. With your feet more evenly planted on the floor and your shoulders relaxed, your posture and gait are naturally corrected. It can literally give you a new spring to your step.

T'ai Chi helps you loosen your muscles, which can generate considerable personal energy. With the conditioning provided by T'ai Chi, your muscles become strong but they don't become tense. In addition, relaxed muscles and joints help prevent the shrinking of the spinal column, a common problem among the elderly. Students learn to more readily align their body and properly transfer their weight while standing and moving.

In a sense, T'ai Chi gives you an opportunity to rediscover the natural architecture of your body. You stop clenching certain areas, move more freely, breathe more freely, and simply feel more relaxed.

Benefits for All

Osteoporosis is a significant problem for women, especially after they've passed through menopause. T'ai Chi teaches women to more evenly distribute their weight, which helps improve their bone density. Because movements are slow and deliberate, the chance of injury is reduced. T'ai Chi arm movements help women increase circulation to the breast tissue and stimulate the lymph nodes underneath the arms.

For men, especially those who have long believed that high-impact workouts are necessary to maintain fitness, T'ai Chi opens new levels of understanding related to movement, the body, and one's spirit. T'ai Chi also helps everyone warm up cold feet and hands through improved circulation.

Do What You Like

Here's a final observation, this one born of common sense. It stands to reason that, if you enjoy doing a particular exercise or practicing a particular discipline, you're likely to stay with it longer. This means its stress-reducing effects will be greater for you. Because T'ai Chi is both noncompetitive and pleasurable, many people find it easy to commit themselves to its long-term, regular practice.

The Least You Need to Know

- When you like a particular exercise, the odds are greater that you'll stay with it and reap the applicable rewards.
- You can practice T'ai Chi for as little as five minutes and still achieve peace of mind.
- T'ai Chi is an excellent antidote to injury.
- The elderly can gain great benefit from T'ai Chi because of its gentle movements and the benefits that accrue in one's bodily systems.

Part 6

Higher Order Measures

This section offers you the opportunity to really take charge of reducing your stress and managing your life. These are powerful chapters. They'll teach you that you have everything you need to take control—all you need to know is how to use what you've got at your command.

By now, for example, you know that we all play a part in creating the stress we encounter. In Chapter 24, "Do You Believe in Magic?," you'll find powerful, profound questions that will help you get to the root of what might be stressing you. By answering these questions, you'll find the means to dislodge maladaptive behaviors that contribute to your stress.

Another common cause of stress is coping with the multiplicity of choices we all face in everyday life. Chapter 25, "The Roads Not Taken: Choices Large and Small," discusses how you can flourish despite an overabundance of choices. It explains the importance of narrowing your parameters, and it teaches you the art of making effective purchase decisions.

Finally, you'll learn a little-known secret: you can simply choose to have less stress. Chapter 26, "The Ultimate Choice: Choosing Less Stress," offers simple but deceptively powerful choices about your day, week, career, and life that will have a profound impact. Chapters 27 and 28 help you focus on keeping stress in check for the long haul, so that you can make the most of the rest of your life.

Chapter 24

Do You Believe in Magic?

In This Chapter

- Taking responsibility for your stress
- Asking the right questions of yourself
- Finding solutions more easily
- Diminishing stress on the spot

Wouldn't it be wonderful if there was a magic wand you could wave and—Presto!—a big chunk of your everyday stress would disappear? In a way, there *is* magic you can use. You have within yourself a powerful, almost magical means of alleviating your own stress. All you need to do is believe ....

In this chapter, you'll learn the magic questions that, once you've asked them of yourself, will make much of your stress just ... disappear! Once you've asked them, you'll be able to

- Get to the root of challenging issues you face.
- Take more responsibility for the stress you experience.
- Achieve resolution more quickly and easily.

Stress and Self-Deception

Oh, what a web we weave when we proceed to self-deceive. When you're faced with a situation that's undesirable or stressful, have you ever stopped and considered who created the situation? Who was really behind most of what transpired?

More often than not, it's likely *you* did. This means you're the one person with the greatest capacity for doing something to correct the situation. You can only do that, however, if you're willing to do some serious self-examination to discover how and why you might have gotten yourself into a pickle in the first place.

Calming Concept

You often get into stress-inducing pickles as a consequence of your own choices. That's *good* news, however, because it puts the power to change the situation in your hands. Once you acknowledge how your choices contribute to your stressful situations, you can amend those choices and can cut down on your stress.

How Did I Arrive at This Point?

When you've gone down a path that has led to considerable pain and gnashing of teeth—a condition otherwise known as stress—you're probably tempted to look around and find someone to blame for the situation. A better, more productive approach would be to ask, "How did I get into this?" The answer to this question often is far more involved than initially meets the ear.

When writing this book, for example, I found myself overbooked. I had some heavy air travel to and from speaking engagements, I also had deadlines for chapters looming before me. While the other passengers were watching the in-flight movie on one memorable trip to the coast, I was mulling over notes, organizing pages, creating new passages, and proofreading old ones.

In my case, finding the answer to the question, "How did I get into this particular jam?" involves understanding a great many different aspects of my personality.

Self-Awareness Is the Key

My personal predicament came from a combination of several causes: my commitment to a career in writing, the personal nature of my involvement in the self-help movement, and my enjoyment of public speaking, especially when I'm able to present a message that can help others. What are the roots of these various elements in my personal makeup?

Early Influences Shape the Adult

My grandparents were blue-collar workers originally of Byelorussian ancestry. They were committed to getting a good education for their children, and both of my parents graduated from college and were highly literate. They met, married, had children, and then moved to Bloomfield, Connecticut, which was blessed with good public schools at the time.

The First Bite of the Writing Bug

As you can see, I gained from my family a strong respect for education and literacy. I myself went on to college (where I majored in marketing) and graduate school (where I earned my MBA).

For all that education, it wasn't until I started my first job as a management consultant that I first learned to write professionally. Following each consulting engagement, I had to prepare a 12- to 30-page final consulting report.

A Personal Journey to the World of Self-Help

In 1977, after the unexpected loss of my father and then in 1978 of my sister, I was thrown into a mental and emotional tizzy for more than a year. In an effort to overcome it, I went on a personal self-help journey. I took every course about health, nutrition, and stress reduction I could. From this experience, I not only managed to overcome my personal distress, I also discovered that I was not alone. There were many more people for whom the lessons I was learning would come as a godsend.

Stressbuster

Develop a clearer understanding of your motivations by charting your personal life-source. Note the influences, events, and ideas that have significantly contributed to the goals and values you cherish today.

Adding Public Speaking to the Mix

During this period of searching, I met an author named Jefferson Bates who inspired me to join an organization known as the Washington Independent Writers. During the course of my involvement in this group, I eventually became an officer—and eventually began to deliver speeches on occasion.

Finding that I enjoyed public speaking, I joined the National Speakers Association where I was exposed to some of the leading thinkers of the day. I began to recognize that there were some topics about which I felt uniquely qualified to speak and write. To be precise, I began to notice that the pace of civilization seemed to be speeding up and that more and more people were in a frenzy more often throughout the day. I wrote a book called *Breathing Space: Living and Working at a Comfortable Pace in a Sped-Up Society*. The book led to speaking engagements and further writing projects.

I eventually caught the eye of the publishers at the Alpha Books division of Macmillan, who asked me to write a book called *The Complete Idiot's Guide to Managing Your Time.* This book came along after that.

It All Comes Together—Somewhat Stressfully

While writing this book, I still had speaking dates to fulfill at conventions and conferences. Publishers' deadlines can't always accommodate an author's private schedule, however, so here I was, winging my way across the continent to give a speech and scrambling to get my manuscript reviewed in time to meet my due date.

I could rant and rail about inflexible deadlines, but that wouldn't change my situation and would just add to my stress. It's far better to look at how I got to this position and to see what insights this will give me to help me avoid future repetitions of this situation. In a nutshell, self-awareness requires that I acknowledge the following.

- I am fully committed to using my knowledge and experiences to develop a message that can benefit others.
- I am committed to carrying that message through my writing career due to personal preference and the values of my upbringing.
- I am equally committed to spreading my message via public speaking when that's the most appropriate way to get it across.

Achieving Self-Awareness

Notice how all these factors reflect my own personal choices? None of them involve coercion by or blaming of outside agencies. It's easy to see that, although juggling deadlines can be temporarily stressful, it's a predictable outcome of the success I've had in achieving all three of the goals I've just stated. It's not something I want to do frequently, but I don't need to view it as a wholly negative experience. Far from it—I can see it as *empowering*! Voilà! My stress level is greatly reduced.

Anxiety Antidote

If you're willing to accept most of the responsibility for the situation in which you find yourself, your quest to reduce any stress you're experiencing will be greatly enhanced.

Stepping on the Brakes

Don't get me wrong. Although it's possible to convert a temporary piece of overscheduling into an empowering event, you don't want to work at this pace all the time. Unfortunately, some people do. Overachievers Anonymous annually bestows the America's Most Overworked Person Award. One year's winner was someone in a powerful enough position that he could set his work limits to suit himself without regard for the demands of others. Nonetheless, his self-imposed workload routinely challenged the limits of human endurance. When interviewed by a major newspaper, the award winner said that he wasn't proud of the title and that he knew he needed to make some changes, but that he didn't know where to begin.

Gosh, and you thought you were the only one!

The Crucial Query

The award winner is not alone. Most overworked overachievers haven't a clue how to put the brakes on their work life. If this sounds like you, here's a simple trick to get the creative problem-solving juices flowing—simply ask yourself:

> "What would a calm person do?"

Answers Abound!

Even if you've been in overdrive for months, posing the question "What would a calm person do?" can open you up to any number of intriguing insights. Depending on the specifics of your situation, possible answers to your question could include

- Do stretches in the morning.
- Always have lunch with a friend.
- See a therapist.
- Read a book about better time management.
- Allocate more tasks to your staff.
- Concentrate on the most profitable activities.
- Schedule more vacation time into your calendar.
- Take more walks throughout the day.
- Brainstorm with your staff.
- Read articles about working at a calm and deliberate pace.

Stressbuster

If you're prone to overwork or overextension, get a blank piece of paper and write "What would a calm person do right now?" at the top. Keep it handy so that, whenever you're stressed out, you can jot down ideas—then *carry them out throughout the day.*

The point I'm making here is a simple—but powerful—one. If you're so overwrought that you can't figure out where to begin to slow down, turn it into a logical exercise. If you *were* calm right now, what would you be doing? When you have the answer to the question, act on it!

Breaking Out of Your Rut

Management sage Dr. Peter Drucker, in his book *The Effective Executive,* tells us that 80 percent of what we do at work is dictated by habit not by need. This means that much of what you do during the workday is done merely because you've always done things that way. Is it, however, the best way?

Calming Concept

The primary difference between people who achieve spectacular career success and those who don't is that the achievers learn from their failures. The primary difference between people who are able to control stress and those who can't is that people who achieve mastery learn from their failures.

If you're so caught up in your routine that you can't easily imagine an alternative approach, try a variation on the question. Take stock of your daily schedule of tasks and ask yourself, "Does this particular task need to be done at all?" An honest answer will probably trim the list substantially. Here's just a partial list of common daily tasks you probably can pare from your work schedule.

- Checking for e-mail messages thrice daily when once a day is sufficient.
- Making a backup hard copy of documents on your hard drive.
- Sending a fax and then sending a follow-up letter that's the same as the fax.
- Reviewing policies and procedures that have been replaced by newer ones.
- Reviewing training manuals and guides that have been replaced by newer ones.

If you carefully assess all the things you do during your day, you no doubt can come up with many more items to add to this list. Imagine how much time you can free up if you break from routine and eliminate them from your schedule!

Your Stress Is Sending You a Message

However unpleasant it is, stress *does* have some value in your life—if you learn to use it constructively. Like pain, stress is a signal that something's wrong. If you listen to the signal, you can learn to fix the problem.

Attending to Your Insights

Stress is a reliable indicator that something is out of balance. This is why ignoring or medicating your stress is rarely the best solution. It doesn't offer you the ability to learn what to do if it reoccurs. Instead, in the face of a stressful situation, your best choice is to ask the question, "What can I learn from this?"

When I sleep for less than seven hours, I simply am not sharp the next day. What can I learn from this? The extra hour I devote to some other activity needs to be directed towards sleep so I can get my minimum of seven hours—and preferably a full eight hours.

Similarly, I've noticed that when I've been plopped down in front of my computer screen for too long, my eyes lose focus and become red, and I begin to feel zoned out. What can I learn from this?

- It is vital to get up from my chair frequently.
- I need to buy a screen that covers my PC or a PC monitor that's not high in electromagnetic waves.
- I need fresh air circulating throughout my office.
- I need to sit more than two feet away from my computer screen.
- My chair might need readjustment.
- I need to look out the window occasionally and focus on something in the distance before looking back at my screen.
- I need to work away from the computer screen several times each day.
- The lighting needs to be at a level at which I can work comfortably.
- I need water nearby to keep me hydrated.

Anxiety Antidote

When stress is unavoidable, you still can reduce it by *attending to the message it's sending you.* Seek out the source of the stress you're confronting and take action to remove it from your environment.

Posing the question sets me in a frame of mind to seek answers. When I find the answers, I can make the changes I need to alleviate my stress. The technique can just as easily work for you!

Reframing Your Stress Away

Let's work with the "What can I learn from this?" question a little longer. Let's say you were passed over for a promotion you were sure was yours, and now you feel quite stressed. What can you draw from this?

- Perhaps you didn't have the skills and capabilities desired by top management.
- Maybe your organization plays favorites.

- Maybe you need to take a course to improve your capabilities in some specialized area.
- Perhaps you are out of touch with the functioning of your department.
- Maybe you are in the wrong organization.
- Maybe you're being groomed for something more special.

Tranquillity Terminology

Reframing is looking at a familiar situation with a fresh perspective.

Notice that these answers aren't as cut and dried as in the previous examples. This doesn't mean they can't be helpful—far from it. By asking this type of question of yourself, you're able to *reframe* the situation to a productive effect.

Reframing often yields a new perspective. You're more objective, less emotional, and more likely to derive creative solutions to the situation at hand. This can be key in terms of career success.

How can this be? Studies show that the most successful people weren't *always* successful. They not only failed but failed often. Their secret to success could be found in how they regarded their failures. Instead of letting a failure get them down, they treated these setbacks as learning experiences.

Certainly, there are many times you'd prefer to not have such "learning experiences," but the phrase is more than a platitude. You get to draw upon the values or critical data you've picked up on the road to where you want to be. This helps you get to where you want to be faster.

Calming Concept

"If at first you don't succeed ..." There's wisdom in this old adage. You can convert your mistakes into triumphs if you take the time to learn from them. As another old saying puts it, after a setback, it's time to "pick yourself up, dust yourself off, and start all over again!"

Oh, What Company You'll Be Keeping

Abraham Lincoln provides a great example of the use of failures as a springboard to success. He lost countless elections for local government, Congress, and the Senate before ultimately winning the presidency in 1860. Noted author James Michener is another prime example. He didn't get a book published until age 42. Al Pacino went home empty-handed in seven Oscar nominations until he finally won Best Actor for *Scent of a Woman*. Susan Sarandon had six such disappointments before she won Best Actress at age 50 for *Dead Man Walking*. Every one of these notables could have given up when they tasted failure. Their tenacity, however, ultimately got them where they wanted to go.

Getting a Grip on Goals

Too often these days, when you attend a Little League game, a parent in the stands is extremely concerned about his son's or daughter's performance. This is the parent who constantly tries to get the manager to move his or her child to a preferred place in the lineup and who yells at the umpire when calls are unfavorable to the child.

Such parents can ruin the joy of the game for their children, not to mention for the rest of us in the stands. It's easy to understand what motivates them to act the way they do, if you think about it. They obviously feel anxious or stressed at their child's sporting (or other performance-based) events. We all have these feelings; these people just take them too far. They—and you, for that matter—should stop for a moment and ask the question, "What experience do I want for my child?" A possible list of answers might include

- To have my child enjoy himself as a member of the team.
- To have my child learn to participate with others.
- To have my child appreciate sports and develop a lifelong fitness habit.
- To have my child know that I am there in support of him or her.

In such situations, however, there's usually more going on than just taking care of your child's interests. An honest evaluation also requires that you pose the question "What experience do I want for myself?" You might come up with answers like

- To enjoy watching my child play.
- To relax.
- To be sociable with other parents and onlookers.
- To show league officials, managers, and coaches that I support them and their efforts.

Taking a Real Holiday

Who would have guessed it? Some people even find it stressful to go on vacation! Are you one of them? Do you fret that things might not be going well back at work? Are you among those people who feel compelled to call in every other hour, even when you're supposed to be taking it easy and enjoying yourself?

Stress Alert

A holiday does you no good if you can't mentally let go of the stressors you've physically left back in the office!

If this sounds like you, you're certainly not getting the benefits that vacations are supposed to confer. After all, the reason you take a vacation is so you'll have a different set of experiences than the daily grind at work. To break out of this syndrome, ask yourself, "What will happen if I don't call?" Some likely answers include:

- Everything will be just fine.
- There'll be some big problems, but other people will take care of them.
- There'll be a few problems that no one but you can handle, but they can wait until you get back.
- Others will miss your input, but they can go a week without you.

When it comes to the vacation-phobic, the fear may be that they won't be missed at all. Frankly, that's unlikely. Sure, there are people back at the office who can fill in for you during your absence, but you *do* contribute your own unique personality and skills to the mix. You'll be welcomed back—*after you've rested and relaxed during your vacation!*

Bless This Stress

Dr. Bernie Seigel, author of *Love Medicine and Miracles*, routinely asks his patients, "What is your illness doing for you?" This question disarms many people. After all, an illness is something you get, right? It doesn't *do* anything for you.

Wrong!

Dr. Seigel's question is designed to help his patients take their condition of illness and turn it into a positive, constructive experience. This works in two ways:

- Illness can bring out your best traits—your ability to cope with adversity and to find creative ways to accommodate your illness while living a full, productive life.
- Illness can spotlight your biggest problems—your deficiencies in diet, in personal care, and in emotional adjustment—so you can take action and correct them.

The same is true with stress.

Shhhh! Listen, Your Stress Is Talking to You

When you ask yourself, "What is this stress doing for me?" you might discover that your stress is telling you some or all of the following:

- I am in the wrong job.
- I am approaching my job incorrectly.
- I need to take breaks more frequently.
- I need to drink more water.
- I need to learn more about tension-relieving techniques that I can self-administer.
- I need to let my boss know that I am over my head right now.
- I need to get more sound sleep each night.

By listening to your stress, you often can discover simple solutions that will help make it—and its symptoms—go away.

Calming Concept

Stress-induced tension headaches account for as many as 75 to 80 percent of all headaches people experience. Yet some people don't get headaches at all. These people listen to their stress and understand what it's telling them to do to keep themselves in balance.

Focus on Something Else

When you're in a seemingly unresolvable situation, sometimes the most appropriate solution is to let it go for a while and turn your attention to something totally different.

Why is this? When you spend too much time focusing on trying to solve an intractable problem, your very *focus* on the problem increases your stress. You need to step back and turn the spotlight off of yourself and your problems. Shifting your focus means finding a less personalized problem or situation to work on for a while. At work, maybe there's a junior person who needs your help. By delving into his or her problems, you give yourself the kind of break you can't muster when you're entrenched in your own stuff.

Helping someone else within your office is stress relieving on several fronts. First, it shifts your focus from your own problems for a while. Second, it gives you the good feeling of helping out a colleague. Third, it inspires others to regard you in a more positive light. After all, if in the midst of your own troubles you're able to turn your attention to someone else … how noble you must be!

Calming Concept

One frequently unanticipated by-product of helping others is the eureka effect. This occurs when, while focusing on someone else's problems, the long-sought solution to your own problem jumps out at you.

When you shift your focus, you're not ignoring your own problem. Your subconscious mind is still working on it for you, although you're not consciously aware of it at the time. This occurs when you get great ideas while shaving or putting on makeup, in the shower, and sometimes while resting in the hammock in the backyard.

Getting in Touch with Your Feelings

One major contributor to stress is the sense that your emotions are beyond your control. You're upset, angry, or frightened, and you think "I can't help it! It's just how I *feel*!"

You're not at the mercy of your emotions—not if you take the trouble to really understand them. When you ask yourself, "How do I feel right now?" with no other agenda and you are being accurate and honest with yourself, a strange and wonderful thing happens. By stopping and *noticing* how you feel, you actually can dispel some of your negative emotions.

Take, for example, being caught in a public embarrassment. If you're focused on how everyone is perceiving you, all you're likely to want to do is run and hide. But if you simply acknowledge your feelings—"Wow! Am I embarrassed!"—the mere act of acknowledging your undesirable feeling helps diminish it.

I'm not sure why this works; I know that it does. Perhaps competing energies cannot occupy the same space at the same time. Feeling stressed and *noticing that you are feeling stressed* compete for the same space.

It's far better to *notice* that you are feeling stressed than to be at the mercy of the feeling itself. When you notice it, you have the option of doing something to alleviate the condition; when you just feel it, you're a passive victim.

Stressbuster

Make the leap from the raw feeling of experiencing to the potentially more beneficial one of noticing how you feel. It's easy to do—just *pay attention*!

From Stress Brilliant Solutions

A co-founder of the Sloan-Kettering Institute, Thomas Kettering was among the most brilliant inventors of the past hundred years, perhaps on par with Thomas Edison. He perfected the diesel engine, automobile ignition systems, chrome painting procedures, and a host of other innovations that virtually transformed the auto industry in the 1920s and 1930s. His approach to problem solving was unsurpassed.

What does he have to do with stress? According to Kettering, problem solving involved a simple change in perception because the solution to the problem must already exist within the problem itself. A problem solver's role is not to master a problem but to make it generate its own solution.

In perfecting the diesel locomotive, for example, Kettering claims his team didn't "invent" the design. Instead, they "offered" the engine six different types of pistons, letting the engine "choose" the one it liked best.

Kettering's insights can be readily applied to the problem of reducing stress. When you experience stress as a result of problems, perhaps long-standing problems, it helps to recognize that, nestled somewhere in the problems themselves, there simply has to be a solution. All you need to do is "ask" the problem to reveal its own solution. If you think about the material we've covered in this chapter, you'll recognize that this is precisely what the questions you've learned to ask are designed to do.

The Least You Need To Know

- Key questions can help you discover solutions to stressful or undesirable situations.
- These key questions focus on how to experience the opposite of what you're currently experiencing.
- Noticing how you feel diminishes the effects of undesirable feelings.
- Solutions to problems come in tandem with the problems themselves. Asking the problem key questions generates solutions.

Chapter 25

The Roads Not Taken: Choices Large and Small

In This Chapter

- Choices, choices everywhere
- Reducing on the choices you make
- De-stressing the shopping experience
- Discovering decision-making shortcuts

The most imposing stressor you face might well be the unrelenting need to keep making decisions. Society today is awash with material goods and service options. There are more brands, features, and options than you can fathom. On the job, you face endless decisions regarding equipment, supplies, subscriptions, which calls and emails to return, what to file and where, what to schedule and when, which tasks to tackle, which tasks to delegate, and dozens of others.

Is it any easier in your domestic life? Suppose you're buying detergent from the supermarket. You're confronted with dozens of brands from which to choose. When buying a tennis racket, you have to choose between different handles, heads, textures, and weights. What about buying a bike? There are men's bikes, women's bikes, mountain bikes, dirt bikes, and trail bikes. And if you're into racing bikes, do you want a 10-speed, 15-speed, or 21-speed model?

You have the power, my friend, to make decisions without collisions. Even if you're confronted with a bewildering number of alternatives, there's welcome news about how to choose, as you'll learn in this chapter.

Choices and Stress: A Not-So-Odd Couple

Too many choices can lead to stress. A wonderful example of how this works can be seen in the Robin Williams movie *Moscow on the Hudson*. In one scene, his character—a defector from Russia—is shopping in a Manhattan supermarket when he spots a dazzling coffee display. There's freeze-dried, rich blend, Colombian coffee, decaf, mountain brew, and so on. And it's packaged in a rainbow display of cans, pouches, canisters, jars, and cartons.

Calming Concept

John Sebastian of the 1960s band The Lovin' Spoonful asked this relevant musical question: "Did you ever have to finally decide? To pick up on one and let the other one slide. It's not often easy and not often kind. Did you ever have to make up your mind?"

Welcome to the Wonderland of Excessive Choices

In Russia, Williams' character was brought up with just two choices: coffee or no coffee. Now, confronted with all different types of coffee and packaging, he has an anxiety attack. He faints, pitches forward, and knocks over the whole display.

On a daily basis, you experience at least a mild form of the same type of anxiety attack whether you realize it or not. The number of choices you face doesn't make your life easier. Instead, it confounds your ability to choose. Don't get me wrong. Having many choices is a wonderful thing in some respects. But too many choices can lead to overload and anxiety. People don't function effectively when they're confronted with an overwhelming number of choices.

Dining Out on Stress

Take a common, everyday situation—dining out. When you walk into the restaurant, you're asked whether you prefer the smoking or non-smoking section. Then you've got more choices. Do you want to sit by the window, in the center, or toward the back? Once seated, your waiter will probably offer water. Do you want it with or without ice? Sparkling or still? With lemon? How about lime? Or maybe just plain? Even after you've dealt with the expected choices of appetizers and entrees, you're still not out of the decision-making woods. Do you want your potato baked, mashed, or French fried? Do you want that baked potato plain, with sour cream, or just butter? If you go with the fries, do you want ketchup? Vinegar? Mayonnaise?

You can be exhausted from all this choosing before your meal even arrives. And after you've eaten, you've got more choices. Dessert? How about coffee? Will that be cappuccino or espresso? Decaf or caffeinated? Sugar or lo-cal sweetener? You go out to dinner to avoid the stress and labor of making dinner at home, but by the time you're done, you're even *more* stressed by the constant need to make choices throughout the meal!

Don't You Want Somebody to Love

You'd think that in something as basic as finding a life partner you wouldn't run into such an overwhelming array of choices, wouldn't you? Wrong. As with any choice today, choosing a mate can easily become overly complex.

Not so long ago, a single person was faced with a limited number of choices. People tended to stay in the community in which they were born, and they also tended to marry someone from within that community. These days, you've got the whole world from which to choose. This makes it hard to settle on any one person today. Who knows if someone better (prettier, more handsome, smarter, richer) might come along tomorrow?

Anxiety Antidote

Having too many choices is just one more manifestation of our information-overloaded society. This is something you've already learned how to address, so you can transfer the techniques you learned in Chapter 11 to the task of mastering the choices in your life.

It's a fact. When you're confronted with too many choices, it confounds your ability to choose. Either you're paralyzed by the fear that you might commit yourself to a choice too soon, or you act as if you have no choices at all.

Cutting to the Chase in Choosing

As the preceding examples should make clear, an overabundance of choices can lead to mental paralysis for many people. Yet it doesn't have to stay that way. If you want to cut down on the number of decisions you make daily, I suggest the following two-step strategy.

- Let go of lower-level decisions as often as possible.
- Let someone else choose when the choice is of no consequence.

Decision via Indecision

When you're swamped with choices, your ability to make decisions is actually diminished. This can cause problems. A popular poster reads, "Not to decide is to decide." The truth of this statement is clear. When you choose *not* to decide, you're still deciding. The only difference is that, in this case, you're making a negative choice—not to take action—rather than a positive one.

Following this strategy of proceeding by indecision only rarely offers desirable results. More often, you'll find yourself facing the world from a passive stance, often at the whim of the decisions made by others.

To avoid this fate, keep yourself limber in handling choices throughout the day. Draw on some of what you learned in previous chapters:

- Set up your desk and office to make decisions.
- Condition your personal environment so it's uncluttered and you have space.

Calming Concept!

Too many choices leads to the perception of a lack of choices. This perception can be highly stressful and can lead you to feel that you have little control over a situation. Never fear—you *can* reduce the choices you need to face. If you so choose!

Why are these steps important? Effective decision making requires focus. All things being equal, if you have a clear desk with one file folder in front of you, you'll have more energy and focus than you if you have that file folder in addition to 20 other piles. Keep a clear desk if you'll be making big decisions. By the same token, when your personal environment is spacious and uncluttered, you have fewer distractions and irritations to get in the way of sound decision making.

Deciding What's Important—and What's Not

Every new day brings a myriad of choices. It's enough to drive you to distraction. There is a way, however, to cut through all this clutter. Of all the choices confronting you, ask yourself which ones are worth making and which can be ignored. The answer is highly subjective but some "must-make" decisions are easy to identify. Generally, they include

- The choice of a spouse.
- The choice of a home (its location and its style).
- Big decisions that affect your business.
- The course of study you'll pursue in school.

The key issue is this: Have you identified, in your own life, the handful of choices that are worth making? If not, now is the time to start.

Identifying the decisions worth making is not always obvious. Is it important to spend time on the color of the next toothbrush you buy? The next movie you see? Such choices might seem important at the time you first confront them, but many are fairly trivial. Of all the movies you've seen, for example, how many have had a profound impact on you? Is it likely to cause serious trouble if you pick badly for your next movie night?

Although you no doubt face a number of important decisions in your life, you also face a host of decisions of no long-term importance. In many instances, they're not even of short-term importance.

You might initially resist this notion, but think about it and you'll see it's true. How long will it matter what restaurant you go to for lunch? How much lasting impact on your life will your next choice of movie have? Even with career-related decisions, you often can go back and change something. Even if you make a bad decision at work, it won't be so bad in the big picture if you're generally producing good work.

Anxiety Antidote

In retrospect, most decisions you make will have no long term or significant impact, however large they might loom right now.

Having to Choose Faster

Sometimes you have to choose fast or lose, such as when you're deciding which way to take your company or department. In the business world, it's getting harder to carve yourself a secure enough position in the market that you can take your time and make your decisions slowly after long and careful analysis. In the current business climate, we experience lucrative micromarkets that explode and then rapidly vanish.

This means that many of your business decisions might have to be made "under the gun"—in the face of serious time pressures. When faced with this phenomenon, it helps to "condition" your decision-making process. You need to take steps to make sure your decision making is consistent with your overall business goals. How can you do this?

Identify where you want your team or organization to be by a certain point in time, and key your decisions to that preestablished goal. (This might mean having the strength to let go of other opportunities to make sure the more important goal is achieved.) Then go after the goal you've identified with vigor. Capitalize on any opportunities that further your goal. Eventually, no matter how sound your plan or how successful your campaign, things will change and you'll have to repeat the process.

The Big Stuff Comes First

Most people have too many priorities, although some seem to have none at all. Both situations can leave you unprepared to make good decisions. Look around you at individuals and organizations that flourish in the face of rapid change. One thing they all have in common is being good at identifying priority issues and sticking with them.

Many people can readily list a number of top-priority goals. But think about it. If you have 18, 20, or 25 goals that you consider important and you consider them all to be top-priority goals, they are, by definition, also all the lowest-priority goals as well!

You can have many priorities, but they can't all be treated as the highest. You have to rank them in order of importance. Otherwise, you can never organize your work effectively and efficiently, and you seriously impair your ability to make good decisions.

After you get your priorities in order, you'll have a clear blueprint of what is important in your life and in your career. This endows you with mental clarity, which in turn makes your decisions come faster and easier with less stress and less energy.

What about when you're faced with too many decisions? Your reflexive action is to try to take them all on. So, when a co-worker asks where you want to go for lunch, your most appropriate response should be: You decide. Of the thousands of times you've gone out to lunch in your career, for example, how many had a lifelong impact? How many can you even recall?

Rationalizing Your Purchasing Protocol

One area of decision-making that presents you with a truly overwhelming array of choices can best be summed up in one word—shopping. Whether you're making purchases for your place of business or for your home, you're confronted with a huge selection of options, prices, and services.

In many organizations, purchases go through an elaborate procedure to make sure the vendor meets a set of predetermined guidelines. Decision-making is made simpler by the procedure. In smaller organizations, however, these procedures often are not well-defined or might not even exist. Households almost never have a predetermined procedure for purchasing merchandise or services.

Tranquillity Terminology

A **spec sheet** (specification sheet) is a list of qualities, attributes, or features you require. When you know the features you need, you're not bogged down in deciding between competing brand names or advertising claims. You can cut to the chase.

The Spec Sheet Solution

Take your cue from big businesses. The next time you consider buying a new VCR, a fax machine, or another domestic purchase, create your own *spec sheet* in advance. Spell out what your looking for, your price range, and other such details. You can hand it to a vendor and let him or her match a product to your specified requirements. If you're concerned about something better coming out later, include considerations of expandability, portability, or trade-in options in your spec sheet. This will ease some of the burden of choosing now.

Itemizing Means Automatic Prioritizing

What do you accomplish by using this strategy? You eliminate the possibility of being sidetracked from your original purchasing goal by the confusing array of other products on the market. You also avoid being confused by a sales pitch that harps on all the other things the product might do (that aren't necessarily relevant to your needs). If you're worried that your list might not take into consideration new features you weren't aware of, this is not a problem. You can use your initial spec sheet as a "talking point" for a discussion with your vendor. If he or she suggests additional, highly useful features you didn't originally request, you can add them to your list then and there.

Stress Alert

Products change extremely quickly these days. As soon as you make a purchase decision, a better, faster, or more economical model hits the market. You can't ever get the perfect item, however, so go with one that suits your needs and leave it at that.

I've Got a Little List...

When you need to make purchase decisions, it's advisable to have a good set of questions in hand at the outset. Ask your vendor about quantity discounts or special terms. If you're making a business-related purchase and you're acting for an educational or governmental institution, you probably already know whether you qualify. If your company buys in large numbers, you might get a corporate discount. Here are some other useful questions to ask.

- Are there weekly, monthly, or seasonal discounts? I know someone who always buys in August, a slow month for many retailers, when they're willing to make deals.
- Will they keep your name off of mailing lists? For me, this has become a key criterion. I'm not interested in being besieged with more catalogs and information than I need.
- Are shipments insured?

Anxiety Antidote

With the rapid changes in technology, it might be to your detriment not to go with newer vendors—they may be the only ones who have the latest and greatest technology. Even new vendors can be checked out, however. Call the Better Business Bureau and talk to their other customers.

- Does the price include shipping or delivery charges and sales tax? Are there any other charges?
- Are authorized dealers or repair services nearby in case something goes wrong with the item?

You want to know about more than just the price and services associated with your purchase. You want to know about the vendor, too. Are references available? Good vendors have them. Are there satisfied customers in your area—real live human beings you can call to ask about their experience with the vendor or product? How long has the vendor been in business?

Making Choices the Checklist Way

The following list contains the questions I use when making an important purchase.

- Are there any quantity discounts?
- Are there any off-peak or odd-lot discounts?
- Is there a money-back guarantee or any other guarantees?
- Is there a guaranteed shipping date?
- Is there a toll-free customer service line?
- Are delivery and installation free?
- Are there authorized dealer/repair services in my area?
- How long will it take for delivery?
- Does the product come with a warranty?

It's possible to choose a service provider without going through elaborate procedures and still have everything turn out fine. When you're dealing with a potential vendor, however, if you can talk to other satisfied customers in your local area, your decision is likely to turn out fine.

Trusting Your Instincts

I came across a study in which two groups of executives were surveyed. Both groups contained individuals facing a purchasing decision. The first group of executives made its decision based on product-review articles, spec sheets, and other data. The second group made its decision based on instinct with little hard data to back it up.

After three weeks, when each group had time to see the ramifications of their decision, everyone was polled again to determine how happy they were with the decision. As it turns out, the second group—those who chose based on instinct and intuition—were happier with their decision than the research-oriented group. How could this be?

Calming Concept

Instinctive decisions aren't made out of the blue. They're based on a complex set of decision-making guidelines that you've developed all your life. You're using these guidelines even though you might not be consciously aware of it.

In his book, *My American Journey*, General Colin Powell said that one of the reasons he was able to make effective decisions in his military career was that he would wait until he had about 60 percent of the data and then make his choice rather than waiting for all the information to come in.

General Powell made his decisions the same way the "instinctive" decision makers did. He, and they, recognized that too much data can be confounding and can lead to more, not fewer, answers. This clearly gets in the way of choosing. By collecting more data than you need, you might be merely defending against a worst-case scenario—wasting all that time and effort on something that most likely will never occur. Or you might simply be seeking out information that confirms or reinforces a choice you've already made but have not yet acknowledged. If so, once again, you're wasting time because your decision already has been made.

Take the Short Way Home

Reaching a decision with less effort is possible! You are three or four phone calls away from any expert on any issue. Suppose you're making a big purchasing decision such as deciding whether to relocate your plant or contemplating terminating half your staff—any big decision.

Can you find an industry expert or someone who maintains a database or has similar case studies you could review? Perhaps you could call a librarian, look on the Internet, or contact someone in your organization. By the third or fourth phone call, you can reach a party who has some gems for you. Perhaps you can find a trailblazer, someone who's gone through exactly what you're up against.

You also might want to become a consultant to yourself. Robert Dole as senate majority leader did this often, referring to himself in the third person. He would ask himself, "Now, what should Dole do next?" This gave him a measure of objectivity he wouldn't have had if he posed the question in the first person. The principle is similar to what you learned to pose to yourself in Chapter 24, where you devised key questions for yourself.

Anxiety Antidote

The type of decision-making protocol you choose doesn't matter as much as actually *having* one. When you've got guidelines for decision-making, the stress is dramatically reduced.

Be Like Ben

Benjamin Franklin often used the "pros and cons" technique. When faced with a decision, he made two lists. One list contained everything favorable about a particular choice; the other contained all its unfavorable aspects. If the pros outweighed the cons or vice versa, the decision was clear.

You can use your computer to aid you in decision making. Certain software lets you assign the pros and cons specific values or probabilities of occurring to make your decision making more objective. You don't need high tech, however, to make effective decisions. As Ben Franklin illustrates, merely writing down what you're up against can help you make your decision.

Go with the Group

Some of the choices you face lend themselves to consensus or majority-rules decisions. Can you employ brainstorming with the right group and the right facilitator? If so, it can lead to a faster decision.

Jimmy Carter, the 39th president of the United States, was an analytical thinker who often devised seemingly practical solutions to tough problems but had difficulty selling them to the American public. He often failed to see that, in addition to logic and analysis, people like to be emotionally swayed to a decision. If your decision making will have an impact on others, you might want to take a lesson from former President Carter's experience and learn to seek consensus.

The Stress of Too Few Choices

So far, this chapter has focused on the stress of an overwhelming array of choices, but that's not the only decision-making situation that can cause anxiety. Too few choices also can stress you out.

In mid-1985, I visited Krakow, Poland while it was still under Communist rule. There, I was hailed by a small man in his 60s at the train station. His major source of revenue came from finding newly arrived Western tourists at the train station who needed a good, clean, inexpensive room and didn't know a word of Polish. I balked at accepting his services at first, but it turned out he and his wife had a nice room indeed—the spare room in their two-room apartment.

During my stay there, I learned that he experienced the stress of too *few* choices in life. He couldn't leave the country. He couldn't travel without presenting a series of papers. He faced many restrictions regarding his residence.

When too much is competing for your time and attention, you might long for a simpler life in a simpler era. When you meet people who, due to social, economic, or political conditions, don't have many choices, you find that they experience equal stress and anxiety about their confinement and about the freedoms they know they're missing. Everyone has their stressors.

Choose and Choose Some More

In your life and the working world you inhabit, you're likely going to face more decisions as life goes on—more than your counterparts in any other generation. You can flourish despite this if you stay focused each day on the few decisions that are vital. You've made many decisions in your life, and many more will face you. You've gotten this far, and you've done pretty well. You can do as well in the future.

The Least You Need to Know

- Most of the decisions you make, in retrospect, don't have any significant impact on your life.
- You're only a few telephone calls away from an expert.
- Look for the trailblazer, the person who's already faced the decision confronting you.
- If you can, try to arrive at an answer by consensus-building or majority rule.
- Make fewer decisions each day but make them the ones that count.

Chapter 26

The Ultimate Choice: Choosing Less Stress

In This Chapter

- Designing a low-stress life
- Choosing to handle change
- Career choices that lead to success
- Focusing on the quality of your life

Imagine you have the power to reduce stress, to be more balanced, and to live life with greater grace and ease merely by choosing to do so. Guess what—you do! If you feel flustered, you can choose to embody grace and ease. If you're swamped with information, you can choose to have clarity.

Making profound choices is a simple but deceptively powerful way to keep stress in check while handling the challenges life throws at you—whether you're learning new technology, surviving a merger, or being laid off. In this chapter, you'll learn how to do all this!

Choosing Wisely: A Strategy for Success

Choosing is not synonymous with positive thinking or any other type of feel-good formula. Every day you are faced with "need to make" choices *independent* of your personal feelings about the subject at hand. Sometimes you are even forced to make choices you'd very much prefer to avoid. You can gain power over your choices and the stress they cause by directly acknowledging this fact of life. It empowers you to

> **Tranquillity Terminology**
>
> **Choice statements** are affirmations of your active involvement in the situations you face in your daily life.

more consistently make the positive choices that will broaden your horizons while keeping stress in check.

How can you accomplish this? In Chapter 21, you learned about the powers of self-talk. Making choices using specific wording is a highly effective and powerful way to give yourself positive, specific self-talk. Let's look at some situations in which these powerful *choice statements* can help. These examples then can serve as models for the specific choices you face in your own life.

The Best Days of Your Life

When was the last time you enjoyed yourself in the present? Do you find yourself constantly preoccupied? Here are some key choice statements to use in your self-talk that will help you get back in touch with your present and your potential.

- I choose to relish my days.
- I choose to enjoy this moment.
- I choose to be fully present to others.
- I choose to fully engage in the activity at hand.
- I choose to proceed at a measured, effective pace.
- I choose to acknowledge all I have achieved so far.
- I choose to focus on where I am and what I'm doing.
- I choose to acknowledge that this is the only moment in which I can take action.

Choosing to Balance Your Checkbook

You can take these general choice statements and tailor them to directly address your particular concerns of the moment. Many people, for example, cite personal finances as a constant source of stress. If this is true for you, perhaps you'd like to put some of these more specific choice statements to work for you.

- I choose to easily live within my means.
- I choose to budget my cash resources appropriately.
- I choose to perform comprehensive cash flow planning.
- I choose to save for the long term.
- I choose to get qualified, professional advice.
- I choose to put away 15 percent of my salary each payday.
- I choose to plan for my child's higher education.

- I choose to provide for my retirement.
- I choose to invest my money with a stable, secure savings institution.

Notice that the first choice statement here contains the magic word "easily." You can insert this word or other modifying words such as safely, effectively, joyously, and so on whenever you feel such modifiers will give your choice even more power.

Anxiety Antidote

The impact of a choice statement can be amplified by incorporating a reference to your desired attitude about the choice.

Happily Ever After?

Marriage, even a happy one, can be stressful. When a relationship ends, however, you're bound to feel stress, even if the ending was your own choice. What positive choice statements can you employ to reduce stress, to make the best of things, and perhaps to move on in life?

- I choose to feel good about my decision.
- I choose to have cordial relations with my ex-spouse.
- I choose to be an effective co-parent with my spouse.
- I choose to maintain a healthy outlook about marriage and relationships.
- I choose to easily and equitably divide our assets.
- I choose to reflect on what I've learned.
- I choose to engage in rewarding relationships.
- I choose to successfully remarry.

Such statements can do wonders to take the inherently stressful situation of a breakup and make it a positive springboard to starting a new life.

Improving Your Tolerance Levels

You're traveling in another dimension, a dimension of sight and sound. That's the signpost up ahead! You're in the *toleration* zone.

Despite your best laid plans, sometimes stuff happens. Often, the best you can do is attempt to anticipate problems to minimize their impact. This means learning to improve your tolerance for stress so it falls within your "toleration zone."

How does this work? Here's a personal example: I frequently experience travel delays, arrive at

Tranquillity Terminology

Toleration, as the term is used here, refers to the capacity of a body (or an individual) to endure or become less sensitive to a substance or condition—in this case, a stressor.

convention halls and meeting rooms only to find they haven't been set up yet, and find myself working with the occasionally unhelpful meeting coordinator, who is more of an obstacle than an aid. Because I can anticipate the possibility of some or all of these stressors whenever I engage to deliver a speech, I've learned not to be unduly upset by them. I simply acknowledge that this is part of my profession—it comes with the territory.

Anxiety Antidote

Most of our stress is time-related—too much to do, too little time. By building more free time into your schedule, you automatically cut your stress down dramatically.

The key word is "anticipation." How can you prepare for the unexpected? It helps to be honest with yourself about the predictable stressors that come with your workplace or personal circumstances. Beyond that, some other strategies can help. The more rested you are, for example, the less upset you will be when something doesn't go as planned and the "wider" your toleration zone will be. It helps to be alert in general.

It's also helpful to keep some slack in your schedule so you've got time to deal with unanticipated problems as they arise. When I am scheduled to speak to a group, for example, I make a point to arrive at the meeting room 45 minutes early. That way, I have plenty of time to cope with unexpected glitches.

Contingency Planning—A Real Stressbuster

If you try to anticipate the likely snafus you might encounter when working on a project or completing a task, you can plan ahead to overcome them. Having spoken to hundreds of groups over the years, I now automatically undertake contingency planning. For example, I now routinely bring along a timer with a large face because I can't count on a clock being in the room. I don't want to make the amateurish move of looking at my watch while I'm speaking.

I try to anticipate multiple scenarios that could cause minor trouble. For example, with regard to your audience: Too few attendees, or too many, can be problematic. If I'm speaking in a large lecture hall that might not fill up, I bring along a roll of masking tape. I can use it to seal off the last several rows so the attendees will sit closer to the front, which always is more desirable for the success of the meeting. At the same time, I anticipate the possibility of a larger-than-expected crowd by bringing extra workbooks or handouts.

What if you're faced with making a presentation? What choice statements are available for you to make?

- I choose to handle this difficult circumstance graciously.
- I choose to easily rise to the occasion.
- I choose to maintain calm in the face of a challenge.

- I choose to feel comfortable speaking before a crowd.
- I choose to take a strategic pause before attempting to respond to tough questions.

Calming Concept

In every industry or profession, you can make specific choices so you're better able to handle situations when things don't go according to plan. Can you identify some that are particular to your own circumstances?

Working with Simon Legree

Good or bad, your boss has an enormous impact on your day. The tougher your boss, the more you need good choice statements. You might need to adapt some or all of these to suit your specific situation, but by all means use them.

- I choose to respect my boss.
- I choose to acknowledge that my boss is fallible.
- I choose to support my boss in ways that he or she hasn't even articulated yet.
- I choose to give my boss space.
- I choose to allow my boss to occasionally be upset.
- I choose to speak well of my boss to others.
- I choose to stand up for myself when necessary.
- I choose to learn from my boss.
- I choose to let my boss learn from me.
- I choose to form a powerful, effective, professional relationship with my boss.

If none of the preceding choice statements does the trick, there's one more you can use if you need it: "I choose to remember that all boss-staff relationships are transitory."

When Stress Is Inescapable

You might be in a tough industry in general and a highly stressful position in particular. Imagine, for example, that you're the head of customer service for an auto-parts department. People call all day with questions, complaints, and off-the-wall requests. Every time you catch your breath, there is another fire to put out.

Calming Concept

They don't call it "The Serenity Prayer" for nothing. Think about all the stress relief borne of Rheinhold Nehbur's words: "God, grant me the serenity to accept the things I cannot change, the courage to change the things I can, and the wisdom to know the difference."

One fundamental choice statement you can make under such circumstances is

> "I choose to learn easily from highly effective people in my profession."

This choice opens doors to greater insight and less stress. It opens you up to observing the behaviors others use to effectively handle problems similar to yours.

Take, for example, a situation in which a new procedure is suddenly introduced within your department, and you have to learn it in short order. You feel scared, burdened, and fatigued. You also feel somewhat challenged and curious. Referring to the preceding choice statement, you might begin by looking around for someone in your department who is well known for being quick to adopt new procedures or technologies and observing how he or she goes about learning this one as well.

This same situation opens the door for other choice statements as well. Rather than resisting change, which will increase your stress, you can make some choices designed to help you gracefully accommodate the situation.

- I choose to feel equal to this new task.
- I choose to be rested and alert before tackling it.
- I choose to easily absorb the new instructions.
- I choose to feel empowered and confident in my ability to master this challenge.

When the Chips Come Marching In

The onslaught of new technology is taking its toll on working professionals everywhere. Does it seem like every time you turn around there's something else to learn? For many people, the main function of their computer has switched from word processing and data crunching to communications and presentations. If you're in this group, undoubtedly you'll feel a surge of anxiety during your attempts to learn new programs, new features, and new ways of proceeding.

These transitions don't need to be tumultuous, however. You can make choices that will help you become more technologically adept without giving up your identity or your soul in the process.

- ➤ I choose to readily take action regarding new ways of doing things.
- ➤ I choose to easily identify and resolve my resistance to appropriate change.
- ➤ I choose to easily discover the opportunities of being online.
- ➤ I choose to be open to new ways of accomplishing my tasks.
- ➤ I choose to feel comfortable with new technology.
- ➤ I choose to identify easily technical mentors.
- ➤ I choose to fully embrace the new changes.
- ➤ I choose to have fun with the new ways of doing things.

Anxiety Antidote

After the meaning of your choice statements sinks in, you'll find yourself almost automatically engaging in behavior that supports your choices.

Creating Your Own Personal Autopilot

Internalization of your choices helps make them second nature—a kind of "autopilot" that allows you to relax your concentration because your subconscious will now keep you on track. What behaviors might kick in as your choices about handling new technology become internalized? Put your dream hat on and let's go for a ride.

- ➤ Each week you learn one new presentation or communications tool, particularly those already part of existing software packages you use.
- ➤ You read at least one article a week related to communications or presentation technology. Perhaps the article is in a PC magazine, a business journal, or your local newspaper.
- ➤ Once a month, you read a book related to technology, but you go easy on yourself. You choose from a variety of books that can help put technology in perspective for you in an understandable, friendly way.
- ➤ You choose one book about using software to navigate the Internet and using a modem.
- ➤ You explore more intently what your clients and customers are doing with technology.
- ➤ You focus on what others in your industry, particularly close competitors, are using. You even ask people how they accomplish certain tasks and what works particularly well for them.

Stress Alert

Resistance to learning a new skill is based on fear of leaving behind the old, familiar ways of doing things. Confront that fear and you'll be able to banish it.

- You join a technology group in your area. The business or calendar page of your local newspaper usually lists who's meeting, when, and where. You find PC and Mac user clubs, bulletin boards, support groups, and the like.

Because you're making choices about technology, one or more of the preceding items occurs almost spontaneously. You also realize that others who once felt even less comfortable than you were able to embrace new technology so it became rewarding for them.

Coping with Constant Change

Many people already feel things are changing too fast right now, but hold on to your hat! The pace of change is bound to accelerate even more in the foreseeable future. You can, however, reduce related stress by adopting some innovative strategies and by reinforcing them with supportive choice statements.

Creative Solutions to Rapid Change

Get a jump on change: Initiate a small part of a new project or activity in advance to gain familiarity for when the project or activity formally begins.

- I choose to readily initiate this project.
- I choose to readily take action on new ideas.

Try total immersion: Surround yourself with everything you need to fully engage in the change process. This might involve assembling resources, people, and space as well as making sure you have a quiet, secure environment that's free of distractions.

- I choose to be a master of the new technology in my profession or industry.
- I choose to smoothly build change into my long-term plans.

Stay abreast of things: Live with the knowledge that change is a constant feature of life. Prepare in advance by reading current literature and by staying in touch with resourceful people who can help.

- I choose to recognize that change is an ongoing process.
- I choose to be open to new points of view.

Learn to leapfrog: Recognize that, although you can't keep up with all the changes in your industry and environment, you can periodically leapfrog over the developments of the past several months and "catch up." Give yourself the time you need to read, study, and absorb what's going on and to make decisions about how you'll apply these new ways of doing things and this new technology to your career, business, or organization.

- I choose to maintain clarity in the face of change.
- I choose to easily pinpoint new opportunities in the face of rapid change.

Stressbuster

Incorporate only one or two new strategies for coping with change at any one time. After all, you don't want your campaign for stress reduction to become a source of stress in itself, right?

More Creative Strategies

If the preceding choices aren't enough to cover all your change-induced stressors, here are a few more to consider.

Look ahead: Cast your eye to a point in the future (say, six months from now) when you want to introduce a new product or service, to have some new technology fully integrated into your operations, or another such goal. This allows you to focus on what's important. You can't ingest every development in your industry or profession simultaneously.

- I choose to easily discover the opportunities in my industry.
- I choose to thrive on constantly changing market situations.

Go cold turkey: This strategy is not recommended for the faint of heart. It takes total immersion to its utmost limits. To do this, you simply suspend normal operations entirely. This frees you to engage in whatever it takes to incorporate a new way of doing things. This is enhanced by making sure you'll have no disturbances, by bringing in outside experts, and by assembling any other resources you need to succeed.

- I choose to be completely open to and readily accept this major change.
- I choose to put my normal, workaday concerns out of my mind while concentrating on learning this new skill or technique.

Designate some days of grace: After deciding to implement major change, build in some *days of grace* (in the words of the late Arthur Ashe) to allow yourself to proceed at half to three-quarters speed. Acknowledge that assimilating the new changes will take time and will involve some disruption. Do not expect to achieve your normal productivity for now. Be gentle with yourself and recognize that you're doing your best.

Tranquillity Terminology

Days of grace are periods in which you ease back on yourself as a reward for successfully achieving a goal.

As the changes you're implementing take effect, you begin operating at a new level. Days of grace taper off as new, unfamiliar tasks become routine for you.

- I choose to implement major change seamlessly.
- I choose to embrace change with grace and ease.

Boosting Your Energy Through Choice Statements

We all have times when we need to increase our personal energy levels. Here are some choice statements to help you draw energy from a variety of sources.

- I choose to be energized from my work.
- I choose to be easily energized by the ideas of others.
- I choose to be energized by my family.
- I choose to be energized by speaking to others.
- I choose to easily attract high-energy people into my life.
- I choose to be energized by life.
- I choose to expend my energy freely.
- I choose to easily replenish my energy.

Recurring Stressors Require Creative Choices

As you can see, you can develop choice statements to address nearly any situation you might face. Here are other possible choice statements that might be of help. These focus on tackling seemingly insurmountable problems.

- I choose to start quickly.

  Sometimes the easiest way to break through a logjam is to get started on something else or to tackle something you've been putting off for so long that it's become a two-headed monster.
- I choose to be more carefree.

  If you're always ready on time and your spouse routinely seems late, what if you do the opposite? What if you stop bugging your spouse and do something else while you wait? Perhaps you could have a magazine by the door, a crossword puzzle, or simply a note pad.

Calming Concept

When working with a team or a partner, try not to stress out over their delays or lack of completion. Try putting the situation out of your mind for a while instead. They might be counting on you to pitch in and do their part, but if they see this tactic won't work, they're likely to come through in the end.

- I choose to share leadership easily.

  Do you have to lead all the time? Similarly, who says you always have to be the one with the bright idea or the one who decides where the group needs to turn next?

- I choose to be lighthearted.

  If you approach what you do as a sort of game, it can make things easier and less stressful. Without getting into Philosophy 101, some people approach their entire lives as if it's a game. They are not whimsical or frivolous; they simply understand that, in the ebb and flow of life (over the span of 70 or 80 years), few things transpire that merit depleting one's health or well-being.

I once fretted whenever I had an unproductive appointment that chewed up half a day and offered little return. Today I realize that, even if out of 240 working days a year I spend 24 of them unproductively, it has little long-term impact on my success. I'm so productive on the other 216 days that I have a built-in compensation for any "down" time. This is probably true for you as well.

Proceeding With Originality

If you're facing the same old same old, it's easy to fall into a pattern of routine responses. This can reduce your capacity to tolerate change. Dr. Roger von Oeck, author of *A Whack in the Side of the Head*, advises approaching challenges with off-the-wall creativity. More often than not, taking a fresh approach to an old problem will bring new, more effective solutions.

A little vignette on originality: It was 5:10 P.M. and the federal courthouse in Suffolk County, New York, was closed. An attorney had missed the deadline for filing suit against a company who caused her client a substantial loss. A partner asked her, "Where would you like to be?" She replied, "San Francisco." Bingo! She made several calls to the San Francisco Bay area and found an attorney who, with 2 hours and 30 minutes before 5:00 P.M., Pacific coast time, could easily prepare and file the papers in the federal courthouse there.

Maximizing Your Level of Success

After all is said and done, we all have the same goal—to maximize our success while minimizing our stress. Here's a chapter-closing superlist of choice statements to help you do just that!

- I choose to feel good about my success.
- I choose to capitalize easily on my success.
- I choose to maintain easily perspective on my success.
- I choose to acknowledge that career success is different from personal happiness.
- I choose to maintain humility.
- I choose to include others in my success.
- I choose to acknowledge those who have made a difference in my life.
- I choose to share the secrets of my success with others.
- I choose to be open to new opportunities for success.
- I choose to acknowledge the accomplishments of others.
- I choose to fully capitalize on my talents and skills.
- I choose to operate with the highest ethical standards.
- I choose to maintain clarity in my work and in my life.
- I choose to be a dynamic person.
- I choose to be widely acknowledged.

Name the stressor confronting you, the challenges you face, or the goals for which you strive. I guarantee there's a choice you can make that will change the way you feel, lead you to appropriate action, and hasten your progress.

The Least You Need to Know

- You can choose to reduce stress, to have more balance, and to live life with greater grace and ease.
- As choices sink in, you naturally engage in behavior that supports your choices.
- Using key words such as "easily" helps boost the power of the choices you make.
- Controlling your personal environment is important, but it's not always necessary.
- For every stressor and every challenge you face, there's a choice you can make to reclaim the driver's seat.

Chapter 27

De-stressing for the Long Haul

In This Chapter

- Settling in for the long haul
- Staying alert, staying alive
- Planning a stress-free future
- A taste of things to come

Did you hear the one about the couple who had been married for more than 70 years, then went to visit a divorce lawyer? The lawyer asked them why, after all these years, they wanted to get a divorce. The couple looked at each other sheepishly and said, "We were waiting for the children to die." This story , told by Dr. Ken Dychewald, underscores the major theme of his book *Age Wave*: You are going to live much longer than you think you will. Perhaps you'll reach 100 years old or even 120.

This tells you two things: You've got a lot more time than you might think you have, and you've got a lot more changes to adjust to in your future. The idea is to make time work for you so you can enjoy all that time to the fullest. In this chapter, you'll get a taste of things to come.

Gliding Along in the 21st Century

The wondrous array of developments in science and technology all but guarantee that, barring some unforeseen catastrophe, you're going to live through many more decades. Medical breakthroughs already in the pipeline, seemingly more akin to Star Trek than planet Earth, promise a new age to astound even the New Agers.

The following breakthroughs appear imminent.

- The effects of aging reversed by growth hormones genetically constructed in laboratories
- New nonoperative ways to treat prostate cancer that work without side effects and are as effective as surgery
- Organ transplants perfected by using immune therapies prior to surgery, without the need of antirejection drugs

What a Concept!

At 85 or 90 years of age, you might decide to run for political office. After all, there will be a large constituency of your contemporaries who will have no problem voting for a fellow octogenarian.

Between 2014 and 2017, look for these breakthroughs.

- Full recovery from spinal-cord injuries via the development of artificial nerves
- The development of artificial body parts that function as well as or better than the original organs and that are visibly undetectable

If you're around in 2035 to 2040, you might see these breakthroughs.

- Replacement of body parts through cloning, which allows perfect genetic substitution of one's own regenerated organs
- The eradication of cancer and heart disease
- Human life spans averaging 100 years or more

With the increased life spans we already enjoy, it's likely you will change careers several times, go back to school at least once (perhaps to get your Ph.D.), start a second or even third family, and start your own business. Even if you can't quite imagine it yet, you might find yourself taking time off to travel the world. Even in your "golden years," you're likely to be active. You might retire and then come out of retirement several times.

Longevity and Stress

Stress can certainly shorten a life span, yet most people still realize something close to their estimated life span. What counts is the quality of your life on the way there. Suppose I told you that you would live to be 115, but with the same amount of stress you experience currently. Would you do it? Would you want to? Although we all want to enjoy a long lifetime, the quest of any rational person is to make those extra years as happy and healthy as possible and to live them with relative grace and ease. In other words, you want to improve the quality of your life—for the rest of your life.

The Straight Dope on Substances

Years ago, a commercial aired on television stating that life got tougher, so the sponsor made its over-the-counter pain reliever stronger. The essential message of the commercial was that the only way to face the workaday world was to medicate yourself at increasingly higher doses.

Popping Pills, Capsules, and Caplets

The rate at which people turn to "medication" as a temporary (or long term!) antidote for the stresses of working in contemporary society is alarming. In a given year, some five billion doses of tranquilizers are prescribed in the U.S. Suppose 150 million adults in the U.S. were to receive such prescriptions; that works out to at least 25 doses annually.

Independent of the vile vial details, all evidence indicates that the levels of dosage and frequency of prescriptions are increasing. This is nothing short of appalling. People increasingly seem to make the progression to more powerful prescription drugs and over-the-counter drugs as a matter of course.

Calming Concept

Popping pills or swigging potions belies the majesty of your human potential. Your body is a wondrous mechanism, and it gives you the clues you need to stay healthy—if only you will listen to it.

Your Body Knows the Score

Here is the secret of the ages: Your miraculous body lets you know what it needs. If you're stressed to the max and have pounding headaches by the end of the workday, your body is sending you a definite message. Popping a pill might bring predictable, temporary relief, but as a strategy for getting through the day, it can't compete with the simple, tried-and-true measures discussed throughout this book. Why? Chemicals can only ease your symptoms; they can't address the root causes of your stress.

The scariest thing about chemical dependency as a vehicle for handling stress is that, sooner or later, you'll be left with nothing. In most cases, you develop a tolerance to medications. It's even possible that maximum doses of pills or drugs will eventually fail to do the trick. When that day comes, your stress returns full force, but this time there's no chemical crutch to lean on.

Stress Alert

The need for quiet in this hyperstimulating world can be overpowering. Indulge your body's demand for calm whenever you can.

No Way Out?

William R. Maples, Ph.D., is a forensic scientist—he diagnoses how and when people die. In his book *Dead Men Do Tell Tales*, he poignantly observes, "Many of the skeletons that come into my laboratory belong to suicide victims who behaved like shy hermits in their final hours. Usually they are found in remote out-of-the-way places. People often go to some hidden place to kill themselves, whether from a desire to act alone and unhindered, or because they wish simply to disappear in solitude, spending their last moments in reflective silence."

I have to wonder, would these people have killed themselves if they could have attained reflective silence throughout their days? Was their quest to die alone simply an ill-chosen solution to the stresses they faced?

Breaking Away from the Pack

You might have noticed that many recommendations in this book involve learning not to follow the crowd. Instead, you're encouraged to find your own, individual ways to reduce the stress in your life. This is only good sense: The masses race though their days. The masses gobble down fast food. The masses take pills by the boatload. The masses, by and large, live lives of tension and turmoil. Stress has become the malady of the modern age.

You don't have to do what everyone else does. It's far better that you learn how to be true to yourself. Being true to yourself means doing what *you* need to do to stay healthy, balanced, and relaxed. It means having inner direction; developing the ability to call upon your knowledge, experience, and instinct to carve your own path; and, ultimately, living with less stress because you are less swayed by popular or prevailing norms.

You are true to yourself when you fully acknowledge the circumstances and events as your life unfolds and when you fully acknowledge your ability to make choices before, during, and after such events occur. You achieve this state by basing your thoughts and actions on an internal guidance system that constantly evolves in response to change. You learn what works in your life and improve upon it. You identify what doesn't work and avoid repeating it.

Advice from the Experts

I've had many opportunities to visit and talk with people who are highly respected in their fields, people who have spent their lifetimes being true to themselves. All are still working, including two who are in their mid-70s. They work by choice because they are committed to their professions, and they choose to remain actively involved—they don't have to. They all are financially secure many times over.

My question to each of them was: "How can the typical working man and woman become a high achiever while keeping stress in check?" They agreed that high on the list of things to do was learning not to let yourself feel compelled to go along with the crowd, particularly when the crowd is taking a seemingly easier road that results in unacceptable outcomes. In addition, they offered several other useful suggestions, including

Anxiety Antidote

When you're true to yourself, you are the ultimate judge of what is appropriate to you and what is not.

- Pace yourself, especially if you've got big goals.
- Don't be afraid to aim high. At the same time, make sure you approach tasks with a realistic notion of what it will take to be successful.
- Take frequent breaks, however short in duration.
- Anticipate setbacks. Nearly everyone faces a long and winding road on the way to real breakthroughs. Everyone is subject to mistakes. The people who recover quickly are the ones who achieve success.
- Follow up. When it looks as if you're near the goal line, don't make the mistake so many people make and coast the rest of the way. Put in a little more time and effort to make sure your quest will pay off.

For your eternal enlightenment and funny bone, I've listed some of my own "Eternal Truths" about handling stress. How many of these can you relate to?

- The hardest step is simply doing something differently from the way you've always done it.
- You don't know how a stress-reduction technique will work for you until you commit to putting it into practice.
- The best results start to come at least a day or two after you thought they would.
- You never quite get all the time you want to engage in a technique.
- It's hard to feel stressed when you're looking good.
- The quiet space you have found will soon be found by others, so find several quiet spaces.
- Break times feel best when you need them the most.
- The less you enjoy doing something, the more potentially stressful it can be.
- No one wants to hear about your stress, unless of course you're paying them to do so.
- No matter what techniques you discover, someone will always suggest that they know a better way.
- It's almost impossible to be the most stressed person in your organization.
- A stressful day seems the worst in the middle, when it feels like it's never going to end.
- When your mother says you look tired, it means you're highly stressed.

Stress Alert

Working with stress day after day is an unnatural act, but that doesn't seem to stop anyone from doing it.

You don't necessarily get better at handling stress with age; it all depends on what you learn and what you put into practice.

Becoming Alert to the Changes in Store

The insights you develop for yourself—and what you learn about handling stress in general—can be bolstered by becoming more fully aware of the changes occurring in society. Understanding that changes are inevitable, and anticipating them before they arrive, can help you become better prepared. This is the best way to reduce some of the stress related to rapid change.

Anxiety Antidote

Reducing stress is a stage you pass through on the way to becoming a more fully balanced person.

For several years, I've been regularly compiling a roster of emerging trends as I see them or become aware of them. My goal in this enterprise has been to diminish the chance of being caught off-guard should they occur. I call these my "soft" forecasts because they all refer to phenomena not based on known technological developments.

Here's the Jeff Davidson lineup of near-term soft forecasts arranged by subject area.

My forecasts for relationships

- There will be more single adults as a percentage of our population. More people will "marry" their work and mistakenly accept the idea that there isn't enough time for a spouse, friends, or a social life. Choosing to avoid intimacy is, in part, a reaction to feeling overwhelmed.
- The divorce rate will stay high. It takes significant time and energy to develop and grow an intimate relationship.
- The notion of limited-term marriage will be introduced for periods of 5, 10, or 15 years. The fundamental issue surrounding term marriages will be whether the couple intends to have children.

Social forecasts

- The gulf between the information "haves" and "have nots" (actually, I call them the "wills" and "will nots") will get wider and wider.
- There will be a movement to return to standards socially and educationally. People won't condone disruptive behavior, illiteracy and innumeracy, or fabrication of the truth to reach public office.

Economic forecasts

- Corporations will continue to undertake mass remedial education efforts. In effect, they will educate greater numbers of people more efficiently than U.S. secondary schools.
- There will be an increase in the servant class—the fast-food worker in the $6 to $8 per hour category. Many of these people will be forced to take on two jobs; many will never become part of the economic mainstream.
- The entrepreneurial economy will continue to come into full bloom. Starting one's own business is a logical, creative response to the confining straitjacket of the 9-to-5 world.

Stressbuster

Avoid letting changes take you by surprise. Start a clippings file of articles that point out trends for the future. You'll be able to anticipate and accommodate changes likely to impact your own life.

- The work-at-home movement will hyperaccelerate.
- The typical American household will own its own fax machine, and soon all phones will have advanced multicommunications capabilities. More consumer

orders will be placed via the Internet and by fax, and more companies will offer 800 fax numbers.

- The proliferation of orders by fax and secure email will prompt a dramatic increase in overnight and second-day delivery of goods.
- The proliferation of toll-free numbers will continue. It will be commonplace to call any business toll free, especially as competition to serve specific targets multiplies.
- Long-standing associations will fall by the wayside as members opt to join smaller, more temporary groups that meet specific needs.
- More edge cities will develop around major metropolitan areas—not because anybody wants them but because the virtual community is replacing real communities. The long-term planning and care in developing mixed-use land in suburbs will diminish.
- Inflation will return in the U.S., prompting people to begin hoarding goods and precipitating a boom in real estate buying and selling.

Calming Concept

Many probable future trends involve the restructuring of work so more and more people will be telecommuting from home. This can be a very positive change, allowing us to more smoothly integrate our personal and workaday lives.

Information/communications forecasts

- Books will be regarded as commodities and will be packaged with software, microchips, videos, and other media. It will become common to email authors who serve as direct long-distance coaches.
- CD-ROMs, videos, CDs, and other entertainment vehicles will all come with ratings labels.
- The emergence of the flat-screen TV will enable people to hang them on walls. Thereafter, "smart homes" will be built in greater numbers. Such homes will have computers built into the walls that respond to English-language requests, freeing people from handling keys and TV remote controls.

- Ultra-friendly software will proliferate, marking the end of instruction manuals. For many applications, the PC will leave the desktop and be totally voice-activated. "Smart" appliances and equipment will be available everywhere.
- The information superhighway will exacerbate information overload as people learn to sort out what they need and when. The Internet eventually will become the preferred and dominant entertainment, information, and communication vehicle.
- Concurrently, we'll need new types of software and ultra-powerful filters to protect us from the explosion of online messages and communications competing for our attention.
- Due to its extensive grip on the global entertainment industry, every country will have American English as its second language.
- Conspicuous recycling becomes commonplace. Regions, states, communities, and individuals will seek to outdo each other, seeing that everything that can be recycled is recycled.

Stressbuster

Here's an environmentally friendly trend: As more vendors recognize the power of reaching customers online, snail mail will mildly decline. This means fewer paper-based communications—perhaps we'll save a few trees!

Political forecasts

- As worldwide temperatures increase, ecology becomes the single biggest issue confronting humankind. The green entrepreneur, conspicuous recycling, and a Green political party will all flourish. People's deep instincts for self-preservation will finally allow them to see the necessity of biodiversity.
- Provinces, states, and sections of nations will seek to secede from their nations of origin. This will be true even in the United States.
- The states will continue to grow in power and autonomy, with the federal government handling more administrative tasks while making fewer policy decisions.
- A black or Hispanic male or a female will be elected U.S. president sometime before 2016.
- Islam will become more influential in the West.
- The breakdown of national borders continues. Yuppie U.S. expatriates try Canada, Iceland, Ireland, Brazil, Thailand, Switzerland, Germany, and Italy (among others) in their search for countries in which the pace will be more conducive to living a sane, comfortable life.
- The notion of bilingual education falls out of favor everywhere as English predominates.

The Least You Need to Know

- Being true to yourself means having inner direction and carving your own path.
- Being true to yourself will help keep stress in control.
- Pace yourself, especially if you have big goals.
- Understanding social changes helps you prepare for them and reduces some of the stress related to rapid change.

Glossary

anticipatory stress Worry or concern with endless stressful possibilities.

asanas A Sanskrit term meaning "posture" or "position."

burnout An umbrella term used to describe a particular type of stress manifested by diminished personal accomplishment, emotional exhaustion, and depersonalization.

call-waiting is a technological innovation that caters to our fears of "missing out." While you're on the phone with a client (or friend, or colleague), anybody else who chooses that moment to call you interrupts your current conversation. Speaking on behalf of your interrupted caller: "How rude!"

catastrophize To commit the common error of emotionally inflating simple negative events into major setbacks.

choice statements Affirmations of your active involvement in the situations that you face in your daily life.

chronic stress Stress that builds over time, possibly stemming from a tough experience over which you have no control except to endure or accept, such as the loss of a loved one, an illness, accident, or other trauma.

completion Every action that you finish is a completion, as can be each activity, each task, even each thought. Getting complete means coming to terms with an issue, or perhaps actually achieving resolution or closure; a mental state that frees you to move on.

contrarian A person who bases his or her lifestyle on personal choice and taste, not the preferences of the crowd.

days of grace Periods in which you ease back on yourself as a reward for successfully achieving a goal.

delegating Handing off of a task and its attendant responsibilities to another. Efficient workers and managers know how to prioritize their tasks and turn low-level ones over to helpers so they're free to concentrate on the high-level problems.

diaphragmatic breathing Breathing through your abdomen!

distress A response to some type of pressure, which can be both external and self-imposed, that prompts psychological and real physiological changes within you of an undesirable nature. It results in your being anxious or irritable, can dampen your spirits, and possibly shorten you life.

downsizing The current corporate trend to improve profits by reducing or eliminating much of a company's regular workforce. It has significantly eroded the old employer-employee relationship and has mightily increased job insecurity throughout commerce and industry.

dress down day A day when formal office dress is not required, and employees are allowed to come to work in casual clothes. It's a popular innovation among employees, and often results in higher productivity than normal "formal" office days.

enclaving The term used to describe the rapid growth of closed communities in American societies. Walled off from the rest of the world, they are closed to all but residents and their guests.

etymology Study of the origin of words.

eustress Stress that provides stimulation and challenges; is essential to development, growth, and change; and helps to make your life enjoyable, even interesting.

fax-on-demand is a system that unites telephone, computer, and fax technology in such a way that a caller can simply dial into a voice-mail system, select an informational topic of interest from a menu, and—with the touch of a few buttons—set up an automated info-retrieval system that faxes back the data requested with no human, customer-service, intervention.

feng shui An Asian term that refers to the power of your surroundings to achieve harmony and prosperity, and incorporates skills in decorating and landscaping to provide a nurturant environment for the people who use a space.

fertility In demographics, refers to the probable number of live births likely to occur within a given generation in a given population.

free radical cells Substances that latch onto normal healthy cells and corrupt them, mutating their DNA. Yuck—sounds like cellular warfare.

gridlock Occurs when too many cars are traveling the streets. When a traffic light turns red, A few cars try to scoot through, blocking the intersection so that the cross traffic can't proceed.

hyperventilation A condition wherein a person begins to take faster, and ever more shallow, breaths. At a certain point, the breathing becomes so inefficient that the victim is pulling inadequate amounts of oxygen into the lungs and may even pass out.

incompletions Worries and emotional reactions that you carry with you long after they have lost their utility or appropriateness. They are inherently stress inducing.

insomnia Sleeplessness.

Luddites People who look upon the intrusion of technology in everyday life with disdain. Those who would prefer to have society return to an era in which technology was not so intrusive.

meditation A stress-reduction technique and a way of focusing on deeper thoughts and feelings by turning away from the distractions and tensions of everyday living.

megalomania The unrealistic desire to be in control and on top of everything within your grasp.

micro-sleep A 5- to 10-second episode where your brain is effectively asleep while you are otherwise up and about.

mismanaged stress Nonadaptive ways of coping with stress, such as relying on drugs or alcohol.

modus operandi A Latin term still in use today, which translates to the standard way of doing things.

narcolepsy A malfunction of the central nervous system that results in daytime sleepiness including sudden, temporary losses of muscle control and brief paralysis when falling asleep or waking. Sleep attacks may occur while driving, operating dangerous equipment, or simply in midsentence.

neo-Luddite Those who believe that the best chance of social survival is via the abandonment of modern technology and a return to a more harmonious relationship with nature. Neo-Luddites loathe television.

overwork quotient The total number of extra hours—beyond your normal workday and workweek—that you can comfortably put in before your work begins to suffer.

oxymoron An unlikely pairing of two words or concepts, such as "government efficiency."

population density The ratio of people to the land area that they live on.

presenteeism Being at work, appearing to be productive, but in reality, being too tired or too unfocused to be effective.

rapid eye movements (REMs) A crucial part of your overall sleep cycle. If your REM pattern is disrupted, even eight hours of sleep may not yield the benefits you need to be effective.

recomplicating Making something more complicated than it was originally. For example, technology was developed that would enhance the process of making, say, fare changes and new reservations in the airline industry; instead, the process has become more confusing and more involved.

reframe Looking at a situation from another perspective.

replacement principle "Zero population growth" for clutter: Simply put, it means that for every new acquisition, you discard, recycle, or donate to charity an item you already own of similar type.

residual stress Stress of the past representing an inability or unwillingness to let go of old hurts or bad memories.

self-talk A way to use internal dialog to empower yourself, reinforce positive goal qualities, and tighten you focus on your goals.

sensory deprivation A technique whereby the various senses (sight, sound, touch, taste, and smell) are masked so that the subject can focus more completely on his or her inner state.

shallow breathing A popular term for chest breathing.

sharp attention The close, careful attention you pay to the details of a task. You can't spread such close focus on several things at once.

situational stress An immediate threat, challenge, or agitation; something that demands attention now.

sleep apnea The cessation of breathing during sleep, usually due to obstruction. Usually, the sufferer is aroused from sleep by an automatic breathing reflex. Thus, he may end up getting little sleep at all.

spec sheet (or specification sheet) A list of qualities, attributes, or features you require. When you know the features you need, you're not bogged down in deciding among competing brand names or advertising claims. You can "cut to the chase."

strategic pause Taking a few moments to collect yourself, gain composure, take a breath, or simply reflect, before proceeding with what you were doing.

stress A by-product of pressures (real or perceived), changes, demands, and challenges that one faces.

stress response When you experience the consequences of exposure to stress such that you suffer some adverse effect.

structural tension The energy arising from confrontating two opposing visualizations of the same circumstance—one of how it is at present, one of the way you seek to change it to.

tickler file A filing system that provides the user with an automatic prompt to follow up on projects or problems.

toleration The capacity of a body (or individual) to endure or become less sensitive to a substance or condition—in this case, a stressor.

type A personalities The designation for hard-driving workaholics.

type B personalities The designation for people who have a laid-back approach to life.

unconditioned personal environment An environment wherein there are no protections in place to keep unwanted intrusions and distractions from interrupting your peace and quiet.

vacation deficit disorder The inability to take time off even when you've earned it and it's offered to you.

yin and yang The opposite but complementary male and female principles that underlie all of life.

yoga A Sanskrit word meaning "union." It signifies the fundamental link between mind and body.

Sources

Achterberg, Jeanne Ph.D., et al. *Rituals of Healing: Using Imagery for Health and Wellness.* New York: Bantam, 1994.

Alessandra, Tony Ph.D. *Charisma.* New York: Warner, 1998.

Alessandra, Tony Ph.D. *The Platinum Rule.* New York: Warner, 1996.

Ashe, Arthur. *Days of Grace.* New York: Balantine, 1994.

Bennis, Warren. *Organizing Genius: The Secrets of Collective Collaboration.* New York: Addison-Wesley, 1997.

Benson, Dr. Herbert. *The Relaxation Response.* (Reissue) New York: Avon, 1990.

Benson, Dr. Herbert. *Timeless Healing.* New York: Fireside, 1997.

Blankenhorn, David. *Fatherless America.* New York: Basic Books, 1995.

Bridges, William. *Job Shift.* New York: Addison-Wesley, 1995.

Carnegie, Dale. *How to Win Friends and Influence People.* New York: Simon & Schuster, 1937.

Charles, C. Leslie. *Why is Everyone So Cranky?* New York: St. Martin's, 2000.

Chungliang, L. *Tai-ji: Beginners Tai-ji Book.* Berkeley, CA: Celestial Arts, 1989.

Davidson, Jeff. *Breathing Space: Living & Working at a Comfortable Pace in a Sped-Up Society.* Portland, OR: MasterMedia, 1991.

Davidson, Jeff. *The Complete Idiot's Guide to Assertiveness.* New York: Macmillan, 1997.

Davidson, Jeff. *The Complete Idiot's Guide to Managing Your Time.* New York: Macmillan, 1999.

Davidson, Jeff. *The Complete Idiot's Guide to Reaching Your Goals.* New York: Macmillan, 1998.

Davidson, Jeff. *The Joy of Simple Living.* Emmaus, PA: Rodale, 1999.

Davidson, Jeff. *Marketing For the Home-Based Business.* Holbrook, MA: Adams Media, 1999.

Davidson, Jeff. *Marketing Yourself and Your Career.* Holbrook, MA: Adams Media, 1999.

Donald, David H. *Lincoln.* New York: Simon & Schuster, 1995.

Drucker, Dr. Peter. *The Effective Executive.* New York: Harper & Row, 1967.

Drucker, Peter. *The New Realities.* Boston: Heinemann, 1989.

Dychewald, Dr. Ken. *Age Wave.* Los Angeles: Tarcher, 1989.

Dyer, Dr. Wayne. *Pulling Your Own Strings.* New York: Harper Collins, 1991.

Dyer, Dr. Wayne. *You'll See it When You Believe It.* New York: Avon, 1990.

Dyer, Dr. Wayne. *Your Erroneous Zones.* New York: Harper, 1993.

Fanning, Robbie. *How to Get it All Done and Still be Human.* Radnor, PA: Chilton, 1979.

Farrell, Dr. Warren. *The Myth of Male Power.* New York: Berkley, 1994.

Frankl, Dr. Victor. *Man's Search for Meaning.* Boston: Beacon Press, 1963.

Fritz, Robert. *The Path of Least Resistance.* New York: Fawcett Columbine, 1989.

Goleman, Daniel. *Emotional Intelligence.* New York: Bantam, 1997.

Gross, Martin L. The Psychological Society. New York: Random House, 1978.

Hardison, O.B. *Disappearing Through the Skylight.* New York: Viking, 1992.

Hardy, Dr. Charles. *The Age of Paradox.* Cambridge, MA: Harvard Business School Press, 1994.

Helmstadder, Shad Ph.D. *What to Say When You Talk to Yourself.* New York: Pocket Books, 1990

Herzberg, Frederick, et al. *The Motivation to Work.* New York: John Wiley, 1959.

Kanter, Rosabeth Moss. *The Change Masters.* New York: Simon & Schuster, 1983.

Klein, Allan. *The Courage to Laugh: Humor, Hope, and Healing in the Face of Death and Dying.* Los Angeles: Tarcher, 1998.

Liang, T.T. *Ride the Tiger to the Mountain: T'ai chi for Health.* Reading, MA: Addison-Wesley, 1977.

Lively, Lynn. *Managing Information Overload.* New York: AMACOM, 1996.

Mantell, Michael. *Ticking Bombs: Defusing Violence in the Workplace.* Burr Ridge, IL: BusinessOne-Irwin, 1994.

Maples, Dr. William R. *Dead Men Do Tell Tales.* New York: Doubleday, 1994.

McGregor, Douglas. *The Human Side of Enterprise.* New York: McGraw Hill, 1960.

Maslow, Abraham. *Motivation and Personality.* New York: Harper & Row, 1954.

Meyer, J.F. *T'ai chi Ch'ung for Health and Self-Defense.* New York: Vintage Books, 1991.

Moore, James F. *The Death of Competition.* New York: HarperBusiness, 1996.

Morris, Desmond. *The Human Animal.* New York: Crown Publishing, 1995.

Ohmae, Kenichi. *The Borderless World.* New York: Collins, 1990.

Posner, Gerald. *Case Closed.* New York: Random House, 1993.

Powell, General Colin. *My American Journey.* New York: Random House, 1996.

Reisman, Dr. David. *The Lonely Crowd.* New Haven, CT: Yale University Press, 1969.

Rich, Penny. *Practical Aroma Therapy.* New York: Paragon Books, 1996.

Roszak, Dr. Theodore. *The Cult of Information.* Berkeley, CA: University of California, 1994.

Sachs, Judith. *Nature's Prozac.* Paramus, NJ: Prentice Hall, 1997.

Schor, Dr. Juliet. *The Overspent American.* New York: Basic Books, 1998.

Schor, Dr. Juliet. *The Overworked American.* New York: Basic Books, 1991.

Sisken, Bernard. *What Are the Chances?* New York: Crown Markers, 1989.

Taylor, Frederic. *The Principles of Scientific Management.* New York: Harper & Row, 1911.

Taylor, Frederic. *Shop Management.* New York: Harper & Row, 1903.

Siegel, Dr. Bernie. *Love, Medicine, and Miracles.* New York: Harper Perennial, 1990.

Von Oech, Roger Ph.D. *A Whack on the Side of the Head.* New York: Warner, 1998.

Index

Symbols

A

B

C

D

E

F

G

H

I

J-K

L

M

N

O

P

Q-R

S

T

U

V

W